U.S.-Cuban Relations in the 1990s

Published under the auspices of the
Center for International Affairs, Harvard University,
and the Centro de Estudios sobre América, Cuba

U.S.-Cuban Relations in the 1990s

EDITED BY

Jorge I. Domínguez
HARVARD UNIVERSITY

Rafael Hernández
CENTRO DE ESTUDIOS SOBRE AMÉRICA, CUBA

Westview Press
BOULDER, SAN FRANCISCO, & LONDON

Copyright © 1989 by Westview Press, Inc.

Published in 1989 in the United States of America by Westview Press, Inc., 5500 Central Avenue, Boulder, Colorado 80301, and in the United Kingdom by Westview Press, 13 Brunswick Centre, London WC1N 1AF, England

Library of Congress Cataloging-in-Publication Data
U.S.-Cuban relations in the 1990s / edited by Jorge I. Domínguez and
   Rafael Hernández.
      p. cm.
   Includes index.
   ISBN 0-8133-0883-6.   ISBN 0-8133-0884-4 (pbk.).
   1. United States—Foreign relations—Cuba. 2. Cuba—Foreign
relations—United States. I. Domínguez, Jorge I., 1945–   .
II. Hernández, Rafael.
JX1428.C9U18 1989
327.729′073—dc19   88-26998
                                                                                         CIP

Printed and bound in the United States of America

The paper used in this publication meets the requirements of the American National Standard for Permanence of Paper for Printed Library Materials Z39.48-1984.

10   9   8   7   6   5   4   3   2   1

Contents

About the Editors and Contributors

Carlos Alzugaray Treto, a career officer in the Cuban Foreign Service, is now Professor of Cuban Foreign Policy and Vice Rector for Research and Graduate Studies at the Instituto Superior de Relaciones Internacionales Raúl Roa García. He has published articles on U.S. and Cuban foreign policy.

Alfonso Casanova Montero, an economist, is Assistant Professor of International Economic Relations at the University of Havana and a member of the research staff at the University's Centro de Investigaciones de la Economía Internacional.

Michael Clough is Senior Fellow at the Council on Foreign Relations. In 1986-87 he was Study Director for the U.S. Secretary of State's Advisory Committee on South Africa. From 1980 to 1987 he was Associate Professor in the National Security Affairs Department at the Naval Postgraduate School. He is the author of many publications, among them "Southern Africa: Challenges and Choices," *Foreign Affairs* (Summer 1988); "Beyond Constructive Engagement," *Foreign Policy* (Winter 1985-86); and *Reassessing the Soviet Challenge in Africa* (1986).

Miguel A. D'Estéfano Pisani, Professor of Law at the University of Havana and at the Instituto Superior de Relaciones Internacionales Raúl Roa García, is the author of numerous works, among them *Historia del derecho internacional* (Editorial Ciencias Sociales, 1985, 1988, two vols.); *Cuba en lo internacional* (Editorial Ciencias Sociales, 1988, vol. 1); *Cuba, Estados Unidos, y el derecho internacional contemporáneo* (Editorial Ciencias Sociales, 1983); *Derecho de tratados* (Editorial Pueblo y Educación, 1977).

Jorge I. Domínguez is Professor of Government and member of the Executive Committee of the Center for International Affairs at Harvard University. A past President of the Latin American Studies Association, his most recent book is *To Make a World Safe* *for Revolution: Cuba's Foreign Policy* (Harvard University Press, 1989).

Armando Entralgo, an historian, is Director of the Centro de Estudios de Africa y Medio Oriente and Professor at the University of Havana. He has written at length about African issues and is a former Ambassador to Ghana.

David González López, international relations specialist, is Head of the Department on Subsaharan Africa at the Centro de Estudios de Africa y Medio Oriente. He has written at length about African issues.

Rafael Hernández, a political scientist, is Head of North American Studies at the Centro de Estudios sobre América and a member of the faculty of the University of Havana. An author of numerous articles on international relations, he is a founding member of the Editorial Board of the *Revista Cuadernos de Nuestra América*.

Kenneth P. Jameson has researched and taught in many countries of Latin America and the Caribbean. His most recent work is on internal financial arrangements in the western hemisphere. With Charles Wilber, he is at work on the second edition of *An Inquiry into the Poverty of Economics*. His articles have appeared in *The Quarterly Journal of Economics*, *The Review of Economics and Statistics*, *Journal of Developing Areas*, and *World Development*, among others.

Pedro Monreal González, an economist, is a member of the research staff at the Centro de Estudios sobre América and Adjunct Professor of the University of Havana and of the Instituto Superior de Relaciones Internacionales Raúl Roa García. He has published articles on the U.S. economy, the international economy, and technological affairs.

James P. Rowles, Lecturer on Law at the Harvard Law School, has taught previously at the Law Schools of the Universities of Costa Rica, Pittsburgh, and Kansas. In 1985-86 he was Visiting Scholar at Harvard's Center for International Affairs. He is the author of *El conflicto Honduras-El Salvador (1969) y el orden jurídico internacional* (EDUCA, 1980); *Law and Agrarian Reform in Costa Rica* (Westview Press, 1985); and *Contempt of Court: The*

United States, Nicaragua, and International Law (Princeton University Press, forthcoming).

Gregory F. Treverton is Senior Fellow at the Council on Foreign Relations and Director of its Europe-America Project. He worked on the staff of the first Senate Select Committee on Intelligence (the Church Committee) and as staff member for western Europe on the National Security Council during the Carter administration. He was Director of Studies of the International Institute for Strategic Studies in London and taught for six years at Harvard's Kennedy School of Government. He is the author of *Latin America in World Politics* (International Institute for Strategic Studies, 1977); *Nuclear Weapons in Europe* (International Institute for Strategic Studies, 1981); *Making the Alliance Work: The United States and Western Europe* (MacMillan, 1985); and *Covert Action: The Limits of Intervention in the Postwar World* (Basic Books, 1987).

Juan Valdés Paz, a sociologist, is Head of the Central American Studies Department at the Centro de Estudios sobre América and member of the faculty of the University of Havana. An author of numerous articles about Latin America and Cuba, he is a founding member of the Editorial Board of the *Revista Cuadernos de Nuestra América*.

Howard J. Wiarda is Professor of Political Science at the University of Massachusetts-Amherst, Associate of Harvard's Center for International Affairs, and Adjunct Scholar of the American Enterprise Institute for Public Policy Research. A prolific author, his most recent books include *The Democratic Revolution in Latin America* (Holmes and Meier for the Twentieth Century Fund, 1990), *Foreign Policy without Illusion: How Foreign Policy Works and Fails to Work in the United States* (Scott Foresman/Little, Brown, 1990), and *Finding Our Way: Toward Maturity in U.S.-Latin American Relations* (University Press of America, 1988).

Introduction

Jorge I. Domínguez and Rafael Hernández

The purpose of scholarship is to shed light on issues, not to settle disputes that lie properly in the domain of government officials. However, scholars can respond to moments when officials review issues to confirm existing policies or to change them. The inauguration of a new U.S. president in 1989 as Cuba examines its foreign and domestic policies opens a window of opportunity to consider the relations between the two governments.

In fact, the future arrived early. In 1987, the U.S. and Cuban governments turned a page in the history of their relations. In July, Cuba became a direct participant in talks over the future of southern Africa, talks that had been carried out between the United States and Angola. In November, Cuba and the United States agreed to reinstate the migration agreement (first signed in December 1984) to make possible more normal migration relations between the United States and Cuba. In 1988, the U.S. and Cuban governments took steps to improve other aspects of their bilateral relations, ranging from better treatment for their respective diplomats to the beginnings of an understanding on the mutual inspection of nuclear power plants.

Also in 1987 and 1988 the war in southern and southwestern Angola intensified, reaching a climax with the defeat of the South African forces that had laid siege to the strategic town of Cuito Cuanavale. Thereafter, the negotiations over southern Africa accelerated and bore fruit. A cease fire was agreed to between South Africa on one hand, and Angola and Cuba on the other hand. Within the framework of the negotiations, South Africa withdrew its troops from Angola. These three governments reached a complex agreement to grant Namibia independence, to station a United Nations force in Namibia to oversee its transition to independence, and to schedule a full withdrawal of Cuban troops from Angola, which began early in 1989 and would be completed in mid-1991, after Namibia becomes independent. In addition, the three governments agreed not to support insurgent forces trying to overthrow any of the signatory governments. Should the governments of the United States and Cuba choose to continue on the path of negotiations in the 1990s, they will be able to say that they are building on the policies that they agreed to launch during the closing eighteen months of Ronald Reagan's presidency.

Our purpose in this book is to sketch where and why the United States and Cuba differ; to identify the issues where differences are likely to endure because they stem from the central values and interests of such different political and economic regimes; and to point to those other issues where skillful diplomacy might find joint interests to settle disputes in accord with these countries' respective national goals.

We had three premises when we launched our project. First, we had no illusions about the past or the future of U.S.-Cuban relations. We know that the differences that divide the countries and their governments are real, and not just matters of misperception or of occasional ineptitude of some officials (although both of these factors have, at times, mattered). We do not presume that all of these substantive differences are subject to solution. Indeed, some of the differences in values and principles might not even be subjects for negotiation; we expect that at least these differences, and probably others as well, will continue.

Second, we wanted to affirm that discussion is superior to shouting, and that parties to a dispute ought to search for noncoercive alternatives to address the conflicts between them—to solve them if they can, and to pursue them effectively but peacefully and honorably, if they must, without foregoing, of course, their respective rights to national defense.

Third, we wanted to address the topic of U.S.-Cuban relations by drawing upon both U.S. and Cuban scholars to analyze policies, reflect on current circumstances, and consider possible alternatives, based on their prior research. This book is a binational endeavor. The chapters are intended mainly as "thought pieces," not as an exercise in generating a full complement of scholarly citations.

The scholars whom we invited to join our project do not agree about the past, the present, or the future of U.S.-Cuban relations. Such disagreements are evident throughout the book. This was not a mistake on our part as editors; it was a deliberate decision to represent a spectrum of often sharply diverging views subject only to the constraints of civil discourse. We thought it misleading to attempt to create the illusion of agreement between scholars in the United States and Cuba when, in fact, we differ.

No one, therefore, should presume that any statement in this book is endorsed by anyone except the person making it. Quite the contrary; readers should presume the existence of vigorous disagreement among the authors. Out of those disagreements, we hope, readers will be able to discern the issues that divide the United States and Cuba, to identify areas where agreements are most likely, and to situate themselves on a spectrum of views.

To understand U.S.-Cuban relations, bilateral issues are an important part of the agenda but only one part. Consequently, we have selected several grand themes around which we organized our joint inquiry. These are ideology, security, relations with "third parties" in Latin America and Africa, economics, and international law. We asked the authors not to limit themselves to those topics that are uniquely pertinent to the bilateral relations between the United States and Cuba; instead, we asked them to identify and discuss the major issues for each grand theme, and only then to situate the U.S.-Cuban relationship in that theme.

Similarly, we did not think it useful to focus on very detailed and specific topics in U.S.-Cuban relations. Instead, we wanted to emphasize each topic's broad considerations that are significant for each country. A practical effect on both sides was that we invited to write for this project scholars whose main work has been on the grand themes under study, not necessarily on the particulars of U.S.-Cuban relations.

The project also emphasizes the importance of understanding the "lenses" through which we seek individually to make sense of events. Therefore, for each topic, we asked for two full chapters, one by a U.S. scholar and one by a Cuban scholar. We preferred this strategy to simply asking for comments in the form of only one chapter per topic; we hoped to signal that there is necessarily a difference in how the substance of a topic is approached, and often in what conclusions are reached, depending on one's initial point of departure. The book demonstrates, in short, the utility of being aware of different national, ideological, and analytical lenses.

We used the following procedures in this project Our criteria for author selection were scholarly quality, seriousness of purpose, openness to discussion with persons of quite different orientations, and ability to pair up usefully on a given grand theme. We gathered in Havana in April 1988 for a week-long workshop, at which outlines and some draft chapters were presented. We were joined by Miguel Alfonso, Richard Bloomfield, Raúl Gómez Treto, and Luis Suárez. The discussion was contentious at times, but also cordial, respectful, and always illuminating (as is summarized in the next section of this Introduction). The workshop's purpose was to sharpen the authors' analytical skills and substantive understanding, and to get a better grasp on the issues on which we agree and disagree. The workshop was hosted by Cuba's Centro de Estudios sobre América (CEA).

Funding for the work and travel of U.S. participants, and for aspects of the production of the book in the United States, has come from the Heinz Endowment. Jorge I. Domínguez's work on Cuba has also been supported by a grant from the Ford Foundation and by the general research support of Harvard University's Center for International Affairs (CFIA) and Department of Government. Other costs for the Havana workshop were paid by the CEA, which supports the work of its own researchers, and which has also been responsible for the translations of all chapters into both languages. This book is being published simultaneously and with the same content in English in the United States by Westview Press, and in Spanish in Cuba by the CEA, in both cases under the auspices of the CEA and of Harvard's CFIA. The authors of each chapter have the sole responsibility for their content. For the English-language version, the authors are in debt to Darlene Bordwell for her fine editorial work, and especially to Jean Shildneck, who administered and carried out the actual production of this book with characteristic effectiveness and good cheer.

Convergences and Divergences

In the United States, there is inadequate knowledge about Cuba, just as in Cuba there is inadequate knowledge about the United States. This mutual ignorance is a result of the hostile and markedly ideological character of the two countries' relations. To a certain extent, the lack of positive contact between the two countries over time has also led to the growth of stereotypes, which—though they may contain partial truths—mainly distort both realities. The knowledge that does exist highlights the negative in both countries, and it has contributed to preserving a framework of mutual hostility. Therefore, the intellectual exchange among Cuban and U.S. participants writing this book is, in itself, an interesting reflection of these factors that have shaped the nature of our knowledge. This was so, even at our April 1988 workshop, which was marked by a real commitment to understanding each other and to thinking jointly about topics of mutual interest.

We now summarize the main points of convergence and divergence that emerged from the discussion, not just between the two national groups, but also, as is appropriate, among authors from the same country.

First, two sets of different and, to some degree, contradictory values consistently tend to separate the United States and Cuba. On one hand are the liberal values that prevail in the United States and that have shaped its political culture since the revolution of 1776; a great many U.S. citizens identify with these values. On the other hand are the nationalist, anti-imperialist, and internationalist values that are a part of the Cuban tradition and that have been emphasized by policies prevailing since the revolution of 1959; a great many Cuban citizens identify with these values.

Second, the prospects for change in U.S.-Cuban relations are moderately good. But this potential could just mean that the relationship might go from terrible to merely less so. According to some U.S. and Cuban participants, this situation might occur because the large differences between the sets of values and interests of both countries narrow the scope for changes in relations. According to other U.S. and Cuban participants, the terms that the United States would set as a condition for improved bilateral relations—particularly with regard to what Cuba calls the practice of internationalism—would be unacceptable for Cuba.

Third, the question of national security is at the heart of the foreign policy motivations on both sides. To analyze this topic objectively, the basic asymmetry between the two countries must be one starting point. From this shared premise, both sides infer divergent propositions.

Some U.S. analysts infer that this asymmetry ought to lead Cuba to acknowledge a certain U.S. hegemony—this might be called Cuba's "finlandization" or "mexicanization." According to this view, Cuba would set the external and domestic policies that it deems appropriate, so long as they would not adversely affect U.S. national security. In accepting those premises, Cuba would at the same time acknowledge that it could not expect symmetrical responses from the United States, even as mutual confidence-building measures are adopted. According to some U.S. security strategists, the Soviet military presence in Cuba and Cuba's own military capabilities, on an island that borders the sea lanes that are significant for U.S. communications and supplies, amount to a permanent potential threat to U.S. security. From this perspective, the degree of direct threat that the United States constitutes for Cuba is lessened considerably by the fact that there has not been a U.S. act of war directly against Cuba itself since the 1961 Bay of Pigs expedition and the 1962 U.S. physical blockade of Cuba during the missile crisis; nor since the 1960s have there been U.S. government-sponsored attempts to assassinate Cuban leaders.

On the Cuban side, the emphasis is on the United States' extraordinary power, as well as on Cuba's vulnerability—geographically so near to the United States and so far from the Soviet Union, Cuba's main external economic and military supporter. Cuban analysts believe that U.S. policy represents a direct threat to Cuban national security because the United States has been so hostile and because it continues to consider a change in Cuba's regime as a legitimate objective for U.S. policy. Although Cuba acknowledges that the United States has security interests, most of the time—in the view of Cuban analysts—those are but ways to assert U.S. hegemonic and geopolitical interests. To compensate for the existing asymmetries, Cuba believes that it must have a substantial military defense that would suffice to deter the United States. This deterrence also requires the maintenance of military collaboration with the U.S.S.R.

Fourth, both sides agreed that the notion that Cuban policy responds mainly to Soviet dictates is a gross oversimplification. However, there were differences between both groups with regard to the extent of convergence or correspondence between Soviet and Cuban policies, especially with regard to the Third World. Similarly, some expressed the view that the U.S.-Soviet negotiations would substantially affect U.S.-Cuban relations, although the majority of participants from both countries believed that other international factors might matter more, such as events in southern Africa and Central America.

Fifth, U.S. policy toward Latin America, according to many participants, had paid little attention historically to human rights and democracy issues, while it emphasized certain ideological premises and rested upon the U.S. capacity to intervene in other countries. U.S. policy had also been marked by lack of planning.

Although Cuba does not feature centrally in Latin America's international relations, most Latin American governments no longer consider Cuba a threat, as they did in the 1960s. This acceptance of Cuba bears on the relations between Latin American countries and the United States, and on the growing Latin American activity in world affairs. Cuba and the United States clash the most over

Central America and the Caribbean; they clash less over South America.

Some U.S. participants expressed the view that the United States has made progress in its policies toward Latin America. While maintaining its desire to retain its primacy, the United States has focused more on issues of human rights, democracy, economic interdependence, trade, and international labor markets. Other U.S. participants, however, believed that substantial differences remained between the United States and Latin America on such topics as the debt, development, and attitudes toward social and political conflicts.

Some Cuban participants expressed the view that the circumstances of U.S. policy in Latin America are shaped less by the East-West conflict and more by the erosion of U.S. hegemony over the region, and by the need to respond to the growth of nonalignment, Third World solidarity, and the convergence among Latin American foreign policies. Other Cuban participants agreed that it was possible to coexist with what might be called a U.S. "positive hegemony" in the region.

The main point of disagreement between the two groups emerged over the question of the legitimacy of providing material support to insurgent or irregular forces. U.S. participants believed that Cuban assistance to the revolutionary movements in El Salvador and Guatemala can be considered a form of intervention comparable to U.S. support for the Nicaraguan Resistance (commonly called the contras). Many U.S. participants advocated that both Cuba and the United States stop providing material support to all such insurgent forces.

Cuban analysts called attention to the fact that the United States had not been an active participant in the Esquipulas Accords that launched an intensive process of negotiations in 1987 and 1988 in several Central American countries (including Nicaragua and El Salvador). Therefore, the United States does not consider itself bound by those accords. The rationale of Cuban policy is as follows: peace would be guaranteed only if all the parties—including the insurgent forces in El Salvador and Guatemala—are taken into account as participants or interlocutors in order that they be actively engaged in the forging of a peace agreement. Cuba would set no conditions of its own to contribute to an agreement, although other parties may.

Sixth, southern Africa shows that it is possible to work jointly to solve regional conflicts based on both U.S. and Cuban interests, as shown by the agreements signed in 1988 as a result of U.S.,

Cuban, Angolan, and South African negotiations. Most U.S. and Cuban participants agreed that the South African regime and its policy of fostering regional instability are the main threat to an enduring peace in the region. With regard to South Africa, most U.S. and Cuban participants agreed that it was important to recognize the black leadership of the African National Congress as a necessary partner in any negotiation. They also agreed that fundamental changes should be brought about in South Africa's political regime. There was also agreement in the need for collaboration among the parties, including the United States, to respond to the high material and human cost of the conflict in Angola and, to a certain extent, in Mozambique. With regard to the latter, there was agreement that the U.S. acceptance of the Mozambique government was also an example of convergence with Cuba.

In general, the question of the legitimacy and political worth of the armed struggle provoked differences among U.S. and Cuban participants. Nonetheless, there is also a range of opinion—even among some U.S. participants—with regard to the possibility that Cuban military forces might have played a constructive political role in southern Africa.

Both sides believe that the differences between their governments are greater with regard to domestic politics in the countries of southern Africa. In particular, the United States and Cuba differ on the question of conflict or reconciliation between the governments and the armed oppositions in Angola and Mozambique. Cuban and some U.S. participants believed that U.S. aid to UNITA does not contribute to regional stability, nor to limiting South Africa's aggressiveness. Other U.S. participants believed that such aid may be right in itself, and is at least a likely outcome of domestic U.S. politics.

Seventh, economic motivations play a secondary role in the prospects for improvement in U.S.-Cuban relations. Political factors are paramount. There was agreement, however, that some private firms might foster those relations for nonideological reasons. According to both some U.S. and Cuban participants, the weight of these economic interests is not just secondary to political interests; the weight of economic interests is modest in itself. Other U.S. and Cuban participants argued that, although the U.S. economy as a whole would be little affected by improved economic relations with Cuba, certain firms or individuals could have substantial marginal gains, were bilateral relations to improve. Some Cuban participants noted that the subordination of economic to political issues need not mean that all political problems on the bilateral agenda would have to be solved before economic relations could develop, although they also believed that the latter would develop gradually and marginally for both sides.

Eighth, with regard to legal issues and to a framework for negotiation, there was a sense that international law could provide an appropriate way to resolve some bilateral disputes. However, the United States might not wish to address all issues in this way unless there were at the same time some *quid pro quo* on Cuba's part.

With regard to a process of negotiation, many thought that it would be advisable to begin with technical (and politically less complex) issues on the bilateral agenda in order to reach agreements that lead to early gains. Some U.S. and Cuban participants called for the possible inclusion on the agenda for bilateral negotiations, based on international law, of aspects of the question of sovereignty (e.g., U.S. intelligence flights over Cuba), the renunciation of the use of force, the formal ratification of the 1962 understandings, and the issue of human rights. This would be better, they argued, than to leave them on the political-ideological agenda. Among some U.S. participants there was doubt concerning whether a code of conduct based on international law could be agreed upon because such concepts as "international consensus" or "democracy"—which are often claimed by states as the basis for their policies—are not well defined, nor are their terms universally accepted.

Participants from both countries argued that the legitimacy of insurgent movements cannot be discussed only with reference to international law. The varying political cultures prevalent in the United States, Cuba, or other Third World countries often refuse to accept the right of certain governments to remain in power, or may, instead, legitimize the right of the political opposition to exist and, at times, to take up arms against such governments.

According to some Cuban participants, Cuba's policy finds its main legitimacy in the regional and international consensus and within the terms of international law. In this way, Cuba seeks to compensate for the asymmetry that it faces with regard to the United States. In this view, Cuba should not accept the consequences of geopolitical imbalance because doing so would result in involuntary and substantial reductions in the sovereign rights due Cuba under international law. From this perspective, it would be, in the long run, counterproductive for Cuba to bargain with the United States unless the United States were to accept the principles of reciprocity and equality under law in its relations with Cuba.

The Chapters

The chapters that follow are best read in pairs, for each pair focuses on the same set of questions, though often reaching different conclusions. Moreover, the chapters' authors often address and supplement each other's points. Because most of the chapters by Cuban authors were written after the first drafts of the chapters by U.S. authors, the logic of the texts has led us to put the chapters by U.S. authors first (the exception is the last pair, where Chapter 11 by a Cuban author develops the history, and chapter 12 by a U.S. author looks ahead). Nevertheless, the chapters by Cuban authors often include a more detailed and extensive discussion of the history of U.S.-Cuban relations than is found in the chapters by U.S. authors; readers who prefer to examine that historical record first should begin with the chapters by Cuban authors.

Jorge I. Domínguez and Rafael Hernández (Chapters 1 and 2) provide overviews of the relationship between the United States and Cuba during the past thirty years, and explore some of the larger themes that have marked them. They agree that the United States and Cuba differ for truly serious reasons—namely, each country's government rests on and embodies contrasting sets of interests and values. At times, each author addresses the reader in each country by asking for a difficult intellectual activity: to see the problem from the perspective of the adversary. The authors agree on the utility of fostering what Hernández has called a "dialogue regime" that would encompass norms, procedures, and commitments to consult before acting unilaterally, and both believe that such a regime can best be built by undertaking a series of more specific agreements. However, Domínguez, more than Hernández, may see more merit in the intrinsic worth of agreements about technical topics. The authors differ the most in that Hernández believes that the United States bears the major responsibility for the origins, content, and prospects of U.S.-Cuban conflicts, whereas Domínguez believes that the governments are co-responsible; Hernández also believes that Cuban foreign policy has been more successful at achieving its goals, whereas Domínguez doubts that either the U.S. or Cuban government policies toward each other could be described as truly successful.

Gregory F. Treverton and Carlos Alzugaray Treto (Chapters 3 and 4) focus on national security questions. Their chapters illustrate best how the substance of a dispute, more than the intellectual or theoretical framework of each author, is at the heart of the two authors' divergence. Both Treverton and Alzugaray think as strategists. Both understand well the relationship between symbols, politics, and the threat as well as the use of force. Both are recognizably "realist" and "rational" in their approach to the study of national security questions. However, one writes from the perspective of the United States, the other from the perspective of Cuba, and they differ precisely for these reasons: both the U.S. and Cuban governments believe that the other has posed and still poses a threat to its own security interests. These mutual threats are significant directly in U.S.-Cuban bilateral relations, as well as in the indirect effect that U.S. and Cuban security policies toward third countries have on bilateral U.S.-Cuban relations. The authors also explore the means that might lead to a containment of conflict, and possibly to the resolution of some disputes, but even their visions of a benign future for U.S.-Cuban relations have a pessimistic cast.

Michael Clough, Armando Entralgo, and David González López (Chapters 5 and 6) illustrate the possibility of convergence in both intellectual approaches and in the behavior of governments. As this book project unfolded, the U.S. and Cuban governments engaged each other in constructive negotiations that have led to an important multiparty settlement on several of southwestern Africa's problems. The authors agree that an important explanation of the settlement is that the United States and South Africa in the end changed their policies with regard to the conflicts in Angola and Namibia. However, Clough also believes that Angola and Cuba changed their policies toward the conflict in significant ways; Entralgo and González emphasize the continuity in Cuban policies. Clough also accords lesser weight than do Entralgo and González (and Hernández in Chapter 2) to the military battles in southern Angola in 1987 and 1988 as a means to explain the decisions to search for a negotiated solution to this conflict. The authors agree, however, that the willingness to think pragmatically and creatively, and to take some risks, were decisive factors in reaching a settlement. Clough hopes for further changes in other U.S. and Cuban policies toward Africa, while Entralgo and González emphasize that they consider Cuban policies toward Africa to have been and to remain appropriate.

Howard J. Wiarda and Juan Valdés Paz (Chapters 7 and 8) illustrate perhaps the widest divergences in the book. They agree (though for somewhat different reasons) that U.S. policy toward

Latin America had often been ineffective, but their agreement stops there. Wiarda argues that U.S. policy toward Latin America, and the process of making policy itself, have been changing and that, as result, U.S. policy effectiveness has increased somewhat. Wiarda finds Cuba, at the same time, wedded to a rigid interpretation of Marxism-Leninism, which helps to explain why it has become an increasingly marginal actor in Latin American affairs—a Cuba thirty years ago central to U.S.-Latin American relations, but now being left behind as the march of history unfolds in other communist countries and in a hemisphere headed toward more democratic regimes, pragmatic policies, and eventual economic prosperity. Valdés Paz, quite on the contrary, believes that Cuba's policy toward Latin America has been very successful. In his view, Cuba has situated its policy toward Latin America within a sensible overall foreign policy framework, and it has identified, supported, and advanced key aspirations of the Latin American peoples in the social, economic, and political spheres (including independence, security, national liberation, economic development, and political democracy, among others). Valdés Paz believes that U.S. policy toward Latin America in recent years has continued to fail because it has remained unable to address effectively these central concerns.

Kenneth P. Jameson, Alfonso Casanova Montero, and Pedro Monreal González (Chapters 9 and 10) agree that improved U.S.-Cuban political relations must precede any significant improvement of their economic relations. They also agree that important positive transformations have occurred in Cuba's economy during the past three decades. Their point of analytical departure, however, takes them to different conclusions concerning the prospects for U.S.-Cuban economic relations. Based in the United States, Jameson takes a macroeconomic perspective; as a result, he finds that Cuba's economic importance to the United States is likely to be quite small. Based in Cuba, Casanova and Monreal take a perspective closer to that which U.S. business firms with potential interest in activity in Cuba might have; as a result, they argue that the economic relationship is likely to be quite significant for Cuba and comparably so for many U.S. firms and consumers. Jameson finds Cuba's potential economic significance mainly in the wider context of the Caribbean's international political economy, whereas Casanova and Monreal have little doubt that the direct, bilateral U.S.-Cuban economic relationship can have great importance for both countries.

Miguel A. D'Estéfano Pisani and James P. Rowles (Chapters 11 and 12) illustrate the differing uses of international law while agreeing on its normative worth and empirical importance. The authors also agree on many questions of substance with regard to international law. D'Estéfano emphasizes the use of international law to provide a framework for understanding the pattern of U.S. aggression against Cuba over time, and thus the legitimacy of the substance and the means of Cuba's actions to defend itself. Once the framework is employed, he believes that it takes us inevitably to the appropriate conclusion: U.S. government policy and actions toward Cuba over time are guilty of serious violations of international law. In addition, however, D'Estéfano believes that international law may provide a useful basis to reach particular agreements in future U.S.-Cuban relations stemming from mutual respect under international law. Rowles focuses, in contrast, less on assigning guilt and more on the prospective uses of international law for the improvement of U.S.-Cuban relations. Rowles' interest is to identify both a conceptual approach and a practical means of implementing that approach, which would enable governments that have been adversaries—such as those of the United States and Cuba—to move toward a different relationship. Rowles shows how international law might serve as a common framework from which the two governments can reach substantive agreements. He goes on to sketch two strategic approaches, relying on international law in a narrow and in a broader sense, respectively, and the potential of each to open the path toward a future of U.S.-Cuban relations different from a past of mutual recrimination.

The authors of this book, as do many citizens of the United States and Cuba, differ in values, in experiences, in intellectual approaches, and in the substantive judgments that we reach. But we agree that the respectful, civil, and sustained engagement of our differences is the more appropriate basis for the construction of a better future for the two countries in which we live—as compared to the patterns of the past—as well as a more effective means to identify those issues on which agreement may be possible. That is the basis on which we have written this book.

1

The Obstacles and Prospects for Improved U.S.-Cuban Relations: A U.S. Perspective

Jorge I. Domínguez

Early in 1989, Fidel Castro marked his thirtieth year at the head of Cuba's government, and the United States inaugurated the eighth president to hold office since Cuban revolutionaries overthrew Fulgencio Batista's government.[1] For most of that time, the two governments have been enemies. From southern Africa to Central America, from the United Nations to strictly bilateral issues, by 1989 the United States and Cuba had confronted each other relentlessly for most of the lifetimes of the majority of their citizens. Although the specific issues that have divided these nations have changed over time, some central questions remain unchanged.[2]

This history provides little basis for illusions that the relations between governments professing values so different and pursuing interests so contradictory can suddenly, much less easily, improve. But the inauguration of a new U.S. president as Cuba begins to prepare for the Fourth Congress of the Communist party and for its five-year plan for the early 1990s may permit each government to change its policies toward the other. The goal: to design a relationship that serves their respective interests more effectively, precisely because it is less virulently hostile.

The chapters of this book explore several of the issues at stake between the two countries. This chapter focuses on the objective interests as well as the values in conflict, and on the legacy of mistrust between the governments. Then we examine some issues on which negotiations might be fruitful, and conclude with a speculative look at possible long-term results.

Interests and Values in Conflict

Cuba and the United States have shared a large part of their respective histories. The United States occupied Cuba from 1898 to 1902, and from 1906 to 1909. It held a formal "protectorate" over Cuba from 1902 to 1934, and landed troops in Cuba several times during those years. As one legacy, the United States continues to operate a military base at Guantánamo under a treaty that has no termination date. In addition, the U.S. government and U.S. private firms played a significant role in Cuba's domestic affairs until the break between the U.S. and Cuban governments between 1959 and 1961. Another legacy is that each country continues to weigh on, and at times obsess, the affairs of the other. As a practical matter, a tangle of economic and legal issues remain from the 1959-1961 dispute.

Cuba and the United States are neighbors in the Caribbean. Their policies on many issues thus necessarily affect each other. These policies include their responses to drug trafficking and hijacking of aircraft and boats, sharing information regarding the paths of Caribbean Sea hurricanes, and maritime pollution along the Straits of Florida, among other issues.

Geographic propinquity also means that each country's policies in preparation for war affect the other's national security. Cuba has been acutely conscious of the threat to its national security from U.S. military might, especially during the 1962 missile crisis—when the United States physically blockaded the island—and in 1965 and 1983, when the United States landed troops in the Dominican Republic and in Grenada, respectively, to counter what U.S. government officials perceived as a Cuban threat to its security and to that of its allies. In Grenada in 1983, U.S. and Cuban forces fought each other for a few hours. The frequent U.S. military maneuvers near or around Cuban water and air space, in southern Florida, and on Central America's mainland also remind Cuba of U.S. military might.

The United States has been conscious of direct threats to its security, most notably when the Soviet Union deployed ballistic missiles to Cuba in 1962. Had the U.S.S.R. not been forced—despite the Cuban government's opposition—to withdraw those missiles from Cuba, that country might have become a major Soviet base for nuclear war. The United States has remained concerned over the Soviet navy's relatively frequent use of Cuban ports, worrying especially over the possible use of Cuba by Soviet submarines carrying nuclear weapons.

The United States has also objected to the U.S.S.R.'s use of Cuban territory to gather intelligence about the United States. Cuba provides facilities to Soviet intelligence surveillance BEAR aircraft that spy over the eastern United States, and it allows the Soviets to operate the sophisticated electronic intelligence facility in Lourdes, Cuba.

Since the 1970s, the U.S. government has worried over Cuba's acquisition of submarines and advanced fighter-aircraft that may impede the U.S. capacity to resupply its forces and those of its allies in the event of a general conventional war in Europe. Were Cuba to enter such a war on the side of the Warsaw Pact, of which Cuba is not a member, the United States would have to redeploy some of its forces to take Cuban forces out of combat.

These security issues have surfaced from time to time in U.S.-Cuban relations, most recently in the 1988 U.S. presidential campaign, when Republican presidential candidate Marion ("Pat") Robertson charged that there were Soviet ballistic missiles in Cuba (a charge denied by both the U.S. and Cuban governments).

The United States has objected to the extension of Soviet influence, directly or through Cuba, to the Americas, and also to Soviet-Cuban military collaboration in Africa. A broad political consensus in the United States holds that such Soviet influence is contrary to U.S. interests.

Cuba, of course, considers its relations with the U.S.S.R. to be a guarantee of its own national security in the face of U.S. hostility. And Cuba affirms its sovereign right to choose its allies and friends, and to deal with them as it sees fit.

Most people who call themselves Cubans live in cities in Cuba or the United States. Metropolitan Miami is the world's second largest city housing Cubans. A significant Cuban migration has led to Florida since the nineteenth century (the Cuban-origin community in Tampa is one example). A large, recent emigration has occurred in successive waves that began in 1960 in response to the Castro government's policies.

In the 1980s, Cuba and the United States have been publicly committed to supporting insurgencies against incumbent governments. Cuba has actively supported the POLISARIO insurgency against Morocco in the former Spanish Sahara, the SWAPO insurgency against South African rule over Namibia, the PLO's war against Israel, and the FMLN insurgency in El Salvador. The United States has actively supported the overthrow of incumbent governments in Nicaragua, Angola, Ethiopia, and Afghanistan.

In the past, the U.S. and Cuban governments have used force against each other. In the 1960s, the U.S. government sought Fidel Castro's assassination and, in 1961, it sponsored an unsuccessful invasion of Cuba by Cuban exiles. Cuba has supported Puerto Rico's independence from the United States, in the 1960s giving material aid to armed actions by Puerto Rican revolutionaries.

For years, the United States sought to overthrow the Cuban government. Although military means to do so are no longer used, the United States remains opposed to Communist party rule over Cuba, and to the expansion of Cuba's influence in the world. Many in the United States believe that it is still a legitimate U.S. policy objective to seek to change by peaceful means the nature of the political regime in Cuba. In the U.S. government's judgment, Cuba has sought to overthrow governments friendly to the United States, even liberal democratic regimes such as Venezuela's in the 1960s. In addition, the United States believes that Cuba has sought to exploit existing differences between the United States and many Third World countries.

Cuba, in turn, believes that it is right and prudent to fight against the U.S. government everywhere because the United States is the leading imperialist power, and because the U.S. government fights the Cuban government everywhere. Cuban leaders believe that U.S. power is intrinsically global and aggressive, and that the United States has no right to attempt to change Cuba's political regime by any means. Cuba's security requires a global response to this global challenge. It is right, they believe, for revolutionaries to be internationalists as they discharge their duty to make the revolution and to fight imperialism.

Cuba and the United States are significant actors on the world stage, although not to the same degree. The key change has occurred with regard to Cuba's endeavors beyond its borders. Cuban civilian and military personnel work in three dozen countries in the Third World at the invitation of those governments. Thousands of Cubans also study or are "guest workers" in the Soviet Union and in eastern European countries. Cuban troops have been posted in Angola since 1975, numbering over 30,000 per year during the 1980s and reaching over 50,000 in 1988. Cuba helps Angola's government in its war against the UNITA insurgency, which has been actively supported by the South African armed forces. Relative to Cuba's population, its troop deployment to Angola has been larger and has lasted longer than that of the United States to Vietnam at the peak of that war. (There are, of course, other important differences between the U.S.

engagement in Vietnam and that of Cuba in Angola.) Smaller contingents of Cuban troops and military advisers serve in countries as diverse as Nicaragua, South Yemen, and the Congo. Above all, the United States objects to Cuba's placement of troops to serve at the cutting edge of Soviet foreign policy goals, even if the decision to do so was made entirely by Cuban leaders.

U.S. and Cuban leaders also have profoundly different ideas about the nature of the good society, the organization of the economy, and the structuring of politics. Each set of leaders believes that the arrangements over which they preside are just and appropriate for their people. Each also believes that the arrangements in the other country are unjust and damnable.

A very broad spectrum of U.S. opinion holds that Cuba is governed by a dictatorship that does not permit the free exercise of political opposition, a right guaranteed to everyone under the United Nations Charter, which Cuba is pledged to honor. In practice, critics of the Cuban government and the Communist party have no access to the press, radio, or television; they cannot organize formally to contest elections and are, in effect, denied their electoral rights and excluded from the National Assembly. The state's security organs, in fact, can use their powers arbitrarily. At times, even very modest organized opposition activities in defense of human rights are repressed. The representation of labor rights independent of party and state organs has also been denied. The only criticism at times evident in the Cuban mass media is that authorized from on high; those who are criticized, in turn, are often stripped of effective rights to defend themselves.

The official media organs, along with the publishers and sponsors of works of scholarship and of the arts and letters, have a narrow conception of the utility of the world of knowledge and the imagination, and a fear of ideas beyond their control. Their use of censorship and their fostering of self-censorship has hurt Cuba's intellectual life. Cuba's official newspaper, *Granma*, is a daily insult to the human thirst for unfettered information and lively reading.

Thirty years after revolutionary victory, political prisoners are still held in Cuba. Even today, the treatment of many of these prisoners is inhuman and contrary to internationally accepted standards.[3]

Although many in the United States recognize as well the significant strides that Cuba has made in education, the provision of public health, reducing inequalities, and sharply curtailing the experience of poverty, the concern for the liberal democratic values at the heart of U.S. political beliefs remains a matter of enduring and serious difference between the United States and Cuba.

Many Cubans believe, as certainly their government and party do, that the organization of society in the United States is unjust; that a formal commitment to equality of opportunity is negated by profound inequalities of result; that racial discrimination remains a national blight in the United States; and that a commitment to the procedures of liberal democracy blinds many U.S. citizens to the disproportionate power that elites have over the country's economy, politics, and society. Cuban leaders argue that, in contrast, theirs is an effective democracy, one committed to the practical empowering of ordinary citizens in concrete situations that directly affect their lives. They are proud of Cuba's accomplishments in health and education, and in giving access to such services to all, regardless of income. They argue that Cuba has a regime where the weight of social-class origins is lessened as an obstacle to the full development of human potential within the framework of the revolution. Within that framework, they argue, Cuban government support for science and scholarship, and for the arts and letters, is unprecedented in Cuban history, bringing many people into contact with the world of research, ideas, and the imagination.

Many Cubans also believe, as certainly do their government and party, that the values motivating Cubans are nobler than those that prevail in the United States. Although many Cubans are motivated by a desire for material comforts, many are also motivated to work for their homeland, the revolution, and the improvement of the life chances of the children of today's Cubans and those of citizens far beyond its shores.

Because of the depth and the diverse nature of these cleavages, U.S.-Cuban relations in the 1990s are likely to remain poor. Neither government should expect the other one to ignore or to sacrifice the serious differences in interests and in principles between the two countries. To note that Cuba and the United States are likely to remain adversaries, however, does not mean that they must be so in the same way as during the previous thirty years. But before changes might occur, we need to examine the legacy of mistrust.

The Legacy of Mistrust

The U.S. and Cuban governments do not trust each other—nor should they, considering the issues and the history summarized above. There are, however, some more specific obstacles to their willingness to negotiate. In both countries, these obstacles arise in part from the past experience with efforts to improve U.S.-Cuban relations.

On the U.S. side, four bases support the charge that the Cuban government is untrustworthy in negotiations. The first refers to the attitude of Cuban leaders—especially President Fidel Castro—toward the United States. In the judgment of many U.S. citizens, no other political leadership in the world is as hostile as Cuba's is to the United States.[4] Evidence of the especially aggressive nature of Cuba's policy toward the United States: Cuba's decision in 1980 to send thousands of common criminals from its prisons through Mariel Harbor to the United States. Beyond this gut hostility, many in the United States believe that Cuban influence in the world rests heavily on its being the premier standard-bearer of anti-imperialism; reconciliation with the United States would weaken Cuba's international appeal. As a result, not even pragmatic Cuban leaders would retreat from strongly anti-U.S. policies.

Second, many in the United States doubt that Cuba would ever suspend its claim to the right to support revolutionary movements seeking to overthrow certain governments, especially U.S. allies in the Third World. On these first two grounds, there is much skepticism that Cuba would accommodate serious U.S. policy concerns.

Third, Cuba is deemed to be untrustworthy even in the midst of a negotiation. Examples are the policies it followed during the two main prior efforts at improving U.S.-Cuban relations during the Ford and Carter administrations. Cuba committed 36,000 troops to Angola in 1975-1976, despite the secret talks that had been under way between the United States and Cuba since November 1974 to improve their relations. Cuba's Angola decision aborted the effort to improve U.S.-Cuban relations, and it indicated that the Cuban government accorded a much lower priority to their improvement than U.S. officials had thought. Cuba deployed troops when U.S. foreign policy seemed "weak" in the immediate aftermath of the fall of Saigon.

Similarly, in late 1977 Cuba committed troops to Ethiopia in the Horn of Africa war against Somalia. That decision lends itself to a similar interpretation: Cuba accorded low priority to its improvement of U.S. relations. In both cases, Cuba made a clear choice: Improving relations with the United States mattered less than its pursuit of other foreign-policy goals.

There is a fourth, more specific reason to doubt the Cuban government's trustworthiness in negotiations. Cuba has terminated three important bilateral agreements with the United States. In 1976, Cuba gave notice that it was terminating the formal agreement reached three years earlier with the United States with respect to hijacking. In 1982, Cuba terminated formal collaboration (begun in 1978) between the U.S. and Cuban coast guards on search-and-rescue missions and drug interdiction. In May 1985, Cuba suspended the migration agreement that it had signed the previous December. In both 1976 and 1985, Cuba based its decision on factors outside the framework of the agreement being terminated. In 1976, termination came in response to Cuba's unproven allegation that the United States was involved in the sabotage that blew up a Cuban civilian airplane over Barbados. In 1985, it was in response to the first broadcasts of the Radio Martí Program of the U.S. Voice of America. (Cuba's 1982 decision was partly related to the agreement being ended: a Miami grand jury had indicted several Cuban officials for collaborating with drug traffickers). From the U.S. government perspective, the Cuban government cannot be relied upon for long to honor obligations it may at a given moment incur with regard to the United States.

On the Cuban side, four bases uphold the charge that the U.S. government is untrustworthy. The first and most important is that the U.S. government does not recognize Cuba as its sovereign equal. Therefore, the United States demands that Cuba accede to restraints that the United States is unwilling to impose on itself. For example, the U.S. outrage over Cuba's commitment of troops to the Angolan war in 1975 hid the fact that the United States had also been intervening in that war, backing forces that undermined the Alvor agreement (which sought a negotiated solution among the contending Angolan forces in anticipation of the November 1975 independence from Portugal). The United States sought to keep Cuba, but not itself, out of Angola. A similar situation occurred during the Horn of Africa war. The United States—just as did Cuba—claimed to oppose Somalia's irredentist ambitions with regard to Ethiopia's Ogaden region. But the United States did little to stop Somalia. Had Cuba not sent troops, the policy goal—to maintain Africa's boundaries—that the United States claimed to support would have been defeated. The U.S. government was simply unwilling to see its Cuban and Soviet adversaries gain in war and politics.

A second charge is that U.S. policy is too often internally inconsistent. For example, the Carter administration warned Cuba in November 1977 not to send troops to Ethiopia, and it reacted strongly to Cuba's ultimate intervention. Nonetheless, in mid-January 1978, at the peak of Cuba's troop deployment to Ethiopia, the U.S. and Cuban coast guards reached a cooperative agreement. And, later in 1978, the two governments agreed to allow former political prisoners to depart from Cuba for the United States. However much some U.S. officials may have tried to communicate to Cuba that the fate of bilateral relations hung on the Ethiopian decision, Havana did not hear it that way. After all, bilateral relations had improved again in 1977, even though Cuban troops had been dispatched to Angola in 1975 and still remained there. In retrospect, the Horn of Africa war proved to be a turning point in U.S.-Cuban relations, but it did not feel that way at the time to the Cuban government.

A third charge is that the United States is too unpredictable with regard to Cuba. In May 1978, Shaba exiles invaded Zaire from bases in Angola. President Carter blamed Cuba (with some, though not much, justification). However, in his anger, he did not accept Cuba's offer to join with the United States in defusing the crisis. In August 1979, the U.S. government discovered the presence of Soviet military personnel organized as a brigade in Cuba. At issue was a longstanding U.S. intelligence failure to keep track of Soviet military personnel left in Cuba since the 1962 missile crisis. The U.S. government accused the U.S.S.R. and Cuba of violating the security understandings first reached in 1962. The main casualty was the U.S. Senate's refusal to ratify the SALT II treaty. More generally, U.S. policy toward Cuba is often subject to the unpredictable vagaries of domestic politics in the United States, especially at election time.

The final charge is that the U.S. government is hypocritical, tearing its vestments over Cuban support for some insurgencies, while the Reagan administration supported other insurgencies. The U.S. government accuses Cuba of dealing with protectors of drug traders like Panama's General Manuel Antonio Noriega, while U.S. government agencies have long dealt with, and funded, the same individual. The gap between U.S. government rhetoric and behavior is at times so wide that foreign governments have difficulty grasping what is the "real" policy of the United States.

In sum, many U.S. citizens believe that an improvement in U.S.-Cuban relations would be bad for the United States because the Cuban government would take advantage of the U.S. "lowering of the guard," and would eventually betray U.S. trust. Many in Cuba believe that an improvement in U.S.-Cuban relations would be bad for Cuba, especially for the maintenance of the political and social values that the revolution has sought to foster.

In my judgment, these contending charges are in many respects correct, and must give pause to those who wish to improve U.S.-Cuban relations. No U.S. government has in fact considered the Cuban government as its sovereign equal: the United States insists on getting Cuban troops out of Angola, but would not even consider discussing with Cuba a withdrawal of U.S. forces from Korea or Germany. U.S. policy is also often inconsistent, unpredictable, and hypocritical. Moreover, the Cuban government has not restrained its international behavior on issues that the United States deems very important. Cuba was particularly militant during the Carter administration—the U.S. president who most attempted to change U.S. policy toward Cuba—by sending troops to the Horn of Africa and common criminals into U.S. cities, and by reactivating support for Central American insurgencies. Cuba has displayed a visceral hostility toward the United States. Cuba erred in terminating the hijacking, coast guard, and migration agreements.

Policies for the 1990s

In a broad strategic sense, U.S. policies toward Cuba have failed. Punitive U.S. policies toward Cuba have not deterred the Cuban behavior to which the United States has objected, and have often rallied Cubans to support their government. Punitive U.S. policies have justified the Cuban government's call on its citizens to struggle to defend the homeland, and on the Soviet Union to defend its ally. Cuba's policies have changed on many specific questions over the years, but those changes can rarely be explained in terms of U.S. influence over Cuba. For example, unrelated to U.S. policies, Cuba has stopped support for some insurgencies in other countries, typically as a result of negotiations with the governments of such countries. Past U.S. punitive policies toward Cuba have not brought down its government nor changed those Cuban policies to which the United States has most objected. Periodic U.S. efforts to punish other countries for their economic relations with Cuba have usually created more burdens than benefits for U.S. policy.

The Reagan administration put to the test whether punitive U.S. policies would change Cuba's behavior. The record shows the failure of that approach and the possible benefits of its alternative. The Reagan administration's initial unwillingness to negotiate with Cuba over migration did not force Cuba to accept those who had entered the United States from Mariel Harbor in 1980 but were unacceptable under U.S. immigration laws; that became possible only when the U.S. government agreed to negotiate with Cuba and to respect its government's interests. In Nicaragua, U.S. policy was in a shambles at the end of the Reagan administration, with Managua's government close to a military victory over the Nicaraguan Resistance; the Reagan administration's reluctance to negotiate with the Nicaraguan government (or with Cuba over Central America) had as its main effect that Nicaragua had not agreed formally to any restraints on its external behavior.

In southern Africa, the Reagan administration at first sought to force the departure of Cuban troops from Angola and, later on, it provided financial support for the UNITA insurgency fighting against the Angolan government. Such U.S. policies could not prevent a major Cuban troop deployment to Angola in late 1987—a deployment to Angola under the Reagan administration as large as that undertaken by Cuba to Ethiopia under the Carter administration. Thanks to that deployment, Cuba defeated South African and UNITA forces in the long battle for Cuito Cuanavale in 1987-1988 and Cuba forced South African troops to withdraw from southern Angola.[5] The prospects for Cuban troop withdrawals from Angola improved only after the United States agreed to direct Cuban participation in negotiations over southern Africa, and only after South Africa suffered these serious military setbacks in southern Angola.

In a similar broad strategic sense, Cuban policies toward the United States have not succeeded enough. To be sure, Cuba's regime has been consolidated and it has projected its power overseas. But the costs at home of relentlessly hostile U.S.-Cuban relations have been very high. Cuba's economy remains underdeveloped, its people still lead an austere life, its society is routinely disrupted by military preparedness, and its young men have died in wars overseas. Cuba depends enormously on the Soviet Union and other eastern European countries. Less hostile relations with the United States would open the prospects for a peace and prosperity not known by a large majority of Cuban citizens. Cuba would also have more diversified international relations while remaining faithful to its socialist partners, who are also improving their relations with the United States.

A strategy to improve U.S.-Cuban relations must begin by understanding the legacy of mistrust. It rests on conflicts of interests and of values between the United States and Cuba, and on widely divergent perceptions of each country's place in the world.

Such a strategy must seek to reduce aspects of this mistrust and must search for partial convergences in each government's understanding of its interests, or at least for mutually beneficial bargains. In that way, a process of mutual accommodation would rest on mutual learning about mutual gains. The two governments need to adopt policies to strengthen their respective credibility. They can begin by reaching agreement on discrete issues that can be implemented readily and monitored easily. In all of these instances, mutual interests are served. The following are some examples.

In late 1987, Cuba reinstated the migration agreement first signed three years earlier, and both governments began to implement it. In early 1988, the United States modified its visa policy and began to allow visits to the United States by some Cuban scholars and officials. The restrictive U.S. visa policy had been justified in part as retaliation for Cuba's earlier suspension of the migration agreement. Various scientific, educational, and technical agreements could be reached to facilitate access by scientists, other scholars, and some students to the respective countries, building on existing interest in both countries. More complex might be to collaborate to contain the pollution of the Florida Straits, protect migratory animals, improve technical exchanges between weather bureaus, and so on.

The United States can also reinstate the fishing accord (signed in 1977), which it allowed to lapse in 1982, while Cuba can reinstate the hijacking agreement. Although in 1976 Cuba formally terminated the bilateral agreement on hijacking, it has behaved as if the agreement were in force. The agreement's reinstatement would publicize Cuba's anti-hijacking policies, thereby deterring hijackings.

For the United States, three safeguards would also be needed. First, there should be less expectation than in 1977 that these small steps would have more comprehensive results. Ultimately, they may, and it is reasonable to aim that they should. But the sum of the small steps will not automatically solve more complex problems that require attention on their own. Second, credible demonstrations of continuing U.S. support should be made to those governments friendly to the United States (especially in Africa, Central America, and the Caribbean) that continue to distrust the Cuban government. This support could dissipate the belief among such U.S. allies that they cannot trust U.S. policy. Third, ongoing monitoring of Cuba through technical means (satellites, signals intelligence, and aircraft surveillance around and over the island) should continue at a level no lower than prevailed in the 1980s.

Cuba as a sovereign government will continue to protest about these violations of its air space, but Cuba cannot prevent the U.S. use of such means. As a practical matter, such U.S. surveillance of Cuba is Cuba's price to be paid for benefits it might receive from a changed U.S. policy. Moreover, such surveillance has a value to Cuba as well, publicly recognized by the December 1984 Communist party Central Committee Plenum. The Plenum asserted that Cuba's national security required that "Pentagon and CIA strategists should know that we are strong in every respect" because such knowledge would deter a U.S. attack on Cuba.[6] A procedure that might be acceptable to both sides is for Cuba to accept U.S. aircraft surveillance over the island in exchange for U.S. adoption of some confidence-building measures derived from the U.S.-Soviet experience in Europe: advance notification to Cuba of U.S. maneuvers in the region, invitation to some Cuban officers to observe some U.S. maneuvers, and so on.

The steps sketched above are only a beginning. Subsequent chapters of this book explore the particulars of other important issues. Here we turn to explore some general concerns that span issues and regions.

For the United States to accomplish a more ambitious policy agenda in its relations with Cuba and with Third World countries close to Cuba, it must accept and accord respect to the regime that has governed Cuba for three decades and to many aspects of its foreign policy. For the Cuban government, such a change in U.S. policy would constitute a considerable victory. For many U.S. observers, of course, any U.S. "acceptance" of Castro's government is offensive. Therefore, it is worth spelling out the scope and limits of such acceptance.

The United States would need to accept that the overthrow of Cuba's government is unlikely; that Cuba's relations with the Soviet Union—within the framework of the evolving security understandings first reached in the settlement of the 1962 missile crisis—are a privileged basis for Cuba's domestic and foreign policies; and that Cuba's right to deploy *civilian* personnel to many countries in search of influence, and occasionally of hard currency, is not necessarily at odds with vital U.S. interests. Such acceptance may be less costly than might at first appear because the United States has been trying unsuccessfully for thirty years to overturn these circumstances. Such acceptance would not commit the United States to agree to the worth of the values embodied in

Cuba's institutions and policies; the United States would continue to criticize Cuba's domestic affairs.

For U.S. policy toward Cuba to change fundamentally, in practice Cuba would need to forego new troop deployments to other countries, end existing troop deployments, and forego providing material support for insurgencies. Cuba would remain free to sharply criticize the United States and its allies and to affirm its general solidarity with insurgencies, short of material support.

The change of both countries' policies would be enhanced if they were to undertake bilateral discussions on security issues to clarify their respective interpretations of the understandings (begun in 1962 and amended over time) reached between the United States and the Soviet Union over the Soviet-Cuban military relationship. Such talks might also explore means to prevent the accidental outbreak of military conflicts between the United States and Cuba, exchange information on nuclear power plant developments of mutual interest, and provide timely communication and reassurance as both the United States and Cuba modernize their future defense postures with regard to each other.

What might be, then, the bases for U.S.-Cuban negotiated agreements on some specific issues? Let us consider three examples. The first (southern Africa) illustrates how both governments may take advantage of a partial convergence of their interests. The second (Central America) illustrates how both governments might bargain despite opposing interests. The third illustrates how values both governments claim to uphold (with regard to drug trafficking) may overcome the pull of other interests.

In southern Africa, a partial convergence of some U.S. and Cuban interests occurs. For years, Cuban troops have protected U.S. oil companies operating in Angola (especially in Cabinda). More importantly, between July and December 1988—thanks to U.S. mediation—Angola, Cuba, and South Africa agreed that Namibia would be independent from South Africa; they further agreed to "the staged and total withdrawal of Cuban troops" from Angola by mid-1991 in the expectation that Namibia will become independent before then and that all South African forces will withdraw from and remain out of Angola and Namibia. They also agreed to stop providing military support to insurgencies (UNITA and the African National Congress) committed to the overthrow of one or another of the signatory governments, and to observe "non-interference in the internal affairs of states."[7]

To provide incentives for Cuba and Angola to complete the withdrawal of all Cuban troops, the U.S. government should stop overt and covert military assistance to UNITA guerrillas fighting against the Angolan government. Even though the United States is not required to do so by the agreements that it brokered, such a decision would be consistent with them. U.S. support for UNITA had been prohibited by U.S. law from 1976 to 1985. In addition, the U.S. government would need to accept an appropriate, limited presence of Cuban civilian personnel in Angola.

For Cuba, these policies would secure Namibian independence, effect South Africa's withdrawal from Angola, and help to consolidate its Angolan ally. By its stated rationale to deploy troops to Angola, Cuba's mission would have been accomplished. Cuban civilian cooperation personnel would remain in Angola to advance Cuba's political and economic interests. This outcome would end Cuba's casualties from war.

For the United States, these policies would also secure Namibian independence, and would end the major remaining Cuban troop deployment in Africa (Cuban troop presence in Ethiopia was reduced earlier in the 1980s by Ethiopian and Cuban accord). In the longer run, the United States may greatly improve its relations with African countries, especially with Angola, whose trade has continued to depend mainly on non-communist countries and whose government shows evidence of seeking to broaden its ties with the West.

In Central America, little convergence exists between U.S. and Cuban interests. No bargain would be possible were the U.S. government to remain committed to overthrowing Nicaragua's government, and Cuba to supporting those seeking to overthrow the governments of El Salvador and Guatemala. Yet the key security provisions of the various proposals for a negotiated settlement in Central America are the same: All governments must stop material assistance to insurgencies, and all governments must engage in discussions with the opposition. U.S. and Cuban agreement to move away from their competing insurgency-supporting policies of the 1980s would require each to give up something of considerable value to the other and, as a result, make a bargain possible. Each side would gain something short of its maximum goals. Each of the diverse regimes that rule Nicaragua, El Salvador, and Guatemala would also move closer to consolidation.

With regard to narcotics, the U.S. and Cuban governments are firmly on record against the individual consumption of drugs; their laws and practices severely punish drug traffickers that are caught. From 1978 to 1982, both governments collaborated in drug interdiction by sea and air. Yet both governments have had close relations with persons known to profit from the drug trade, the most notable being Panama's General Manuel Antonio Noriega. Each government's interest in dealing with Noriega was the same: He provided intelligence and the use of some Panamanian facilities to both the United States and Cuba. Each government overlooked Noriega's involvement in drugs.

Apart from particular cases, neither government can justify to its people—or to the values it claims to uphold—a continuing relationship with persons who have a diversified international illegal portfolio: They traffic in weapons, information, drugs, and so forth, although each has justified temporary tactical relations with such persons. U.S.-Cuban relations would improve, and the values in which both governments claim to believe would be fostered, were the United States and Cuba to agree to restore the 1978 coast guard interdiction agreement and to sever ties with those in the international narcotics business.

These policies would facilitate the removal of the remaining legal and economic U.S. sanctions on Cuba that are explored in other chapters of this book, including the U.S. embargo. As a tactic, these U.S. policies can be dismantled gradually to reward Cuban behavior that the U.S. government finds constructive. That action would at last draw some practical use out of a policy legacy that otherwise outlived its usefulness long ago, as indicated at the beginning of this section.

The dismantling of U.S. policies of economic denial toward Cuba might also unlock the gridlock of mutual claims for compensation for past economic injuries. The United States demands compensation for the property Cuba seized from U.S. citizens and firms. Cuba demands compensation for the costs of past U.S. policies. A rational resolution of these competing claims is possible only in a climate of greater trust and shared policy gains. It is unlikely, however, that any U.S. government would settle the contradictory compensation claims unless a net transfer of funds occurs from Cuba to the United States. So, too, would a longer-run agenda enable a reopening of discussions over the status of the Guantánamo naval base in order to formulate the additional military safeguards that the United States would expect from Cuba and the Soviet Union, were the Guantánamo base to be returned to Cuba.

In sum, the content and style of U.S.-Cuban relations can change. Both governments can achieve jointly some policy objectives, ranging from southern Africa to Central America to specific bilateral concerns. Yet they would still compete for influence, and their values would still greatly differ. But the chances of military conflict directly or in third countries would recede greatly.

Concluding Speculations

The United States is likely to find it difficult at first to live in peace with a government so near and so different as that of Cuba, even if one assumes that Cuba becomes less hostile. The United States has never lived in peace with such a government. U.S. adversaries have either been distant or, as in Cuba's case, have never been accepted as legitimate sovereign interlocutors. In addition, less hostile relations with Cuba would signal acceptance of a communist regime in the Americas as well as the fact of—though not the approval for—a significant Soviet role in this hemisphere. Many U.S. citizens would bitterly oppose such accommodation. It offends their values and, in their view, it threatens U.S. interests. They believe that the United States should never agree to conciliate regimes such as Cuba's.

The end of a history of bitter conflict might embolden revolutionaries elsewhere to attempt to replicate Cuba's experience, not because they are the creatures of Cuban power but because they would come to believe that the Cuban experience proves that revolutionaries prevail in the end. This outcome would fortify their Marxist beliefs that the march of history is on their side and would justify their Leninist commitments to give that history a helping hand. From the perspective of these revolutionaries, the foreign-policy constraints by which Cuba would need to abide are minor compared to the affirmation of Cuban sovereignty, the projection of its image worldwide, and the transformation of Cuba's domestic life.

Cuba is also likely to find it difficult at first to live in peace with the United States, even if one assumes that the United States becomes less hostile. Revolutionary Cuba has never made that assumption. The existence of the enemy just beyond the horizon has required and justified the buildup of its armed forces, given Cuban leaders credibility as they exhort citizens to sacrifice, and forged a national identity in combat with that enemy. There would be much less need for a large Cuban military establishment, or even for drafting so many youngsters into military service.

There would also be much less need for mass mobilization and less acceptance of economic hardship and scarcity. Cuban troops abroad would return home. With real enemies, Cubans overseas have been capable of heroic deeds on several of the world's battlefields. Those same Cubans at home have been much less heroic in the daily routine of production and productivity—the unexciting tasks of peace.

Cuba's past response to political relaxation has created problems for its leaders. The influx of 100,000 visiting Cuban-Americans in 1979 generated discontent with conditions inside Cuba. It turned out that those exiles (long-called "worms") seemed to have enjoyed more prosperity than those who remained in Cuba. The belief that gold grew on the streets of Miami fostered the discontent that led to the 1980 rush into the Peruvian embassy and the emigration through Mariel. Cuba's response to economic prosperity has also been problematic. In each of the three world sugar price booms since the early 1960s, Cuba has mishandled its economic policies, over-imported, and generated the foundations of a subsequent economic crisis.

In short, Cuba has at times been very resourceful and successful in moments of combat and scarcity. Can the Cuban revolution survive peace and prosperity? Will Cuba become just one more island in the sun once its overseas troops are back home, and once it no longer backs insurgencies militarily? Can Cuba survive the flow of ideas, intellectual as well as consumerist? Can it make do without the powerful motivation of U.S. hostility? In the mid-1980s a specter haunted Cuban leaders: that their people were secret capitalists. Will a Cuba at peace in the 1990s be haunted by a new specter—that Cubans stop being revolutionaries, and that the rest of the world will come to consider Cuba boring? If so, the Cuban revolution's foreign-policy victories might spell a historic defeat.

Each country's leaders can find reasons not to change policy, but their countries have much to gain by building a common future in peace. They can reduce the likelihood that Cuban and U.S. citizens will die in combat; they can accomplish shared, or at least not incompatible, objectives; and they can take practical steps to serve their peoples more effectively.

Notes

1. I am grateful to the participants in this project, and to Abraham Lowenthal, Marifeli Pérez-Stable, Robert Pastor, and Mao Xianglin for comments on earlier drafts. The first version of this chapter was presented in Havana at an authors' workshop for the project on "U.S.-Cuban Relations in the 1990s," funded by the Heinz Endowment and co-sponsored by Harvard University's Center for International Affairs and Cuba's Centro de Estudios sobre América. Funding for my other research on Cuba has come from the Ford Foundation. These views are solely my own.

2. For elaboration and documentation, see my *To Make a World Safe for Revolution: Cuba's Foreign Policy* (Cambridge: Harvard University Press, 1989).

3. Institute for Policy Studies, "Preliminary Report of U.S. Delegation to Cuba," March 1988.

4. For example, speech (May 1988) by the U.S. Department of State's Coordinator for Cuban Affairs, Kenneth Skoug, "Cuba: 'Our Last Adversary'," in U.S. Department of State, Bureau of Public Affairs, *Current Policy*, no. 1085 (1988).

5. Military analysis in *New York Times*, August 24, 1988, p. A10.

6. *Granma*, February 4, 1985, p. 2.

7. U.S. Department of State, Bureau of Public Affairs, "Principles for a Peaceful Settlement in Southwestern Africa," *Selected Documents*, no. 31 (July 20, 1988); *New York Times*, December 18, 1988, p. IV-3; *Granma Weekly Review*, December 18, 1988, pp. 1, 3-4.

2

Cuba and the United States: Political Values and Interests in a Changing International System

Rafael Hernández

Ninety years ago, Captain Alfred T. Mahan stated certain concepts with a clarity and precision that would make today's strategists pale:

> Between nations long alien we have high warrant for saying that interest alone determines action. . . . The United States are just about to enter on a task of government—of administration—over regions which, in inhabitants, in climate, and in political tradition, differ essentially from themselves. . . . And it is our interest to do so. Enlightened self-interest. . . . [O]ur new possessions, with their yet minor races, are the objects only of solicitude. . . . The inhabitants may not return love for their benefits—comprehension or gratitude may fail them; but the sense of duty achieved, and the security of the tenure, are the reward of the ruler.[1]

Exactly ten years before Mahan wrote those words, José Martí said:

> . . . There is in America a nation that, due to geographic morality, has proclaimed its right to crown itself ruler of the continent and has announced . . . that it is entitled to all of North America and that its imperial right should be acknowledged south from the isthmus. . . . It is stated as a prevailing and tactical concern . . . that nobody regards as immoral, nor as armed robbery . . . . Why then invoke, to extend its domination over America, the Monroe or Canning doctrine, to

> prevent foreign domination in America and ensure a
> continent's freedom? Or is the dogma to be invoked
> against one foreigner to attract another? Is the
> foreigner—with its foreign character, foreign
> interests, foreign objectives—to be eliminated in the
> name of liberty, of this same liberty eliminated *de
> facto*—or because the foreigner also brings the
> poison of loans, of the canals, of the railways?[2]

Mahan's lucid speech underlines that when dealing with countries with values different from those of the United States, the United States should be guided only by its own interests. Bearing in mind that although these backward nations (described with exaggeration as minor races) are not capable of adequately carrying out their role as objects of domination, the United States should be enlightened enough to implement its new imperative. To do so, it must base its policy not on the consensus of the dominated, but on guaranteeing the possession of its new dependencies in which its security resides. This not only constitutes a duty fulfilled, but also the reward of its dominating power.

Martí's approach is just as revealing. Translated into today's less expressive language, Martí asserted that there is a moral and political duality in the geopolitical vision (the Monroe doctrine) by which the United States will preserve the freedom of Latin America against extra-hemispheric powers at the price of asserting its exclusive rights over the region. The values and interests of the United States are as distant from those of Latin America as they are from the European powers. It is senseless for Latin American countries to back a U.S. custom-made freedom foreign to their nature and interests under the pretext of technical progress and the credits that will flow from the North.

Besides the intellectual merits of both texts, they are exemplary, for they represent two paradigms as well as an agenda of problems. Furthermore, their weight on the respective national traditions justifies their being taken as starting points for a wider analysis. We now discuss—without being all-inclusive nor repeating what is said in other chapters of this book—some issues directly linked to the question of values and interests that underlie the conflict between Cuba and the United States, characterizing both approaches. We then consider the limitations that these same values and interests impose on the prospects for change.

Some Clues to Cuban Foreign Policy

Cuba has a political process defined by its own values and interests and corresponding to its history and political system, which converge with those of other nations within the international system. In contrast to its economic power and physical size, Cuba has one of the most global and comprehensive foreign policies of Latin America, formulated in doctrinal terms and actively implemented at diplomatic, strategic, and economic levels.

The most complex feature of Cuba's foreign relations is its policy toward the Third World. Taking into account its condition as both a socialist and underdeveloped country, it is obvious that Cuba's alliances with some Third World countries are not based exclusively on ideological affinities. A very notable example is that most Latin American countries, despite very clear ideological differences with Cuba, have interests that have led them to carry out concerted actions with Cuba, even on very sensitive political issues.[3]

Cuba's position, disproportionate though it may seem compared to its economic power, is not an anomaly in the context of world trends—the internationalization of the Third World's critical agenda—nor is it foreign to these countries' will to develop their political resources, fostering their capacity to coordinate policies on a regional and global scale.[4]

Thus, it follows that Cuba's foreign policy cannot be rationally explained simply as an answer to U.S. activities; however, there can be no doubt that the main events that take place in Cuban foreign relations are interwoven with its relations with the United States. This occurs not only because the United States and Cuba maintain hostile relations, but also precisely because of the complex agenda of Cuba's foreign policy. It would be very difficult to find another small country with so many variables in its international equation, or one that operates in so many different parts of the world in which the United States also operates, such as Latin America, Africa, and the socialist countries.

Cuba's alliances with Third World countries are not simply based on confronting U.S. policy, even though they eventually converge with the policies of those countries that have conflicts with the United States and that, often, have more normal relations than does Cuba with the United States—such as is the case with the large majority of African countries. In truth, these alliances are based on cooperation to face real economic, social, and political problems—such as the foreign debt—that form part of the North-South conflict. Even in the cases of such alliances that have a military component, their aim is not to develop an anti-U.S. crusade on a global level. Even though Cuba has stationed numerous troops or advisors in some countries—such as Angola, Ethiopia, or Nicaragua—it has abstained from engaging in direct hostilities against U.S. allies, such as Zaire or Honduras, in those regions.

Nonetheless, it is a fact that Cuba's foreign policy has rivaled that of the United States not only with respect to Latin America but also in other regions of the Third World. But on many occasions this confrontation has been the result of Cuba's fulfillment of foreign policy objectives and commitments that are not directly related to its differences with the United States—for example, Cuban policy toward Africa.

To the astonishment of many Cubans, some have asked why Cuba preferred to send troops to Angola instead of improving its relations with the United States. In the first place, it is highly improbable that the Cuban government even took this as a dilemma. The political and material support to governments and movements allied to Cuba, such as the Popular Movement for the Liberation of Angola (MPLA), has been part and parcel of Cuba's policy since 1960; to have abandoned it while possessing the legitimacy and resources to assist these movements would have meant a sharp change in Cuba's strategy for African alliances. In fact, according to this reasoning, the surprise would have been Cuba's not honoring its established commitments. In any case, had Cuba weighed the political and symbolic significance of these alliances, objectively considered, and compared it with the remote possibility of dialogue with the Ford administration or with Henry Kissinger, proponents of the latter option would have been greatly outnumbered. One could ask whether, in Cuba's shoes, the United States would have acted differently.

A very important aspect of Cuba's policy toward the Third World in the wider context of its foreign policy is Cuba's rejection of the notion of "spheres of influence." Independent from ideological motivations, the very existence of a socialist regime ninety miles away from the United States is undoubtedly a denial of this geographic fatalism. To a larger degree, this location, facing the United States and in the midst of the Latin American community, has conditioned Cuba's approach to international relations, which is different from those of other socialist countries.

Thus, we infer that, for Cuba's policy, peace is a wide-ranging objective that must reach beyond the peace among the superpowers. Cuba fears that a *pax inter pares* would be limited to the prevention of nuclear war, while local wars would remain to settle "ideological disputes." Taking into account that Cuba and its allies have been participants in conflicts that are now called "low-intensity," it is untrue to say that Cuba's motives are only ideological. Particularly on the issue of regional conflicts, Cuba has seen that changes in U.S. policy at the world level do not necessarily imply favorable changes at the regional level. Rather, the opposite has occurred: after the beginning of U.S.-Soviet talks, U.S. aggressiveness has increased at the regional level.[5] Furthermore, a fundamental discrepancy between the United States and Cuba is the clash of their interests in Third World settings. It is worth noting here (and examining in more detail later) that this issue is central to the conflict between the two nations.

Therefore, we can see that the main interest of Cuba's policy is its security in respect to the United States. We will not go into detail because the subject is discussed in the chapters by Treverton and Alzugaray, but let us consider some of the key features of this issue. The main problem of Cuba's national security, though not the only nor the most probable one, is the possibility of a direct U.S. attack, be it against economic or military targets, a blockade, or a surprise mass air raid against Cuba's principal cities. Even though Cuba considers that the 1962 agreements that ended the missile crisis are still in force, at that time the Cuban government did not consider that its national security could depend upon the word of the Kennedy administration. The inconsistencies expressed by the United States—in 1978, in 1979, and, afterwards, on several occasions under the Reagan administration—in reference to the degree of its commitment and of the terms the fulfillment of the agreements by both sides have justified this lack of confidence.

Still, some ask themselves if by now it is realistic to expect a direct U.S. military operation against Cuba. In fact, it seems that the idea of disposing of Cuban socialism militarily does not prevail now in U.S. thinking. But, let us put it this way: Are there no possibilities whatsoever for crises to break out that would bring about U.S. military actions against Cuba—crises in our region, in other Third World countries, or even in Europe? Can Cuba believe that it is no longer a target of U.S. contingency plans? Can it be assured that U.S. interventions in a Central American country or on a Caribbean island will not imply for Cuba the prospect of equivalent "neutralization measures," that is, military actions for which the "secondary target" is Cuba? It seems clear that Cuban concerns are far from unfounded.

The persistence of U.S. destabilization plans and of the U.S. economic blockade against Cuba, the continued U.S. occupation of the Guantánamo naval base, U.S. military intelligence flights over Cuba—along with other U.S. policies now reduced or cancelled, such as subversion, pirate attacks, or counter-revolutionary bands—and, in fact, the reaffirmation of a policy that seeks to change the political regime in Cuba have all been direct threats to Cuba's national security and to the stability of the Cuban regime.

In reference to covert actions, in these past two years the reactivation of this type of operation within the CIA has been revealed.[6] What Treverton has called the political culture of covert actions is still in force, especially in the field of propaganda ("Radio Martí," "TV Martí"), political actions (support to organizations and groups such as the "human rights committees"), and intelligence activities (maintenance of underground operations in Cuban territory).[7] On the other hand, although the official U.S. position opposes terrorism, the ambiguity latent in all U.S. policies related in one way or another to certain sectors of the Cuban-American community—where terrorist operations against Cuba have been typically implemented—connotes a range of insecurity in this sense. Consequently, most Cubans in Cuba have reason to believe that Cuba actually is a U.S. target.

The other side of this perception—that Cuba constitutes a threat to U.S. security or that it pretends to change the U.S. regime—is unbelievable for most Cubans, no matter what their ideological position may be. Why is the United States more hostile toward Cuba than toward any other nation—excepting only those countries against which it has waged wars, such as Korea or Viet Nam? Why is it more recalcitrant against Cuba than against the Soviet Union or China? Thirty years after the revolution, Cubans perceive from the United States an unending reproduction of gestures of enmity.

These actions also create what could be called the paradox of the negative policy. According to this mechanism, U.S. policy, against its own interests, contributes to strengthening the Cuban perception that Cuba is a besieged fortress, with its corresponding results of mobilization and internal cohesion. For example, from 1981 to 1986, while Ronald Reagan was president, Cuba's military mobilization reached more than a half million reservists and 1.5 million militiamen, in addition to those in the Civil Defense and the Revolutionary Armed Forces regular troops. This figure amounts to 80 percent of the nation's combat able-bodied persons.[8]

The Cuban leadership has insisted that the concern over national security is not limited to the particularly antagonistic situation of relations with the United States during the Reagan administration. Cuban security is defined beyond the prospect for solutions to the bilateral differences. From Cuba's point of view, the "illusions of peace" that could be achieved with the United States would be limited to the contingency of its "many changes of administrations," which could bring about—as has happened—abrupt changes in U.S. policy, affecting directly Cuba's national security.[9]

On the other hand, during the Ford and Carter years, Cuba experienced what Carlos Rico has called "the effect of the schizophrenic giant": the reception of contradictory signals from the same U.S. administration. As is well known, the policy differences between the State Department and the White House or the National Security Council create a structural incoherence. When these differences become overt, as they did in the 1978-1980 period, Cuba simultaneously receives two different messages, creating a situation of fundamental insecurity.[10]

All these factors tend to reaffirm the idea that Cuban security is part of a structural situation into which the country is inserted due to the nature of its regime and its proximity to the United States.

Cuba as a Phenomenon of U.S. Politics

Since 1960, when Cuba became an electoral issue during John Kennedy's presidential campaign, it has become a fetish of U.S. domestic policy over which the "hard" or "soft" line against communism is tested. As Richard Goodwin put it, Cuba became the target of sanctions, propaganda, and all types of "quarantines," while, at the same time, all those who opposed the revolutionary regime became "freedom fighters"—thanks to domestic politics.[11] It is not surprising that after a while, Cuba also became a "Third World Soviet hired gun" or a danger "second only to the Soviet Union."

The "loss" of Cuba turned Latin America—until then ignored by U.S. public opinion and all political candidates—into a field of domestic debate.[12] After the Bay of Pigs (Playa Girón) invasion fiasco in 1961 and the panic of the October 1962 missile crisis, Cuba was transformed into the ghost of the cold war become real, producing a clear and enduring image in domestic U.S. politics. In the field of foreign relations, the Alliance for Progress, U.S. activism within the Organization of American States (OAS), and the counterinsurgency programs during the first half of the 1960s tried to block communism in Latin America, first within the boundaries of Cuba.

Yet, the decrease of U.S. interest in Latin America toward the end of the 1960s and in the early 1970s did not reflect lessened aversion toward Cuba at the government level, but a greater concern for other problems. The new poles of attraction of U.S. foreign policy, such as Viet Nam, U.S.-Soviet détente, and its new policy toward China, did not bring Washington and Havana any closer.[13] Nonetheless, between 1971 and 1973, a dramatic change took place in U.S. public opinion toward relations with Cuba. In early 1971, a Harris survey showed that 61 percent of U.S. citizens opposed a normalization of relations, with 21 percent in favor; in 1973, another Harris survey indicated that those against normalization of relations had dropped to 33 percent, and that 51 percent favored normalization.[14] On one hand, less government attention toward Latin America brought about a general decline of concern over the "Cuban threat." On the other, this change not only reflected the diminished presence of Latin America in domestic U.S. politics, but also the changes in the domestic consensus due to the aforementioned examples, particularly the Viet Nam war. It would be very difficult to demonstrate that any changes in Cuba's behavior at this time would have inspired such changes in the United States.

To what extent have Cuban actions affected these changes in later years? According to a Potomac Associates survey in 1977, more than a year after the dispatch of Cuban troops to Angola, only 25 percent of the U.S. public opposed the renewal of diplomatic relations between the United States and Cuba (59 percent favored it). Even though Cuba's policy is not an insignificant factor, the data tend to support the hypothesis that it is not the main factor that has shaped the predominant attitude of U.S. public opinion. In fact, these changes are associated mainly with the transformations of the U.S. domestic political moods, including those that took place because of the U.S. administrations' ideological orientation. This hypothesis seemed to have been confirmed in 1982, when the Reagan administration's "go-to-the-source" policy (e.g., attack Cuba as the alleged source of revolution in Central America) was at its peak: consensus on a renewal of U.S.-Cuban relations dropped to its lowest point. In 1982, a survey by the Chicago Council on Foreign Relations indicated that 48 percent of the U.S. public was in favor of normalizing relations with Cuba, while an increased 37 percent was against it.[15] In this sense, Cuba has remained an object subject to the laws typical of the domestic U.S. political context—in other words, a fetish.

This fetishism could perhaps explain why U.S. citizens have sustained a worse opinion of Cuba than of Argentina under the military juntas, of Pinochet's Chile, and of El Salvador under the Death Squadrons, according to surveys.[16] The way in which U.S. public opinion receives information and interpretations of events in Cuba can influence the building of such a disproportionately negative image.[17] Furthermore, the U.S. government's own rhetoric constitutes a very important means for communication; the U.S. government is more likely to frequently accuse Cuba of being the source of all the hemisphere's evils than it is to condemn the military dictatorships in the region.

However, U.S. public opinion on Cuba is consistent in general with its opinion on Latin America as a whole. U.S. citizens are more interested and apparently know much more about African problems than about problems of our region. According to the 1987 Interaction and Overseas Development Council survey, 32 percent of U.S. respondents do not have an opinion or say they know nothing about the main Latin American problems. Only 11 percent admit to this ignorance in reference to Africa. Curiously, the 65 percent of the "informed public" on Africa consider that the social and economic problems are the most serious for that continent, while only 21 percent think the same about Latin America.[18] According to the U.S. public, the main Latin American problems are political: bad leadership, unstable governments, civil wars—not communism. Based on this opinion, the following conclusions may be reached:

- Cuba and Latin America are not important issues within U.S. political culture.
- To the extent that the region's problems are perceived, our political systems are deemed to be the root cause of all our problems.
- Communism is to be considered just an epiphenomenon of these problems.

These conclusions suggest that Cuba's image would be the extreme case of what is generally a negligent and ethnocentric analysis of Latin America, perceived as a sort of turbulent suburb of the metropolis.[19]

It has also been stressed that no electoral basis exists to encourage a rapproachment toward Cuba. Nonetheless, despite this negative image, U.S. public opinion—as can also be seen in the surveys—has not been nor is it now against the renewal of relations.[20] This suggests that the determining perceptions during the policy development have been those of the governing elite. Other surveys reveal that most elites also pronounce themselves in favor of a change in U.S. policy toward Cuba; thus, when it comes to decision making, other factors of domestic politics seem to oppose a change.

There is a political basis against the renewal of relations found in some right-wing pressure groups predominant in Miami who have proclaimed themselves representatives of the entire Cuban community. Yet, the interests that have promoted the perceptions of Cuba in party documents and in policy circles in general are not limited to this narrow lobby. These interests have reacted to the Cuban problem as part of the "communist threat" syndrome in Latin America. They reflect what Howard Wiarda would call a "new containment."

To what extent is this phenomenon of domestic politics related to the East-West dynamic and to the relations between the United States and Latin America? U.S. policy usually considers Cuba's foreign policy actions to be adverse to its global interests. This sort of "magnetic effect"—characteristic of the hegemonic features of U.S. policy—tends to "attract" all of Cuba's foreign relations into the field of bilateral U.S.-Cuban relations. In terms of U.S. policy, Cuba is presented as an object of its strategy against the Soviet Union. It can be shown, however, that Cuba's importance for the hegemonic interests of the United States and for U.S. foreign policy have had a fundamental regional effect.

Even though Cuba did not take part in the East-West rapprochement during the years of détente—Cuba was not invited—this factor does not seem to have influenced U.S. public opinion much (as surveys show), nor did it even affect U.S. interest at the time to open a bilateral dialogue following Carter administration policy in 1977 and 1978. As was stated, Cuba was not included in the U.S. détente agenda with the Soviet Union. At that time, the Cuban issue shifted within U.S. policy to the extent that it was explicitly identified as a test case of its Latin American policy.

Of course, the increase of East-West tensions toward the end of the 1970s revived the U.S. anti-communist rhetoric even more spiritedly with regard to Cuba. Yet, this "affinity" between the topic of Cuba and that rhetoric does not necessarily imply that the U.S. government's perception of Cuba was determined by a change of U.S. policy towards the Soviet Union—such as the change that took place after Soviet troops entered Afghanistan. As Robert Pastor has pointed out, Afghanistan or Iran were part of the international context of the turning point that took place in 1979. Nonetheless, "traumatic events" such as the Sandinista revolution of 1979 were more decisive in setting the framework for an anti-Cuban policy toward Nicaragua, and thus, to reactivating hostilities toward Cuba.[21]

The Latin American Conflict Between Cuba and the United States

Since 1959, Latin American policy has become a center of confrontation between the two nations. Nevertheless, in the mid-1970s the concern within the region was not communism; in fact, Latin American countries began to renew relations with Cuba after 1970, and the OAS had to lift sanctions against Cuba in 1975. At the same time, the rebuilding of U.S. dialogue with Latin America during that decade necessarily included a dialogue with Cuba, which was readmitted *de facto* into the regional community.[22]

Still, as a U.S. diplomat accredited to Cuba once said to me, the main issue in the conflict between Cuba and the United States—according to U.S. views and interests—is Cuba's relations with the national liberation movements and the anti-imperialist governments in the region. Nicaragua, Grenada, and the Central American liberation movements were "drawn" as issues into the U.S.-Cuban bilateral conflict, blocking and, finally, stopping the dialogue process in 1979. The logic of Cuba's relations with those governments and movements, and the dynamics of the Latin American regional framework within which it was interacting, were simplified: the United States perceived Cuban actions as directed deliberately toward clouding U.S.-Cuban bilateral relations. According to this view, Cuba betrayed the trust of the U.S. policy makers who had made this dialogue possible.

However, with the exception of the radical right,[23] as of late the majority of the analyses of Cuba's policy toward Latin America have cast aside the simplistic schemes of "export of revolution."[24] The process of Cuba's reinsertion in the hemisphere has become consolidated in the 1980s. The war between Argentina and the United Kingdom over the Malvinas islands, the redemocratization of South America, the negotiations seeking to settle the Central American conflicts, Latin America's debt crisis, and the crisis of the inter-American system have found Cuba in a position similar to that of the rest of Latin America. In some of these topics, as in the search for integration formulas and, above all, in the Third World policy style and in the Latin Americanization of regional foreign policy, this convergence has concrete bases on both sides: for Latin America, Cuba is an important regional actor that cannot be excluded from the efforts and initiatives of Latin Americans to solve urgent regional problems; for Cuba, Latin America is its natural area of insertion and its forum of international activities *par excellence.*[25]

Cuban perception of Latin America is also not the same as it was in the 1960s. The Cuban government acknowledges that Latin America holds a different position in reference to the United States, and considers that the U.S. position in this hemisphere has weakened to the same extent that the Latin American governments are increasingly less submissive.[26] This world view, recently reiterated with increasing frequency, has even taken the form of certain tacit connivance between Cuba and those governments. Cuba has also noted the fact that Latin American countries use their relations with Cuba as part of their political bargaining with the United States.[27]

Moreover, relations between the Soviet Union and Latin America have not been an element of irritation between Cuba and the region, for they have unfolded over time through their own channels. Soviet relations with Argentina, Peru, and, more recently, with Brazil in the economic and military fields have taken place outside of what the United States calls "the Cuban connection." It is well known that Moscow's relations with Latin American communist parties have not been channeled through Cuba either before or after the revolution.

The issues of Cuba's military strengthening and its links to the Soviet Union do not contradict its regional policy, either. To some extent, the legitimation of Cuba's security policy within the Latin American context also shapes Cuba's interests and perceptions as it faces the United States. Cuba has stated that neither its MiG-23 combat aircraft nor its land equipment, nor the Soviet naval visits to Cuba, represent a source of friction with Latin America. Cuba is not preparing itself for a general war, nor for war against any Latin American or Caribbean nation; Cuban military exercises are dedicated mainly to defense against a U.S. attack. Cuba does not use neighboring countries, nor does it deploy forces beyond its territorial waters, to threaten countries like Mexico, Jamaica, or Haiti, some of which are not always friendly.

For its part, the United States has argued that Cuba has a potential capacity to intercept the sea lanes that surround the island, which the United States needs for naval supplies. This peculiarity, common to other countries of the Caribbean Basin, does not necessarily imply that Cuba is a threat against which the United States has to be prepared. In fact, the United States has proven that it has the capacity to deny Cuba the use of its neighboring waters and to blockade the island by sea and air in case of a crisis, as it did in October 1962. In other words, the United States is too near Cuba and the Caribbean nations for it to require its expansion into their neighboring waters in maneuvers more typical of its "show-the-flag" policy.

With regard to backing the revolutionary and anti-imperialist causes, again Cuba is not alone in the region. The Polisario Front in northwestern Africa, SWAPO in southwestern Africa, and the FMLN in El Salvador, as well as the legitimacy of the PLO in the Middle East, have been recognized by an important part of the international community, including Latin American countries that are friendly with the United States. Generally, Polisario, SWAPO, and the PLO are not aiming to overthrow U.S. allies, namely the governments of Morocco, South Africa, or Israel nor is Cuba's political support to the Puerto Rican independence movement directed toward overthrowing the U.S. government. This differentiates Cuban policy from U.S. policy that has given aid to the *contras*—without the consensus support of Latin America—against the Nicaraguan government, or from U.S. efforts to destabilize Cuba. Similarly, Cuba's military aid to Nicaragua and Angola has been free of the essential qualities that characterize U.S. military intervention—in Indochina for example—in many aspects, among them: (1) It is not Cuba's objective to participate in a counterinsurgency war; and (2) there has been no Cuban penetration or attack on the main enemy's positions (South Africa), nor on those of countries allied with the "insurgents" (Honduras).

With regard to the Central American conflict, Cuba's position has been that of trying to prevent, as much as possible, the risks of escalation, favoring strategies that will deter the United States from intervening. Cuba has followed a peace policy, but one that ensures independence, dignity, and justice for the Nicaraguan people and for the other Central American peoples, establishing a regional agreement to end all foreign military presence in the region's countries. In truth, Cuba's position, consistent with the 1987 Esquipulas Agreement, has been nearer to the Latin American consensus than has the U.S. position.

Does it mean that most Latin American governments have become pro-Cuban? Does this imply that most of these governments maintain directly anti-imperialist stands against the United States? An example of the new correlation of forces—with its different shades and complexities—is the continuing confrontation since 1987 in the U.N. Human Rights Commission between Cuba and the United States. Regardless of the diplomatic arrangement achieved and of the characteristics of the issue at hand, the form and meaning of the debate took on great symbolic importance. In effect, the conflict was played out between two blocks—that of the European community, representing the United States, and the Latin American group, representing Cuba. With this alignment, Cuban legitimacy within the Latin American context is accepted as fact. Naturally, Latin American countries prefer not to vote against the United States, but neither do they want to vote against Cuba. Taking into account that the strong pressures exerted on the Latin American governments[28] by the United States in effect reduce the former's room to maneuver, the votes directly favoring Cuba or the abstentions from voting in favor of the U.S. proposal define the extent and limits of the consensus.

In fact, U.S. coercion today does not always obtain what it did in the past, almost automatically and by consent. This change can be interpreted as an objective sign that U.S. domination in Latin America reflects a declining hegemony.[29] In any case, the Latin American factor—in existence since 1959—currently has an increasing significance in Cuban policy.

Is Negotiation an Objective?

According to one approach, the agenda of unsolved problems between the United States and Cuba constitutes the essence of the conflict.[30] This approach—one that we shall call "diplomatic"—states that the main issues in conflict could be addressed through a series of items on the bilateral or international agenda, the eventual solution of which would lead to an accord and a renewal of normal relations. Foreign policy problems—the "Cuban-Soviet alliance," confrontation in Africa or in Central America—would be subject to solution through agreements and commitments between the United States and Cuba. At the same time, paradoxically, it has been stated that the reduction of tensions between the two countries is a requirement to achieve such agreements.[31]

An alternative, opposing model would recognize the fundamental asymmetry of power between Cuba and the United States as the basic factor for any arrangement. From this factor stems the need for Cuba to admit the preponderance of the United

States, agreeing to do nothing that could hamper U.S. interests. In such an arrangement, Cuba would maintain its political system and its economic (but not military) relations with the Soviet Union, even though it would try to increasingly strengthen its relations with and trust in the United States along the road toward normality.[32]

On our part, we have tried to offer elements for an approach based on interests and values as well as on the changing international situation, especially in the hemisphere and on its predominant trends. This logic would establish a structural definition of the conflict and of the obstacles to reducing it. To conclude, we take up the main problems in order to discover their primary elements.

U.S. Policy: Interests in and Limits to Change

U.S. policy toward Cuba does not stem from a particular interest group, nor from the Trilateral Commission, nor from the Committee of Santa Fe, nor from groups from the East or the West. Nor has it differed dramatically between Democrats and Republicans, nor changed radically between liberals and conservatives. There are nuances or degrees—sometimes important—between the tactical paradigms of one or the other group. But these differences do not reflect different perceptions about interests or values; therefore, they are not determinants in the transformation of policy.

First, past attempts to modify these policies have not been the result of the formulation of a new, comprehensive, and articulated policy, as such. They were barely directed toward changing certain features of policy, or they were isolated attempts that were frustrated and weakened since their very conception, precisely because they were restricted and "experimental" policy initiatives, limited to a specific sector of the government and based on the principle of "seeing what happens." Logically, such policies have suffered a lack of fundamental stability. The Cuban answer to these policies has been conditioned by this pattern. In these conditions, destabilizing factors are free to act as they please. At present, the anti-Cuban connection[33] has at its disposal an official covert action potential such as "Radio Martí" and the "TV Martí" project that goes beyond the resources of the right-wing Cuban-American lobby. This connection could easily undermine an ambiguous and incoherent "normalization process."

Second, contrary to a negotiation proposal, the recommendations from the various shades of the U.S. policy spectrum formulate proposals that are either asymmetric or that contradict Cuban interests, such as:

- The United States should normalize relations with Cuba only if the latter is "desovietized."[34] This assertion strangely coexists with the idea that the present Soviet influence over Cuba would be beneficial, for it would bring about the "liberalization" of the Cuban system.
- Discussions should be held about mutual national security concerns, such as the Soviet presence in Cuba and the U.S. military maneuvers in the Caribbean.[35] The quid pro quo between these actions presupposes a symmetry in the worth of their respective national security policies—which is in itself debatable. Furthermore, the United States should begin high-level talks with the Soviet Union with the objective of attaining Soviet military withdrawal from Cuba.[36] That is, what is expected from the Soviets is an attitude similar to that which led to their withdrawal of nuclear missiles in 1962—only now they would withdraw conventional weaponry.
- Cuba should unilaterally refrain from giving aid to rebel movements.[37] In this proposal Cuba is not considered to be part of any multilateral or bilateral agreement by which the United States will agree to stop its arms supply to Central America.
- The United States should widen its transmissions toward Cuba as a means of civic education. "TV Martí," with programs designed to teach the elements of a democratic culture, must begin as soon as possible.[38] This measure, though formulated by conservatives, co-exists with the old liberal strategy of influencing Cuban socialism "from the inside" and, indeed, with the policy of changing the present Cuban system.

Relations with the Soviet Union

Apparently, the new U.S.-Soviet dialogue sponsored by the new thinking would lead to a reduction of tensions all along the East-West axis, as has happened in Europe and in the bilateral relations between the superpowers. However, the extent to which the East-West negotiation as such has determined the reduction of conflicts in the Middle East, southeast Asia, or southwest Africa is subject to debate. Apart from the agreements on arms reduction in Europe and a new approach to bilateral issues, the U.S.-Soviet dialogue has not caused other settlements. It is even debatable whether the Soviet Union's withdrawal from Afghanistan is the result of a new policy toward the West and of a constructive U.S. commitment. Nor does it seem that the issues concerning Iran and Iraq, Viet Nam and Kampuchea, or Angola, Cuba and South Africa have progressed thanks to that dialogue. Until now, the U.S.-Soviet dialogue does not seem to have had a substantial impact in Central America. Even though Soviet policy has reiterated a pledge not to deploy nuclear weapons and has eschewed installing Soviet military bases[39] in the region, this by itself has not reduced the conflict levels, nor U.S. concern over the "Soviet-Cuban threat."

Even though the United States congratulates itself for the new climate of understanding reached with the Soviet Union, when the topic of a new relation with Cuba is mentioned, the issue of the "Soviet military presence" in Cuba is raised. As a hypothesis, let us admit theoretically that the United States requires the maintenance of its military presence, just for deterrence purposes, in order to sustain peace in the region. This would prevent "adventurisms" from other powers in the Caribbean Basin. Likewise, the United States needs to know what is happening militarily in Cuba, which would supposedly be good for peace between both countries. Following this same line of reasoning, given the proximity and nature of the regimes in both countries, Cuba should also be strongly armed and should demonstrate its military power to defend itself, also with the same purpose of deterrence. Indeed, Soviet military aid to Cuba, at the scale accepted since 1962, also has the effect of deterrence.

U.S. aspirations to reduce Soviet military supplies to Cuba would have other counterproductive consequences. This hypothetical step, as well as any other that would make Cubans feel weaker before the United States, would not create the best climate for negotiations. When Cuba began a process of dialogue with the United States during the mid-1970s, it felt sufficiently secure to cut in half the size of its armed forces,[40] which had been modernized and professionalized. Cuba was so sure about its security that it even sent several thousand troops to Angola and Ethiopia, without having such a deployment affect its willingness to carry on dialogue with the United States. All this took place, naturally, at Cuba's initiative. To objectively face such a delicate project as the beginning of these negotiations would require favorable political conditions, including self-consciousness about security. It would be very difficult for a Cuban government that did not feel militarily secure before the United States to be able to count on such needed political conditions, even if it wished to negotiate.

Finally, Cuban-Soviet ties were recently ratified by means of a Peace and Cooperation Treaty, which is to endure for twenty-five years. This treaty constitutes an unprecedented way of shaping relations between both countries, with clear and distinct meaning for the United States.[41] Mikhail Gorbachev's visit to Havana in April 1989 contradicted the predominant expectations in the United States that the differences between Cuba and the Soviet Union over specific policies would cause general discord between these two governments.

Position Within the International System and Relations with the Third World

Cuba's foreign policy has attained in the 1980s a better fit within the consensus of the international community. Cuba's present insertion and location in the international system enables it to display world and regional perspectives that are not limited to its national interests. This has been acknowledged by Cuba's Third World allies as well as by many Western actors, among them the governments of Spain, France, and Sweden, and organizations such as the Socialist International.

The *rectification process*—begun in 1986 in Cuba to change aspects of government domestic policy—has not brought about changes in the strategic bases of Cuba's foreign policy. However, the management and evolution of external economic relations, the cooperation with sources of foreign capital—including firms from western industrialized countries—and the principle of rationality and economic realism have been strengthened. Some rectification policies have also served to adjust the management of the domestic economy to external scarcities, and not the other way around. During the 1980s, Cuba has followed a realistic yet principled foreign policy characterized by the search for practical solutions to international problems.

To what extent has the policy of Cuban alliances—besides fulfilling an ideological motivation—widened, diversified, and strengthened Cuba's international position? Objectively, these alliances have also legitimized Cuban policy, even vis-à-vis the United States. Necessarily, the international alliances that underlie Cuban policy have strengthened Cuba's position in the international arena, especially among Third World countries and across a wide array of ideological positions. In this way, the effect has been to reduce Cuba's disadvantage found in the purely bilateral balance with the United States. As Cuba's position is strengthened, it will be more able to contribute actively to restore the equilibrium of the international system, which has been affected by the inequality among nations and by social conflicts, much more than if Cuba had been focused on its narrow national interests. Furthermore, Cuba has promoted a nonbipolar international security system, one that is not based on "zones of influence" but on the balanced participation of regional actors.

The process of negotiation over the southwest Africa conflict presents a model of realism and the will to cooperate. Various factors have conditioned this process. On one hand, in the last few years, U.S. policy toward the southern cone of Africa has taken into account all the relevant actors. On the other hand, Cuba and Angola reiterated their willingness to negotiate a political solution with South Africa. But, above all, Cuba's military response to the South African challenge in late 1987 and early 1988 forced the latter government to agree to negotiate. To face the South African threat, Cuba increased its troops in Angola to 50,000 by early 1988. This unprecedented reinforcement by the Cuban government, notwithstanding other processes under way in the international arena, stopped the South African offensive to seize the strategic town of Cuito Cuanavale, and also caused a political retreat by the apartheid regime, leading to the success of the negotiations. The agreements reached by Angola, Cuba, and South Africa, enshrined within the U.N. framework, represent an important precedent for other negotiations. But, does this mean that the United States is ready to take on the solution of other conflicts in the same terms? A lesson from the agreements on southwest Africa—in the skeptical language of *realpolitik*—is that, where Cuba has deployed decisive force, the United States has tended to behave as a pragmatic negotiator—and nothing more.

Bilateral Dimensions

The main progress obtained on the bilateral agenda is that of the migration agreements. It may be the only aspect of U.S.-Cuban relations that in practice evinces a normalization regime. The signing of the U.S.-Cuban migration agreement in December 1984 was the guarantee to the United States against the reoccurence of another Mariel. (Cuba suspended the agreement in May 1985 due to the beginning of broadcasting by "Radio Martí"; the agreement was reinstated in November 1987.) The Cuban government has given significance to the migration agreement, setting a precedent that change toward a more rational relationship in conformity with

the principles and norms of international coexistence is possible
The signing of this agreement fulfilled a political interest on both
sides, leading to a reasonable and realistic result. Most important
was that the United States negotiated with Cuba on an equal
footing over a topic of common interest, acknowledging Cuba as a
sovereign in the international arena and binding their mutual
relations over migration by means of a treaty.

At the level of a bilateral agenda, the reinstatement of the
migration agreement shows the usefulness of dialogue in which
both parties have interests and are ready to negotiate on the
premises of mutual respect and without preconditions. Thus, other
specific agreements could be reached on topics such as coast guard
cooperation, mutual assurances over the management of nuclear
power plants, the prevention of air and sea piracy, the control of
communicable diseases, drug traffic, and information services for
air and sea navigation.

In all these cases, as in the migration agreement, the United
States has very concrete interests that may yield comparable
specific benefits, though they would be circumscribed to the
technical issue at hand. Those who support the diplomatic
approach believe that a "step-by-step" chain of agreements would
contribute to restoring a climate of trust; this approach would show
the U.S. public that negotiations are possible and, above all, would
open the doors to discussion of the international agenda, without
preconditions.

In reality, no reasoning explains why both parties necessarily
would shift from the level of specific agreements to that of
discussion about the fundamental conflicts between them. There is
no inherent connection between the nature of bilateral topics and
such issues as regional crises or Cuban-Soviet relations.[42] In
addition, there has been no reason to presuppose that the United
States would be ready to negotiate on an equal footing over other
issues where the United States historically has insisted on an
asymmetric relationship, as has been the case of the Guantánamo
naval base and the economic blockade. Given its pre-existing
material advantages, the United States might reason that it should
seek Cuban concessions over these issues, which would lessen the
bases of equality and reciprocity in any negotiation. It would be
very difficult to conceive of a normalization process without the
possibility of settling these larger issues.

A Dialogue Regime?

In general, Cuban policy could be interpreted as an effort to induce the United States toward a real negotiation, based on equality and reciprocity between the parties. Regretfully, Cuban actions to keep open the road to negotiations are frequently perceived not as pragmatic opportunities, but as signs of weakness. For example, when Cuba eschewed the alternative to respond to "Radio Martí" by means of general interference with radio transmissions in the southern and eastern part of the United States, some in the United States considered this a sign of Cuban impotence. Nonetheless, Cuban policy has never closed the doors to peaceful solutions. There is a difference, perhaps a subtle one, between what Cuba might be ready to discuss and the issues over which it might be ready to negotiate. In fact, with regard to the conflicts in Central America and the southern cone of Africa, Cuba has publicly stated its differences with the United States and has tried to induce the United States to negotiate arrangements with the other regional actors. At times, as in 1978 and 1979, Cuba has addressed U.S. public opinion directly about the terms of its military cooperation with the Soviet Union. It is my view that Cuba's general foreign policy framework permits it to discuss any differences with the United States, but not to negotiate away its sovereign rights in domestic or foreign policies. Particularly, Cuban policy has historically rejected a "negotiation" under circumstances of coercion or hostility, just as the United States ordinarily rejects such circumstances for itself.

Negotiations should be a means to attain a stable regime that governs relations. The idea of normalization would not just end the blockade and raise the rank of "interests sections" to that of embassies; nor would normalization make political sense if one were to seek to build an ideal model of relations to achieve harmony between the two countries. Above all, a policy seeking normalization should bring forth what we will call a *dialogue regime*. Such a policy would establish the norm of resorting to discussions and negotiations instead of acting unilaterally.

This system obviously does not result naturally from reaching isolated agreements whose endurance may be precarious. These agreements would be desirable and could contribute to create "trust" between both parties. But their doubtful stability, for reasons that may even be beyond the will of the signatories, would be a rather weak basis to design policies. The suspension of a specific agreement would have the ripple effect that would hamper the rest, and that might poison the milieu of the relationship itself.

A stable dialogue regime can only be developed on the basis of a series of specific agreements, but it is not merely the sum of such specific agreements. In other words, it does not stem simply from the will to sign specific, isolated agreements, but from the formulation of a policy, which the United States still lacks with respect to Cuba.

The strategic issue is not how to begin to negotiate—there are already many suggestions for that and many more can emerge—but how feasible would such a stable dialogue regime be? We believe that such a regime would need to establish a certain degree of understanding, capable of analyzing, through consultation and other normal diplomatic procedures, the respective actions of each party that may worry the other. A dialogue regime—as a policy and not just as a mere procedure—should permit discussion of problems, the mutual elucidation of policies, the anticipation of possible undesired outcomes, and the verification of issues that are unclear. It would permit to analyze beforehand the prospects for crises. And it would be the first step along a process conducive to negotiations.

As is well known, the lack of a dialogue regime is not due to the absence of a channel of communications or a device for transmitting messages, which in fact already exists in the respective Interests Sections. A dialogue regime would imply rejection of the use of force and unilateralism in bilateral relations. It presupposes that both parties would be ready to consider bilaterally the issues that could affect their respective interests and would establish the political will to do so.

Given its nature, a dialogue regime would not require a process of complicated decisions where the need for consensus in the United States might become a stumbling block—the president can effect the necessary policies without the need of a Congressional vote. In fact, the president did not require the cooperation of other groups from the "opposition" to reach agreements with Cuba over migration and radio interferences; in the same way, should he wish, the president can take measures to reduce the effectiveness of the blockade, without a vote by the Congress.

Nor must one think that just because of this dialogue policy, the United States and Cuba will not be involved in any foreseeable or unforeseeable crises in the 1990s. One must not suppose that Cuba would renounce the basic premises of a policy that, besides responding to a well-articulated view of the world, has brought to it the respect of Third World countries and of many political forces in the West, as well as the support of the socialist countries. On the other hand, one should not assume that the United States will resign itself to the loss of hegemony in the hemisphere, nor that it will go beyond the well-known doctrine of its spheres of influence. The difference that the dialogue regime may make is that crises that might emerge in any Latin American or Third World country for reasons unrelated to Cuban or U.S. actions, but that might come to affect their bilateral relations, could be analyzed bilaterally within a constructive framework.

What has changed U.S. policy toward Cuba in the past and may do so in the future is the need to formulate pragmatic proposals for Latin America. The nuances of Cuban policy toward the United States have been linked more to factors in its Latin American policy than to those in its relations with the Soviet Union.

With a constructive policy toward Cuba, the United States would benefit mainly for pragmatic reasons. It would change a cold war ideological regime that has not been able to influence Cuba's actions in its favor for a negotiation regime in accordance with the existing trends in the region, which the United States could use in a moment of crisis in order to contain it. But above all, it would achieve a concrete political result in the hemisphere, the southern portion of which tends to build its own means of agreement. In any event, the United States may have to face the possibility that Cuba may reinsert itself effectively in the region, though still outside of the old inter-American system. Is there any U.S. interest in keeping itself outside of these emerging trends? Or does the United States prefer that its relations with Cuba be a secondary and involuntary result of its relations with Latin America? The "Cuban case" is today—more than in the 1970s—a test of the capacity of the United States to reformulate and to make flexible its policy toward Latin America. The United States can freeze such policies again, but that move would constrain its capacity and effectiveness to participate at the strategic level in the dynamics of the hemisphere.

Notes

1.   Alfred T. Mahan, "The Relations of the United States to their New Dependencies," *Engineering Magazine* (January

1899), reprinted in *Lessons of the War with Spain and Other Articles* (Little, Brown and Co.), pp. 243-247.

2. José Martí, "Congreso internacional en Washington (II)," *La Nación* (Buenos Aires), December 20, 1889, reprinted in his *Obras completas*, vol. 6 (Havana: Editorial Ciencias Sociales, 1975), pp. 56-62.

3. See the behavior of the Latin American Group (GRULA) in the UN Human Rights Commission, in Geneva, in 1987-89. In this case, the results of concertation are even more conspicuous: the outcome was contrary to the policy advocated by the United States and against its diplomatic pressures.

4. The Cuban case is just a noteworthy one among a group of Latin American and Third World countries that have given priority, in their national interest, to the search for a foreign policy strategy based on concertation to widen their "space" within the international system—e.g., India, Algeria, or Zimbabwe, among the Nonaligned, or Mexico, in Latin America.

5. See the Main Report to the Third Congress of the Communist Party of Cuba, "International Situation" section, February 1986.

6. For a well-documented history of these operations, especially in the Central American arena, see Bob Woodward, *Veil: The Secret Wars of the CIA, 1981-87* (Simon and Schuster, 1987). In 1987, Cuba made public the plans of certain CIA agents that point to covert economic warfare, especially against agriculture and communications.

7. See Gregory Treverton, *Covert Action* (London: I.B. Tauris, 1987), pp. 12-43.

8. See Main Report to the Third Congress of the Communist Party of Cuba, "Armed Forces" section, February 1986.

9. See Fidel Castro's speech at the Fifth Congress of Cuba's Communist Youth Union, *Granma*, April 7, 1987.

10. For a more thorough discussion of the differences between Vance and Brzezinski, see Robert Pastor, *Condemned to Repetition* (Princeton University Press, 1987), p. 62. Pastor states that the first step in the disagreement between the two was their assessment of Cuba's presence in the Horn of Africa.

11. This is an almost verbatim testimony of a close associate of Kennedy. See Richard Goodwin, *Remembering America* (Little, Brown and Co., 1988), pp. 125-126.

12. *Ibid.*, p. 108.
13. Even though the reasoning concerning "Cuba-as-a-U.S.S.R.-satellite" implies the idea that the U.S.-Cuban conflict should have been solved through East-West negotiations, this item does not seem to have been included in the Nixon administration's agenda.
14. See William Watts, *Perceptions of Cuba: Spring of 1988, An Overview* (Potomac Associates, draft paper).
15. *Ibid.*
16. See the attitude scale toward Western hemisphere nations in *The Gallup Report International* (1983) in *Ibid.*, p. 3.
17. Studies of Cuba's image in U.S. mass media reflect distortions that go beyond what may be considered "bad press." See Ed McCaughan and Toni Platt, "Tropical Goulag: Media Image of Cuba," *Social Justice*, 15, 2 (1988).
18. Christine E. Contee, *What Americans Think: Views on Development and U.S.-Third World Relations* (Interaction and Overseas Development Council, 1987), p. 48.
19. Mexico, the most esteemed Latin American country from the U.S. viewpoint, has not escaped this "negative image" in the press and in the U.S. Congress.
20. Watts, *Perceptions of Cuba.*
21. Pastor, *Condemned to Repetition*, p. 277.
22. The Linowitz Commission—which has been transformed into the Inter-American Dialogue—acknowledged Cuba as a test case of U.S. policy toward Latin America.
23. For a peculiar interpretation of Cuban foreign policy based on a psychoanalysis of Fidel Castro's personality, according to the principles of *hubris* (Olympic arrogance) and *nemesis* (punishment and vengeance), see Edward González and David Ronfeldt, *Cuba, Castro and the World* (Rand Corporation, R-3420, June 1986).
24. Among others, see Heraldo Muñoz and Boris Yopo, "Cuba y las democracias latinoamericanas en los ochentas," *Documentos de trabajo PROSPEL*, no. 9 (March 1987); William LeoGrande, "Cuban Policy Recycled," *Foreign Policy* (Fall 1982); and Jorge I. Domínguez, "Cuba in the Eighties," *Foreign Affairs* (Fall 1986).
25. For a more thorough discussion, see Juan Valdés Paz's chapter in this book. See also Muñoz and Yopo, "Cuba y las democracias latinoamericanas," p. 6.

60

26. See Fidel Castro's interview in *L'Humanité*, May 25, 1987, pp. 14-18, and his speech at the Third Congress of the Committees for the Defense of the Revolution.
27. See Fidel Castro's speech at the Fifth Congress of the Communist Youth Union, *Granma*, April 7, 1987, p. 4.
28. Even in cases where Cuba does not have diplomatic relations, even though there is a political understanding, as with Colombia.
29. I follow here the correlation between hegemony and domination established by Perry Anderson—based on the work of Antonio Gramsci—in his book *Las antinomias de Antonio Gramsci* (Editorial Fontamara, 1978), p. 42.
30. See Wayne Smith, *Subject to Solution* (Lynne Rienner Publishers, 1988).
31. *Ibid.*, p. 12.
32. This variant could be called hegemonic pragmatism or, from the Cuban perspective, dependent socialism. It appears in Gregory Treverton's chapter in this book, though he seems to have been inspired by Edward González, who might have taken the central idea from Walter Laqueur.
33. For an assessment of this concept, see R. García, L. Cervantes, and R. Hernández, "La FNCA y la conexión anti-Cubana," *Cuadernos de Nuestra América*, no. 1 (1984): 145-173.
34. Committee of Santa Fe (Francis L. Bouchey, Roger Fontaine, David C. Jordan, Lt. Gen. Gordon Sumner, Jr.), *Santa Fe II: A Strategy for Dealing with Latin America in the Nineties* (August 1988), p. 33.
35. *An Alternative U.S. Policy toward Cuba: Policy Alternatives for the Caribbean and Central America* (PACCA, 1988), back cover page.
36. Committee of Santa Fe, *Santa Fe II*, p. 31.
37. *The Americas in 1988: A Time for Choices. A Report of the Interamerican Dialogue* (Washington, D.C.: Aspen Institute for Humanistic Studies, May 1988), p. 11.
38. Committee of Santa Fe, *Santa Fe II*.
39. See Mikhail Gorbachev's speech at the Cuban National Assembly, April 4, 1989, *Granma*, April 5, 1989.
40. See Main Report to the First Congress of the Communist Party of Cuba, December 1975.
41. See the text of the Treaty in *Granma*, April 5, 1989.
42. Conversely, developments in these relations do not have effects over the bilateral agenda. Mikhail Gorbachev's visit

to Havana in April 1989 would have little influence on the issues pending between Cuba and the United States.

3

Cuba in U.S. Security Perspective

Gregory F. Treverton

This chapter represents the perspective of an American strategist. Its focus is thus on the ways military instruments possessed by or located in Cuba bear on the interests of the United States. It searches for common ground between the United States and Cuba but does so from the starting point of U.S. interests. Given the checkered history of U.S.-Cuban relations, the hard edges of the analyst seem preferable to the warm, fuzzy language of the diplomatist; that practice was the rule in the conference from which these chapters developed, and it served us well.

It would go without saying that a Cuban perspective is different, except that Carlos Alzugaray says it in his companion chapter. He accords "security" a more expansive definition than I give it here. In that perspective, the United States has posed a direct threat to Cuban territory for some of the last thirty years, and may even today in an extreme case. The United States has, depending on one's taste and definitions, threatened Cuban sovereignty for much of the last century and a half.

My perspective does not deny the validity of the Cuban perspective. Nor does it deny that U.S. actions have played a role in Cuban actions; whether Professor Alzugaray is prepared to make a reciprocal stipulation about Cuban actions, I leave to the reader to decide. Understanding the past is crucial to imagining the future. Yet, however the United States and Cuba came to their current pass, that is where they are. Not all the security concerns raised by Americans about Cuba are important or even real, but by the same token, not all are fanciful, and some *are* important.

Hence, this chapter addresses four sets of concerns, by U.S. lights: Cuba as a base for its—and for Soviet—military forces in the Caribbean; Cuban actions in supporting or fighting alongside groups or governments the United States opposes, first within and then beyond Latin America; and more specific aspects of bilateral relations, like narcotics or migration, that have or might have security implications. This chapter asks what steps might be taken, by either country alone or by the two together, to diminish the force of these U.S. concerns and thus their spill-over on bilateral relations.

The Elements of a Security Regime

The Cuban missile crisis, coming a few scant years after Fidel Castro took power, framed the trilateral relationship among the United States, Cuba, and the Soviet Union in which U.S. concerns are imbedded. Viewed positively, the crisis issued into an evolving set of understandings, first tacit or ambiguous, then more explicit, defining which actions were acceptable, which not. Those understandings, primarily between the United States and the Soviet Union, have developed into a crude security regime governing Cuba, a regime in which Cuba is a tacit, if sometimes grudging, partner.[1]

The regime took Cuba out of the U.S.-Soviet nuclear competition—no small achievement. In doing so, it achieved the paramount U.S. security interest in Cuba: assuring that Cuba would not be a base for nuclear attack on the United States. Once achieved, however, that success became less important to the United States than it was in the 1960s. While the missiles in Cuba would have provided the Soviet Union with a gimmicky kind of nuclear parity, within a decade the huge Soviet buildup produced a much more robust parity. Moreover, newer Soviet systems—most notably submarines located close to the U.S. coast and firing missiles on a depressed trajectory—came to pose just the same sort of short-warning threat that the Cuban-based missiles would have. Still, it is hoary to contemplate what U.S.-Cuban relations would look like now, in political terms if not purely military ones, if they were overhung by nuclear weapons.

After the mid-1970s, the focus of U.S. concerns shifted to Cuban and Soviet conventional capabilities in Cuba. The shift reflected both the nuclear success and its limits. It came about because of the sharp increase in Cuban military capabilities and in their deployment in the region and beyond.

The outcome of the 1962 missile crisis left lots of loose ends that later returned to haunt the parties, but it did embody a basic bargain: The United States would not invade Cuba if Cuba did not harbor weapons of a strategic—that is, offensive nuclear—nature.

The basic understanding was reconfirmed in 1970, when the Soviet Union pledged not to construct a facility in Cuba for ballistic missile submarines. In 1978, Moscow reassured Washington that the MiG-23s delivered to Cuba were not carriers of nuclear weapons. And, despite Secretary of State Alexander Haig's language about dealing with subversion "at its source" (that is, Cuba), the Reagan administration also accepted the basic deal.[2]

The defects of these arrangements from Cuba's point of view were, first, that it was not a full party to them, a fact that emerged as a specific problem in the 1979 dispute over what the United States regarded as a Soviet "combat brigade." Indeed, the original deal was struck over Cuba's head, without prior consultation between Havana and Moscow; under the Cuban-Soviet agreements, the missiles remained in Soviet hands. Castro signalled his assent, however reluctant, to a deal in the middle of the crisis:

> If the United States were able to give Cuba effective and satisfactory guarantees with respect to our territorial integrity and were to cease in its subversive and counterrevolutionary activities against our people, Cuba would not need to strengthen her defenses.[3]

The second defect, related to the first, was that the basic bargain was never formally confirmed. When Cuba rejected U.S. demands for on-site inspection of the missile withdrawal, the American administration, while not denying that it had done a deal, could regard itself as not formally bound. In fact, "no invasion" did not equal "no aggression," for CIA-supported anti-Castro operations continued until April 1964. When CIA support ended, the Cuban government may or may not have clearly detected the change. CIA involvement in assassination plotting against Castro continued, even after the spring of 1964. In retrospect, those efforts look feckless, even half-hearted. However, that they should not seem so to Fidel Castro and his government hardly is a surprise.

From the U.S. perspective, later concerns had their origins in the ambiguous resolution of the missile crisis. In 1962, nuclear missiles were the preoccupation; indeed, there probably would have been no crisis had Cuba and the Soviet Union confined the buildup to conventional weaponry. So the resolution put no clear constraints on the presence of Soviet troops in Cuba or on the size of the Cuban armed forces.

Given that, in 1962, the Cuban revolution was struggling to survive in Cuba, not much attention was paid to Cuban military deployments abroad. In his reflections, McGeorge Bundy, President Kennedy's national security advisor, believes that trying to turn the screw tighter during the crisis—seeking Cuban pledges of good behavior in the Caribbean or an end to the Soviet presence in Cuba—rapidly would have eroded U.S. support at home and abroad.[4]

The United States insisted that the nuclear-capable Il-28 bombers, but not the conventional MiG-21 aircraft, be withdrawn. Reluctantly, the Kennedy administration accepted that some Soviet trainers would remain in Cuba, and Moscow made no commitments about its future deployments to the island—unpleasant facts that later American administrations, especially the Reagan administration, sometimes wanted to ignore.

In 1970, the Soviet Union asked the new Nixon administration about the status of the 1962 understandings. In response, the United States unilaterally formalized its commitment not to overthrow the Castro government. On behalf of the president, Henry Kissinger communicated to Moscow that the U.S. defined the understandings

> as prohibiting the emplacement of any offensive weapons of any kind or any offensive delivery system on Cuban territory. We reaffirmed that in return we would not use military force to bring about a change in the governmental structure of Cuba.[5]

The United States had dropped its insistence on on-site verification. Later in the year, the understandings were made even more explicit in covering submarine bases.

In 1975, while moving into Angola, Castro for the first time publicly praised the 1962 understandings as having eased the threat of invasion. In November 1978, the Carter administration invoked the understandings over the newly discovered MiG-23s in Cuba, and was reassured by Moscow that the Cuban versions were not nuclear-capable (some MiG-23s are). Cuba began to display the planes in public.

The "combat brigade" episode of 1979 advanced the understandings to include conventional forces just as it demonstrated how fragile the underpinnings of those understandings were. The residual Soviet troop presence in Cuba, lost by U.S. intelligence, was "rediscovered" by increased efforts in the wake of the fall of the Shah of Iran. The Soviet Union, surprised, agreed not to introduce combat troops or upgrade its presence into a self-sufficient combat force.

Yet, even that relatively successful outcome for the United States derailed Senate ratification of SALT II. Cubans have believed then and since that the rediscovery of the brigade was no accident or bureaucratic happenstance; rather, they consider it a calculated move to embarrass Cuba as it hosted the nonaligned summit. It may be that the precise *timing* had something to do with the summit; certainly administration concern over Cuban actions was increasing and almost all Americans regarded Cuba's claim to nonalignment as a nasty joke.

In my view, however, the more important determinant of timing lay not inside but outside the administration, with those in Congress eager to use whatever ammunition they could to defeat SALT II. In that effort they succeeded, though not without help from the Soviet Union in Afghanistan. For U.S.-Cuban relations, the brigade episode underscored the fact that if the understandings had made the Soviet Union in Cuba less of a security problem for the United States, Cuba itself had become a bigger one.

Fortress Cuba

There is no question that Cuba has become a formidable base for military and intelligence activities. By U.S. statistics, the Soviet Union had in the mid-1980s some 2,800 military advisers in Cuba, plus a mechanized infantry brigade of the same size (the famous "combat brigade" again), plus an equal number of military advisors; 7,000 civilian technicians; and 2,100 technicians at the Lourdes listening post, which enables the Soviet Union to eavesdrop on military and civilian communications in the region, as well as telephone conversations in the continental United States.[6]

Lest readers distrust these U.S. statistics, here is Fidel Castro's own 1986 account of Cuban military strength: "there has been a qualitative improvement" in the air force and navy, "with the introduction of more modern weapons and equipment." Noting that reservists staffed Cuban forces in Angola, "more than half a million reservists have received training...[and] more than 100,000 Cubans have completed internationalist [military] service...In a mere five years 1.5 million men and women were organized into units and trained and equipped to participate in the defense of the country as members of the Territorial Troop Militias."[7]

Certainly, Cuba is convenient for the Soviet Union in these respects. Cuban bases permit it to fly aerial reconnaissance and anti-submarine missions up and down the U.S. east coast, missions that would be extremely expensive absent those bases. The interconnection of Soviet and Cuban intelligence services extends the reach of Soviet intelligence-gathering in the region.

Cuba's own forces rank at or near the top in Latin America, Cuba's small size notwithstanding. The whole range of capabilities need not be laid out here, but Cuba has active duty armed forces of 175,000 (79,500 conscripts) backed by 130,000 reservists. The army has some 950 tanks; while the bulk of these are older T-54/55s, they are not antiquated by the standards of its neighbors. The air force operates more than 250 combat aircraft, including one squadron of 15 MiG-23s.[8]

In sum, the Cuban army is large, and well trained and equipped, with more extensive combat experience abroad than any other Latin American military. The country's MiG-23 aircraft have the range to reach all of Central America plus the southeastern United States.[9] Cuban civil and military transport, in particular its recent acquisition of AN-26 short-range transports, would permit it to deploy 15,000 troops anywhere in the Caribbean within several weeks, and to get some units there within hours—capabilities not matched by anyone in the region except the United States. For more far-flung deployments, Cuba remains dependent on the Soviet Union, as it has been in Africa.

It is at least as interesting—or as worrisome—to recall that the sharpest growth in Cuba's armed forces did not come in the early 1960s, when an American invasion was a plausible threat (indeed occurred). The growth came in the 1970s, when Cuba sent forces to Africa. Cuba had 0.7 percent of its population under arms in 1960, 1.3 percent in 1974, and 2.3 percent by 1980.[10]

Nor is it reassuring to notice that this growth reflected Soviet support, which fell from 250,000 metric tons of military hardware in 1962 at the time of the missile crisis, to 15,000 tons annually for the next ten years, then moved upward again in the mid-1970s, reaching nearly 80,000 metric tons in 1982. It is even less reassuring to note that the 1970s increase coincided with the Ford and Carter administrations, those most disposed to improve relations with Cuba.

It is fair to say, as Cubans do, that some modernization of Cuban forces during the 1970s was in the cards precisely because Soviet deliveries slowed in the 1960s. But it seems fairer to conclude, as most Americans do, that the extent of the modernization in the 1970s and 1980s went beyond any plausible defensive purpose and that its timing was, in the 1970s at least, politically unfortunate.

Plainly, Cuba does not pose a direct threat to the territory of the United States. It could, however, in unusual circumstances, pose such a threat to Mexican or Venezuelan oil fields of interest to the United States. (The U.S. base at Guantánamo is indefensible but strategically of minor importance, despite the sometimes fanciful Cuban constructions of what goes on there; no doubt it would have been closed long ago except for the politics of relations between the United States and revolutionary Cuba, a point on which Professor Alzugaray and I agree.)

Rather, the U.S. security concern is hypothetical but not out of the question. If a major U.S.-Soviet war occurred, in Europe or elsewhere, 60 percent of total U.S. reinforcement supplies in the first sixty days would depart from U.S. Gulf of Mexico ports and transit the Florida Straits between Florida and Cuba.[11] Thus, the United States would have to be concerned about Cuban (and perhaps Soviet) attacks on its supply lines through the Caribbean. That is particularly the case as Cuba acquires more MiG-23s and submarines; even if the latter are old (Cuba now has three of the Soviet FOXTROT class), they could inflict considerable damage.

The point is that military planners now must reckon with their "Cuban problem": At the outset of a war, the United States would have to divert scarce military resources to constrain Cuba. It might take an invasion to do so. These concerns are those of military planners, but they have increasing force in a period when U.S. military resources are perceived to be stretched thinly. In a major war, it is fair to say that Cuba would be a minor problem; yet, in planning American military forces, the "Cuban problem" is a constraint. The United States might ease the problem by gradually moving military resources away from the Gulf coast to east coast ports, but that would cost money and create bottlenecks in wartime. In any event, it only illustrates the point: Fortress Cuba imposes costs and constraints on U.S. military planning.

Cuban Forces in the Third World

The second and third U.S. security concerns derive not from the missile crisis but from thereafter—the foreign deployments of Cuban military power, first in Latin America, and second, in Africa. This chapter is not the place to rehearse Cuba's far-flung military support and combat operations; those topics are detailed in the chapters on Africa and Latin America. The range and size are impressive for a country as small as Cuba: by a conservative estimate, upwards of 40,000 in Angola before the 1987 buildup, including some 8,000-plus technical advisors; 4,000 in Ethiopia; 3,500 in Nicaragua, including civilians; and around 500 each in the Congo, Mozambique, and South Yemen.[12] These numbers are illustrative only, for actual figures vary considerably as forces are rotated. Distinctions between "military" and "civilian" advisors also are, by nature, slippery. Other observers would put the Ethiopian presence as high as 10,000 and add to the list Libya and Algeria (3,500 total) plus small detachments in Zambia, Uganda, Tanzania, Equatorial Guinea, São Tomé e Príncipe, and Lesotho.[13]

These Cuban actions threaten U.S. security interests only indirectly, by putting at risk U.S. allies or supporting groups and regimes opposed to the United States. It is hard to make these threats commensurable with that posed by the simple fact of Cuba as a base for its and Soviet military power. In strategic terms, Cuban actions in Africa rank third, for the U.S. interests there are slender (Angola) or the outcomes ambiguous (Ethiopia). There, the effect of Cuban actions is more political and symbolic, diminishing any chance of more fruitful relations with the United States; that was so even in Angola, where Cuba and the United States shared some interests: independence for Namibia, and Chevron-Gulf oil exports from Cabinda, for instance.

I rank Cuba as a military fortress, an island aircraft carrier, second because it is both hypothetical and limited. If the United States has to reckon with its "Cuban problem" in a major war, it knows it can handle the situation, though at some cost. It is Cuban action in Latin America and the Caribbean that ranks first among U.S. security interests in Cuba. There, the risks are actual, open-ended and uncertain for several reasons:

- Central America, relatively stable and prosperous if not always very democratic until the 1970s, has been and will remain unstable for a number of reasons, among which, to be fair, the past failure of U.S. policy must be counted.
- This instability coincided with—perhaps was partly the result of—a diminished British presence in the Caribbean (whose Anglophone countries do have a democratic tradition) and a reduced U.S. military presence in Central America. The United States had 22,000 military personnel in the Caribbean basin outside the United States in 1960, a figure that rose to 25,000 in 1968 but fell to 16,000 in 1981, principally due to draw-downs in Panama and Puerto Rico

(although more recently the U.S. presence has increased and its capabilities for deploying forces to the region have increased more).[14]

- Even if U.S. interests (in the shape of Central American or Caribbean governments) *per se* are not powerful, those countries are psychologically "near."[15] More important, future outcomes of current instability are uncertain. Just as the past and present of Nicaragua, El Salvador, Guatemala, and Honduras have been interconnected, so will be their futures. Even disbelievers in "domino theories" can worry that minor threats today (for instance, major Cuban or Soviet military bases elsewhere in the region besides Cuba) might, if unchecked, become major tomorrow.

- This instability has coincided with the realization, sometimes exaggerated, that Mexico's political system is creaky, hence its stability may be suspect. In Mexico, the U.S. stake is immense.[16] Domino theories are especially suspect in the instance of Mexico but, still, it is hard to argue that instability or radical regimes in Mexico's neighborhood will help produce the kind of evolution in that country that would minimize risks for the United States.

Thus, my ranking of possible U.S. security concerns about Cuba is:

1. (Soviet) offensive nuclear forces based in Cuba
2. Cuban military deployments in Latin America
3. Cuba as a fortress for its and Soviet military power
4. Cuban military deployments in Africa

Whatever their motivations, Cuban actions both in and beyond Latin America inject that country to the center of East-West, and U.S.-Soviet, relations. Whatever the fact, it is impossible for Americans not to regard Cuba as a kind of Soviet "hired gun" in the Third World, whose actions are in good measure repayment for the billions of dollars of Soviet aid it receives annually. That aspect is enhanced, for those inside Cuba as well as outside, by the knowledge that Angola and other countries that can afford it have paid Cuba for the presence of Cuban personnel. Making money—tens of millions of dollars per year from Angola before falling oil prices dried up Angolan revenues—is understandable in national terms but does make ideological solidarity look more like good business.[17]

Even a measured reading of history gives prominence to the Cuban role. In general, it is arguable whether the Soviets and the Cubans are noticeably more effective at Third World military and intelligence operations than the United States. If Angola in the mid-1970s is counted a success for them, that success derived partly from the availability of the Cuban cadres but mostly from the fact that, once the South Africans intervened, the Soviets and their Cuban allies were perceived in Africa as on the "right" side, the United States on the "wrong."

Soviet influence also increased during a number of decolonization struggles, especially in Africa. Yet, again, that influence derived more from the clear Soviet identification with the "right" side, while the Western nations remained saddled with the colonial legacy, than from the brilliance of Soviet clandestine operations. The primary instruments of Soviet policy in these cases were open, not covert—rhetorical support plus some military assistance.

When coups in the Third World have brought to power regimes more friendly to the Soviet Union—from Egypt and Iraq in the 1950s, to Peru, Syria and Libya in the 1960s, to Grenada and Suriname in the 1970s—most of the time the Soviet role has been marginal. Only in Southern Yemen in 1978 and, more controversially, Ethiopia in the mid-1970s, was the Soviet role central.[18] However, the Soviets have been better at protecting friendly regimes once in power. They have done so through a combination of measures more half-covert than covert: military assistance, support for "vanguard" parties and, most important, Cuban (and sometimes East German) training of intelligence services and militias loyal to the regime.

Indeed, if the Soviet Union has any obvious advantage over the United States in the shadow wars of the Third World, it is the Cubans. Certainly there is an element of unfairness in U.S. complaints about that advantage, for if Cuban internationalism abroad partly repays its Soviet debt, there are also Cuban reasons for its foreign military deployments. However, proximity to the United States and its small size by comparison to its foreign deployments will make Cuba a continuing target of U.S. attentions.

Looking to the Future

In looking to the future, Cuban actions within and, especially, beyond Latin America will be hostage to the course of Soviet policy, especially in Africa and Central America—surely so in U.S. eyes, even if Cuban leaders protest to the contrary. Only time will tell whether Soviet leader Mikhail Gorbachev is truly in the process of liquidating unpromising Soviet ventures in the Third World, of which Afghanistan is the most obvious but also the most special, given proximity.

Yet, whether Soviet actions amount to retrenchment or to a more modest process of consolidation, Americans will expect the Cuban role to diminish correspondingly. Castro has reasons of his own to want to consolidate or even retrench, but history does not suggest that being cast into a supporting role for Soviet policy is Cuba's preferred part.[19] For Cuba, better to be the leading edge of a policy the Soviet Union supports, as with Cuban activism in Africa in the 1970s, than the compliant subordinate.

As Professor Alzugaray notes in his chapter, thus far it seems that when U.S.-Soviet relations improve, U.S.-Cuban relations do not, but when the U.S.-Soviet dialogue cools, so does that between Washington and Havana. Yet, there is little mystery to that pattern. It is not just a matter of U.S. hostility to Cuba; it also reflects Cuban intentions and actions.

When Cuba says it is not merely a Soviet proxy and behaves accordingly, Americans draw the appropriate conclusions. Warming superpower relations after 1963 were also a time of active Cuban subversion in Latin America. Détente of the mid-1970s is a more ambiguous case, since the Soviet Union evidently also was prepared to risk the superpower relationship in African adventures. Yet, in both the 1960s and the 1970s, Cuba gave preference to revolutionary adventures abroad over participating in warming East-West relations.

It may be that if this current period of improving superpower relations persists, U.S.-Cuban relations will also; eventually, those relations might even emerge from the shadow of the superpower interaction. But much will depend on how Cuba acts. The United States will be looking for signs that Cuba, in whatever combination of its own calculations and concert with the Soviet Union, is winding down *its* foreign deployments.

Angola will be the first test, an intriguing one, so far positive with the December 1988 agreement for a Cuban withdrawal linked to Namibian independence.[20] There, Cuba backs a government, not an insurgent movement, so winding down that support will be doubly hard—because it will be visible and because eventually it will compel the government to negotiate with its armed opposition, Jonas Savimbi's UNITA, to which the United States resumed covert assistance in 1986—assistance President Bush promises to continue.

Moreover, reports of Cuban-Soviet differences over Angola have circulated in the past, and it is at least conceivable that, if implementation of the agreement began to break down, Cuba might want to stay on even if the Gorbachev retrenchment argued for the Soviets to scale down their arms supplies to the Angolan government. In an interview, Cuban Vice-President Carlos Rafael Rodríguez stressed that Cuba would not leave if Angola did not desire it, even if the Soviet Union did.[21]

On the other hand, Cuba has reason (apart from Angola or the Soviet Union) to want to withdraw. Over the last five years, Cuba's military role has become more prominent; first Cuba began to control the tactical operations of the war, and more recently Cuban units have begun to replace Angolan in the battlefields of the south.[22] The cost, in money and manpower, has risen accordingly; with some 50,000-plus soldiers in Angola and a badly stretched economy at home, Cuba is hard pressed to try to reward returning *internacionalistas* with good jobs and housing.

It will be especially intriguing to see what happens if South Africa still tries to frustrate a settlement in Namibia—still a possibility though a less likely one than most would have estimated two years ago. Throughout, Cuba has insisted that there could be no formal link between its presence in Angola and South Africa's in Namibia, although *de facto* that link has emerged. Indeed, the irony of the agreement is that it came about, in considerable measure, precisely *because of* the Cuban build up in 1987. South Africa was bloodied at the siege of Cuito Cuanavale, and so seems to have concluded that its strategic interest no longer justified the cost of holding Namibia.

In Central America, the Soviet Union—and perhaps especially Cuba—seem to have decided that any more-than-modest role in support of insurgents in El Salvador or elsewhere is too costly, too risky, or both. The U.S. invasion of Grenada in 1983 confirmed Cuba and the Soviet Union in a line of policy on which they already seemed decided.[23] Both Cuba and Nicaragua reduced their support for the FMLN in El Salvador after its 1981 offensive failed and after the Reagan administration raised the temperature of the issue.

While Nicaragua remains deeply intertwined with Cuban military and intelligence agencies, there, too, the Cuban role seems to have been a cautionary one from early on, and especially after 1983.[24] What Fidel Castro really thinks of the Sandinista leaders will make fascinating memoir reading, but a stream of Latin American visitors to Havana has reported him as concerned about those leaders as hot-headed, capable of bringing down a U.S. intervention on the region. He began to caution them in public soon after they took power in 1979 and continued to do so throughout 1980. After Grenada, the lesson seems to have been explicit: Like Grenada, Nicaragua could not count on Cuba to go to war to defend its revolution.

Central America will remain the focal point of the U.S.-Cuban relationship into the 1990s. Much will depend on the peace process and how both regimes and oppositions in Nicaragua and El Salvador fare in it. Most likely, peace will not break out, and outcomes will be ambiguous. If agreements are achieved, charges and counter-charges of violation will continue. Verification will be weak if the United States is not central to it, and perhaps suspected of bias if it is; more important than verification, mechanisms for inducing compliance, too, will be either weak or unilateral.

These circumstances will be unpromising for increasing U.S. confidence in Cuban restraint. Even if Cuba is restrained in providing aid to kindred movements, it will not be easy for the United States to be sure of that fact or of its continuing. Turbulence in the region makes it all the harder to draw tidy lines between what is permitted and what not: witness past arguments over the famous runway on Grenada.

New "Security" Issues

Two eminently political sets of issues, narcotics and migration, now have security implications. They have become important in their own right and, from a U.S. perspective, because of their effect on views of whether Cuba can be trusted. (Airline hijacking would have been on the list some years ago, and it might return. However, that seems unlikely, thanks to a combination of better airport security in the United States plus a changed Cuban attitude toward hijackers, never mind formal U.S.-Cuban arrangements.) Both narcotics and migration bear on whether the United States will regard Cuba as a responsible international citizen or a troublemaker, even a security threat. They are "sleepers" in the realm of security.

The recent history of migration is the most bizarre example. In 1985, Cuba suspended the agreement it had signed the previous December; Radio Martí's first broadcasts were the announced justification. Then, in 1987, when the steps toward reconstructing the agreement began, their first fruit was U.S. prisons taken over and burned by Cuban prisoners who feared their forced return to

Cuba. In the combination of sympathy for the Cuban prisoners and outrage at what they had done, any credit to Cuba for taking a constructive step was lost. In addition, the reminder that migration can result in domestic violence was not lost.

In the short run, narcotics may be even more serious because, for all the side effects, more immigration from Cuba retains its tug on Americans' self image as a bastion for the oppressed and its specific constituency among Cuban-Americans. Cuba has been accused by the United States from time to time of being involved in a network of drug trafficking and anti-government guerrillas. Thus far, such charges have turned out to be exaggerated, the networks more complicated than portrayed, and Cuba's role less than imagined.

Now, both the United States and Cuba seem to have supported a government led by a major trafficker, Panama's Manuel Noriega. (So, too, have the Sandinistas, at least for money and investment-laundering purposes.) For the United States, the evolution of the relationship seems straightforward: The CIA sustained contact with Noriega for intelligence purposes over several administrations, while evidence of his drug trafficking accumulated. The Reagan administration, in particular, fixed on Central America, was inclined to disregard that evidence until a public storm made it impossible to do so.

For U.S.-Cuban relations, the point is that the sensitivity of the narcotics issue in the United States will remain dramatically higher than in the past, for the near term at least. Handled well, the moment could be an opportunity to resume specific anti-drug cooperation. Handled badly, it could dramatically inject narcotics, with the security connotations of anarchic behavior, into the relationship between the United States and Cuba.

Negotiated, Tacit, and Third-Party Arrangements

In conceiving of future U.S. security policy toward Cuba in the new administration and beyond, two themes stand out. One is *explicitness*: Does the path to actions that would enhance U.S. security and be acceptable to Cuba lie through explicit negotiation or through tacit accommodation and mutual observance of third-party agreements? The second is the future of *Cuban-Soviet relations*, for the core U.S. security concerns derive from that relationship. From an American perspective, absent change in it, specific, small accommodations between Cuba and the United States are imaginable, but movement toward normal state-to-state relations is not.

From a strategic perspective, logical next steps would seem to be building on the emerging security regime and doing so through explicit U.S.-Cuban negotiations. After all, if the United States can negotiate with the Soviet Union, and even reach agreements like that on intermediate nuclear forces (INF) that involve Soviet inspectors outside U.S. missile factories, why cannot the U.S. and Cuba negotiate? In these negotiations, the United States would seek commitments about Cuban military actions and would agree to constraints on its own actions in return.

Yet, consider the obstacles. Imagine explicit U.S.-Cuban negotiations over the issue of most concern to the United States: Cuban support for kindred governments and movements around the world. Central America would be the obvious focal point of such negotiations. Could the two parties agree on "rules of the road" governing the behavior of both there? It seems unlikely. Any agreement would be difficult to verify; money, in particular, moves easily across national borders. As has been the case with arms control, formal agreement tends to magnify the importance of small violations, and so makes verification more central.

More to the point, particular rules are all ambiguous or controversial between the United States and Cuba. The allies and opponents of the two in Central America are the mirror image of each other, yet both say they act in the name of "democracy," so that will not do as a criterion. What, then, about recourse to international law, distinguishing between governments in power and their armed opponents? On such a distinction, both parties seem ambivalent. For Cuba the ambivalence is explicit: it must reserve the right to aid its ideological kin in opposition to established governments even if tactically it might refrain from doing so.

Nor is the United States everywhere prepared to enshrine the status quo. While aid to the Nicaraguan contras has been controversial in the United States, most opponents of aid still would not accept that the Sandinistas deserve to be distinguished from the contras merely because the former managed to shoot their way to power while the latter could not. The same seems true, though more vaguely, of the Angolan government.

Similar problems would bedevil explicit agreements on other rules—limitations on kinds of support to, say, "nonlethal" or "defensive" weaponry or to "nonmilitary advisors." Verification would be difficult and its object ambiguous: The defender's tanks look defensive to it while its opponents' appear offensive; if the flow of battle changes and the defender counterattacks, the perceptions reverse. "Military" personnel are not easily distinguished from "civilian" ones, as demonstrated by the Cuban "civilians" on Grenada, who could fight as well as advise.

For the near future, it will be more fruitful to think about pursuing further what is already the practice of indirect limitations. In the Central American peace process, the parties directly involved sought to limit foreign military assistance and military activities across borders. Outside powers, especially including the United States and Cuba, could not easily oppose the provisions. If they actually went into effect, the two could be bound without explicit bilateral negotiations and without having explicitly to abandon principles or embrace distasteful regimes.

Third parties also would be in charge of verification, a mixed blessing from the U.S. perspective. On one hand, verification would not be a matter simply of taking Cuba at its word, and the verification arrangements would be at one remove from the politics of the U.S.-Cuban relationship. On the other, Americans would worry about verification and more about compliance, as they already have about the Central American peace process. Technically, verification would be weak without U.S. satellites, sensors, and other technology. Worse, Americans would fear that violations, even if detected, would be dismissed as trivial lest they reveal the fragility of the whole process.

It is also worth exploring how tacit or reciprocal but not negotiated limits could be expanded. Grenada demonstrated one tacit limit on Cuban behavior, one both imposed and self- imposed: if the United States attacks Cuban allies in Latin America, those allies can expect no increase in support from Cuba. In other areas, the limits of tacit measures have been apparent. In fact, Cuban and Nicaraguan support to the FMLN insurgents in El Salvador seems to have been relatively limited after 1981. Yet since both were unprepared unilaterally to renounce their right to provide such support, their limits were dismissed by the United States as merely tactical.

Jorge Domínguez has made the intriguing suggestion that Cuba undertake to remain aloof from a NATO-Warsaw Pact war.[25] However, this aspect of Cuba as a security problem for the United States is rooted in the nature of the Cuban-Soviet relationship. Given the history of Cuban-Soviet military cooperation in Cuba and beyond, no such Cuban undertaking would be credible so long as the basic structure of that relationship remained intact. No matter what Cuba said, U.S. military planners would still have to reckon with the possibility that if war came, Cuba would be compelled to make common cause with the Soviet Union.

At the same time, unilateral Cuban measures both before and during a U.S.-Soviet crisis might hold some promise. Before the crisis, Cuban restraint in acquiring anti-shipping capabilities would help; already, Cuba tacitly cooperates in U.S. intelligence-gathering about MiG-23s and submarines. In the heat of a major crisis it might be possible, though hardly easy, for Cuba to visibly demonstrate restraint (keeping submarines above water in a few ports and planes on the ground) with the U.S. prepared to reciprocate by not attacking Cuba.

So, too, Cuba might refrain from acquiring long-distance military transport. Doing so would at least ensure that any major deployment beyond Cuba's immediate region would take time and require Soviet assistance.

In general, the more Cuban openness about its military forces, the better. In his chapter, Professor Alzugaray makes an issue of the U.S. surveillance flights around or over Cuba, and in terms of national pride his concerns are understandable. The flights also may be interpreted as violations of international law, although it is interesting that satellite overflights have been tacitly accepted while airplane overflights have not. The grounds for the difference are *not* that nothing can be done about satellite overflights, for both superpowers could do something about photo reconnaissance satellites in low orbit; rather, ten miles up is unacceptable, but a hundred is not.

From the perspective of building confidence between the United States and Cuba, those flights should be welcomed by Cuba. In a crisis, the flights would be all the more important as a way to clarify Cuban intentions.

It does not seem out of the question, even if explicit U.S.-Cuban negotiations prove difficult, that the two countries might agree around the edges of other talks to a series of confidence-building measures—exchanges of observers to try to sharpen distinctions between military and civilian advisors, exchanges of information on military forces, and the like.

"Mexicanization" and the Soviet Connection

Beyond specific questions, a more general issue arises. From a U.S. perspective, it seems both strategically unlikely and politically impossible for U.S.-Cuban relations to become anywhere near normal until Cuba grants some deference, at least tacit, to U.S. preponderance. Plainly, the United States has and will continue to apply a double standard, presuming that major powers have room to maneuver that small ones do not. Such deference is labelled "hegemony" when it is disliked, "accommodation" by small countries to large neighbors when it is sought.[26]

This would mean, if not the "finlandization" of Cuba (the term is unfair to Finland, but it is worth remembering that it was first coined, by a Brazilian foreign minister, to describe a model for Cuba), at least the "mexicanization."[27] Cuba would, in effect, say whatever it wanted but limit its actions in cases where the United States felt itself to have powerful stakes. It would not be explicitly compelled to do so, but rather would choose to do so on the basis of calculations of its own interest.

In particular, Cuba would have to make clear that it would not go beyond rhetorical support for fellow revolutionaries in or beyond Latin America. ·That would mean no military support or advisors and sharply reduced technical missions, especially in Latin America and especially where conflicts were in progress. It would also imply that, over time, Cuba's own military forces would be scaled down to reduce, if not eliminate, the threat posed to the United States by fortress Cuba.

Cuba could continue its economic connections to the Soviet Union and retain its existing political system, just as Finland retains its trade links west and its democratic polity. However, whether Cuba could retain its military alliance to the Soviet Union is more doubtful. Notice that Finland is a treaty ally of the Soviet Union, partly through choice and partly through the lack of it, and it buys most of its military hardware from the Soviet Union. Mexico cooperates fairly closely with the United States in police and intelligence matters.

U.S.-Soviet relations will remain competitive in the best of cases, and the history of the Cuban-Soviet connection is, in U.S. eyes, a lot for Cuba to live down. As suggested above, an agreement to remain neutral in a European war could not be taken seriously by the United States so long as the Cuban-Soviet alliance remained intact. Nor is it easy to imagine that Cuban military deployments could be "transparent" enough to reassure the United States if the bulk of its equipment and advisors were Soviet.

This "mexicanization" may not be within this Cuban generation's imaginings for Cuba. It would imply voluntarily circumscribing Cuban options in order to pursue other objectives: relations of normality and confidence with the United States. It would overturn thirty years of Cuban history, and Cuba's leaders may calculate that the price is too high. Indeed, the history of

Cuban approaches to the United States suggests such a calculation: each approach has stopped short of any Cuban concessions that would have been interesting to the United States, and well short of the kind of implicit deference suggested here.

Little has indicated that Cuba is really interested in better relations with the United States except on Cuban terms. From a U.S. perspective, the leadership shows little sign of willingness to change the pattern of a revolution built on hostility to the United States.[28] Perhaps it cannot afford to, for a combination of external profile and the internal politics of the revolution.

However, Soviet calculations may not match those of Cuba; should Gorbachev remain in effective power, who can tell? At some point, the Soviet rethinking of foreign commitments is bound to touch Cuba. New realities in Cuban-Soviet relations might change Cuban calculations over time. If Gorbachev pulled back from unprofitable Soviet adventures, in Angola for instance, the costs and risks of Cuban deployments inevitably would change. That rethinking might make, first, for less activism in Central America, and second, eventually, for a fresh look at Cuba's position with regard to the United States. What has been unthinkable might slowly become conceivable.

In any event, the Cuban-Soviet relationship is fundamental to the question of security in relations between the United States and Cuba. Until it is addressed, U.S.-Cuban relations are doomed to no more than partial relief of a hostile status quo.

Notes

1. Jorge I. Dominguez has done the most thinking about these security bargains, and my discussion owes much to him. For a discussion of security regimes, see Robert Jervis, "Security Regimes," *International Organization*, 36, 2 (Spring 1982), pp. 357-378.
2. Alexander M. Haig, Jr., *Caveat: Realism, Reagan, and Foreign Policy* (New York: Macmillan, 1984), pp. 98, 128-129.
3. As quoted in *Revolución*, October 24, 1962.
4. McGeorge Bundy, *Danger and Survival: Choices about the Bomb in the First Fifty Years* (New York: Random House, 1988), p. 408.

5.   Henry Kissinger, *White House Years* (Boston: Little, Brown and Co., 1979), p. 634.

6.   These numbers are from U.S. Departments of State and Defense, *The Challenge to Democracy in Central America* (Washington: June 1986), p. 10ff. Cuba has not seriously disputed them and so, implicitly, has confirmed them.

7.   *Main Report: III Congress of the Communist Party of Cuba* (mimeographed English-language edition, February 1986).

8.   From International Institute for Strategic Studies, *The Military Balance, 1987-88* (London: IISS, 1987).

9.   Effective combat radiuses could be smaller depending on the profile of the mission and the armaments the planes carried.

10. Joseph H. Stodder and Kevin F. McCarthy, *Profiles of the Caribbean Basin in 1960/1980: Changing Geopolitical and Geostrategic Dimensions*, N-2058-AF (Santa Monica: The Rand Corporation, December 1983), p. 57.

11. U.S. government estimate, in U.S. Departments of State and Defense, *The Soviet-Cuban Connection in Central America and the Caribbean* (Washington, March 1985), p. 5.

12. These figures are from a careful, non-American source, *The Military Balance, 1987-88.*

13. See Pamela Falk, "Cuba in Africa," *Foreign Affairs*, 65, 5 (Summer 1987), p. 1086-1087.

14. The figures are from Edward Gonzalez, *A Strategy for Dealing with Cuba in the 1980s*. R-2954-DOS/AF (Santa Monica: The Rand Corporation, September 1982), p. 5.

15. I try to distinguish different interests in my "Strategy in Central America," *Survival*, 28, 2 (March/April 1986).

16. See my "U.S. Interests in Mexico Beyond Drugs: Discussion Paper," prepared for a Harvard-El Colegio de México Conference, April 1988.

17. See Falk, "Cuba in Africa," p. 1095; and Juan M. del Aguila, "Cuba's Military Involvement Overseas: The Domestic Reaction," unpublished paper, January 1987. Falk's estimate of Angola's payments is a half billion dollars. I have used a more conservative number because of the uncertainties about how much Angola paid and for which Cuban services, and how much the Cuban state benefited.

18. See Steven R. David, "Soviet Involvement in Third World Coups," *International Security*, 11, 1 (Summer 1986), pp. 3-36. Afghanistan in 1979 might be added to the list, but having to send 100,000 troops hardly seems like a "success" and certainly not a covert one.

19. Edward Gonzalez and David Ronfeldt, *Castro, Cuba and the World*, R-3420 (Santa Monica: The Rand Corporation, June 1986), p. 98.
20. The text of the agreement was printed in the *New York Times*, December 14, 1988.
21. April 6, 1988.
22. Falk, "Cuba in Africa," pp. 1091ff.
23. On the ebb and flow of such support, see Gordon McCormick and others, *Nicaraguan Security Policy: Trends and Projections*, R-3532-PA and E (Santa Monica: The Rand Corporation, January 1988), pp. 17ff.
24. On those entanglements, see McCormick and others, pp. 13-15.
25. See Chapter 2, "The Security Regime," of his *To Make a World Safe for Revolution: Cuba's Foreign Policy* (Cambridge: Harvard University Press, 1989).
26. For a stimulating Cuban view, see Rafael Hernández, "La lógica de la frontera en las relaciones E.U.-Cuba," pp. 6-54.
27. For an earlier use of the Finland analogy in U.S.-Cuban relations, see Gonzalez, *A Strategy for Dealing with Cuba in the 1990s*, pp. 100-102.
28. See Gonzalez and Ronfeldt, *Castro, Cuba and the World*.

4

Problems of National Security in the Cuban-U.S. Historic Breach

Carlos Alzugaray Treto

Cuban and U.S. citizens can agree—as both Dr. Gregory Treverton (see preceding chapter) and I do—on the recognition that national security lies at the heart of the dispute between our countries. Nevertheless, this agreement probably goes no farther, and both chapters give evidence of it. The definition of "national security" itself leads to broad differences of opinion. From Arnold Wolfers, who wrote in 1952 about the ambiguity of the term as a symbol, to the United Nations, which in 1983 requested that the general secretary organize a study to define the concept, "security" has remained a category of international politics many times referred to but seldom defined, even by those who most often appeal to it to legitimize a certain policy.[1]

U.S. literature on national security problems is a case in point. Since the end of World War II, a national security interest has been used a number of times to justify a certain course of action. Nevertheless, it is only seldom that both international relations scholars and U.S. foreign policy makers take the time to define what they mean by the country's national security and why something that takes place thousands of miles away from U.S. borders can constitute a real threat to its security (and not to the security of other countries). The reader can judge whether Dr. Treverton has succeeded in defining these terms of the debate on the security perspective of the Cuban-U.S. breach.

Of course, the Cuban approach to national security cannot be the same as that of the United States. Dr. Treverton argues that my concept of the term is expansive. I admit that it is broader, but certainly not expansive; had that been the case, I might have affirmed that U.S. support of Great Britain during the 1982 war with Argentina in the South Atlantic represented a threat to Cuban national security, which I do not.

If Cuban national security is given a conceptualization beyond strictly military dimensions to also include economic, political, and even social aspects, it is precisely because Cuba, as a small country, is more vulnerable than a big superpower like the United States to all kinds of pressures. For example, it would have been not only utterly ridiculous but also counterproductive for the Cuban government to have imposed on the United States an economic blockade (or trade embargo as it is euphemistically called by the U.S. government) in retaliation for the one that the United States imposed on Cuba in the early stages of the breach.

But this asymmetry is not the only, nor even the most important, reason for the differences in approaches to national security in Cuba and the United States. I agree with Dr. Treverton in the sense that, in discussions about national security, what is perceived becomes what is real. In the Cuban perception, the most important thing is that throughout history, our national security has been the object of a permanent military, political, economic, and ideological threat by the government of the United States; at the same time, it seems totally irrational to Cubans for the United States to believe, as it seems, that Cuba could constitute an ever-present threat to U.S. security.

In this chapter, I hope to contribute to an understanding of how topics related to national security are approached in Cuba, the role attributed historically to the United States in Cuba's conception of its security, the measures that Cuban leaders have had to take to confront the U.S. threat, how we view Cuba's situation with regard to global security problems, and, finally, what prospects are perceived for the Cuban-U.S. historic breach as regards national security.

Conceptual Issues

The Cuban and U.S. concepts of national security are plagued with asymmetry and contradictions. The first instance of asymmetry lies in the fact that, although the concept of national security in the United States has been widely developed and even regulated by law and there is a government agency that tries to coordinate all policy on the subject, in Cuba the term as such is hardly ever used—which does not mean, of course, that the government does not have a national security policy.[2] One of the reasons why Cubans are reticent about using the term is because *national security* has a pejorative connotation for most Latin Americans. It is perceived, first of all, as a doctrine of U.S. origin drawn up to serve U.S. interests of domination and hegemony in Latin America. Moreover, some rightist dictatorial regimes (which Jeanne Kirkpatrick calls "authoritarian") have installed systems of internal repression against the people's liberation movements under the slogan of "national security." Both aspects of the problem have been widely studied by Latin American specialists. One of them, John Saxe-Fernández, has compared national security in Latin America to a kind of "hemispheric counterreform."[3] Therefore, it should be clear that Cuba's *national security* has nothing to do with that doctrine as it has been tragically transferred to some other Latin American countries. Much less does it have anything to do with the concepts of security as designed by U.S. scholars.

A first approximation to the topic of national security as a political category from the Cuban point of view requires a conceptual and content definition. We could agree with Raymond Aron that security is one of the eternal goals of states and that, in fact, it becomes the primary goal of all their domestic and foreign policies.[4] Nevertheless, this concept would not be sufficient, for, though according "national security" a place in a scale of values, it does not specify what is meant by security.

Another commonly used definition is the one Walter Lippmann proposed in 1943: "A nation has security when it does not have to sacrifice its legitimate interests to avoid war, and is able, if challenged, to maintain them by war."[5] On stressing that the fundamental content of security is to safeguard the "legitimate interest" of a nation, and, introducing in the definition the contradictory element between that safeguarding and the need to avoid war, Lippmann made an important contribution that brings out the dilemma with which all states are confronted in their national security policies. On criticizing Lippmann, I would have to say, however, that he does not clarify that the use of force is only justified in the case of legitimate defense, and that such defense is generally associated with territorial integrity and national sovereignty, and not with other concepts, no matter how legitimate they may be considered by the ruling groups of the country in question.

However, the concept of national security in contemporary times requires greater precision concerning the definition of "legitimate interests." The Polish specialist Andrzej Karkoszka has suggested that the concept of security "seems to be related to the likelihood of survival, to confidence in the maintenance of the state's boundaries and of its territorial integrity, and to the nation's prosperity and to the preservation of its cultural and ideological integrity."[6]

Moreover, among the underdeveloped countries, the concept of security is linked ever more closely to that of development. Paradoxically, in 1966, in the midst of the Vietnam War, Robert McNamara recognized this link by stating that security meant development and that, without development, there could be no security. The then secretary of defense in the Johnson administration warned of the danger of approaching the problem of U.S. security from an exclusively military point of view, adding that, on the contrary, it was largely dependent on the security of the developing countries. Viewed in this framework, McNamara's thesis had an evident interventionist edge; nevertheless, it is no less true that he recognized that for Third World countries security was part and parcel of development.

The national security of any country, large or small, is based on both permanent and nonpermanent factors. These last may be of a varied nature, such as the socioeconomic regime or the political superstructure. Those of a permanent nature play a very important role. Geographic location, availability of natural resources, and the country's size and population are aspects that cannot be transformed, at least in the short run, and all statesmen should keep them in mind when formulating national security policy for their countries.

Even though there are objective factors that determine national security, it is also true that from the point of view of international relations, this is an eminently subjective political category. In today's world, above all, it is very common that what one state considers a legitimate interest may be perceived by another as a threat to its national security. Therefore, a unilateral approach to one's own national security may constitute a permanent threat. This paradox of national security leads us to another phenomenon that is an integral part of that problem, which Karl Deutsch has described as a kind of Parkinson's Law of national security, according to which the big power's feeling of insecurity increases to the same extent as its power grows in the search for security, even though it is not clear who is seriously threatening its national independence.[7] This expansive nature of the national security of some states is extremely risky; carried to its ultimate consequences, it may lead to the false concept of absolute security.

Naturally, all these interpretations of national security that give it a unilateral, absolute, and expansive nature are simply explanations that tend to justify a course of action that facilitates interventionism beyond a nation's borders—as has been the case with the United States, time and again. Henry Kissinger himself (while referring to the Soviet Union) has warned that "absolute security for one country means absolute insecurity for all others; it can be achieved only by reducing other states to impotence."[8]

In contrast to the national security doctrines that stress the unilateral, expansive, and absolute approach, there is the thesis of national security as an ever more interdependent phenomenon, and of the need to include within this concept the categories of indivisibility and equality, which means that any country that aspires to security should link its own security with that of others, and that all nations have the same right to security.[9]

This brief examination, though incomplete and limited, may constitute a first approximation to some doctrines of national security, and at the same time propose some bases for the study of its problems from the Cuban point of view. I suggest that these bases include the following elements:

1. Every state has the legitimate right to preserve its national security.

2. National security includes not only safeguarding national sovereignty and territorial integrity, but also guaranteeing other component elements of a nationality: economic development, political self-determination, cultural and ideological identity, social justice, and international stance.

3. National security is indivisible from international security, and vice versa. All states should respect the national security of the rest, and the international or global security as a whole. No state that acts against the national security of another may demand that the latter respect the former's security.

4. National security is the responsibility of each state. However, when national security is threatened, the state in danger may, on the basis of its right to legitimate defense, ask another state for help without threatening the national security of third parties by so doing.

5. When applying its policy in the sphere of security, a state such as Cuba should keep in mind permanent conditions that affect its national security such as its geographic size and location and its history.[10]

National Security Themes in the History of U.S.-Cuban Relations

Geography and history have determined that Cuba is a small country with a powerful enemy only 160 kilometers from its northernmost point—which has been the main threat to its existence throughout the nearly two centuries of the history of the Cuban nation. Authors of the most diverse points of view have conclusively shown that throughout the nineteenth century, the U.S. government was one of the main obstacles to all Cuban attempts to join the concert of American nations as a free and independent state.[11]

The U.S. threat to Cuba was the subject of discussion among the most advanced Cuban political thinkers in the colonial period. Little by little, the criteria that José Martí expressed most clearly were crystallized: Cuba must be independent of Spain and of the United States, not only to serve its interests as a nation but also "to win Cuba's independence in time to stop the United States from expanding through the Antilles and falling with even greater force on the lands of our America."[12] Martí was aware of Cuba's strategic importance, not only to its powerful neighbor to the north, but also to the security of the rest of the Latin American nations.

Geography made the Cuban archipelago a coveted possession throughout the seventeenth, eighteenth, and nineteenth centuries. At the threshold of the twentieth century, it acquired an even greater strategic importance when the United States, impelled by the need to acquire markets and raw materials for its growing industry, launched its imperial expansion toward the south, with Cuba as part of the northern boundary of its future sphere of influence.

Cuba's subsequent history is well known: military intervention in 1898-1902, when the Platt Amendment was imposed; establishment of a U.S. naval base at Guantánamo; intervention and U.S. "protectorate;" large and concentrated land holdings and reliance on a single crop; underdevelopment and dependence—in short, economic and political domination.[13]

This economic and political situation brought about crises several times in the next fifty-seven years. The succeeding Cuban administrations acted as faithful servants of their U.S. master and of the domestic oligarchy. Only in 1933, as the result of a revolutionary movement, did a progressive sector reach power; for 100 days, it took some measures to rectify the country's ills, even nationalizing some U.S. companies. Nevertheless, thanks to

Washington's manipulations through U.S. Ambassador Sumner Welles, this government was quickly overthrown. From this spurious process Fulgencio Batista came to the national spotlight. For the next twenty-five years, he was the most faithful servant of U.S. interests.

The crisis of the semicolonial regime in Cuba produced the revolutionary process of 1953 through 1959. Because of the close links between U.S. interests and the oligarchy in power and the role that U.S. economic penetration played as the main cause of Cuba's underdevelopment, it was inevitable that the revolution that emerged victorious in 1959 should be anti-imperialist.[14]

In the first few years, Cuba's anti-imperialist position was expressed in the following terms:

1. The revolutionary leadership was aware that a process of initial radical transformation would necessarily imply the adoption of an agrarian reform, which inevitably—because of the nature of Cuba's dependent economy—would adversely affect the interests of large U.S. companies and of Washington's main Cuban stooges.

2. Thus, the U.S. government could immediately become the main threat to the security of this national liberating revolution. The history of Cuban-U.S. relations showed that, in the past, intervention by Cuba's powerful northern neighbor had frustrated every process of national renovation.

3. Keeping in mind the relative strengths of Cuba and the United States, it was clear that, without making any concessions in its principles, the revolutionary government should avoid any situation that would lead to direct intervention by the U.S. armed forces. However, since this was a foreseeable alternative, the country had to be politically and militarily prepared to put up firm resistance in a balance-of-power situation that was extremely unfavorable.

4. An important element in the defense of revolutionary Cuba would have to be the solidarity of other American peoples, including the people of the United States. Moreover, the Cubans felt solidarity with other Latin American peoples that were suffering in situations similar to the one in Cuba before 1959.

5. In the tactical implementation of this line, the revolutionary leadership, headed by Fidel Castro, decided that it was

important to make it immediately clear that it was determined to carry out revolutionary transformations without making any concessions, and that Washington should understand that, even though Cuba did not seek a direct confrontation, it would not avoid one were the United States to persist in endangering Cuba's national security.

These conclusions are drawn in Fidel Castro's main statements in 1959 and 1960, especially during his April 1959 trip to the United States.[15]

The agreement on the Guantánamo Naval Base was a perennial, concrete reminder of what political dependence on the United States had meant for Cuba. The presence of a foreign military installation in its territory not only wounded Cuban national pride, but also constituted a serious threat to the security of the country, which was preparing to take radical measures. Nevertheless, the Cuban government has always avoided any statement or action that could be interpreted as a threat to that imperial enclave. This was an example of the firm yet serene and realistic approach with which Cuba confronted security problems with the United States in 1959.

In one way or another, most U.S. authors—including some who support a more realistic policy toward Cuba—have upheld the thesis that, ever since the Cuban government attained power, it has sought a confrontation with the United States, adversely affecting U.S. security interests. This is not true; precisely in order to guarantee its national security in the midst of transformations that would inevitably have an anti-imperialist character and would harm U.S. economic interests, Cuba tried to carry out this process in a climate of at least minimal mutual understanding with the United States in the first few months of 1959.[16]

However, the United States reacted against the Cuban revolution in an irremediably hostile way. In March 1959, the National Security Council in Washington began analyzing ways to overthrow the Cuban government.[17] Those measures began to be put into practice during the first year of the revolution, thus confirming the Cuban leadership's worst fears. It is not necessary to summarize the subsequent history of U.S. actions against Cuba; this has already been done exhaustively in countless works by U.S. and Cuban authors.[18]

With reason to spare, the Cuban government has considered that all U.S. policies in the past thirty years have been aimed at destroying the revolutionary process, violating Cuban territorial integrity, destabilizing its political structures, strangling its economic development, isolating Cuba in the world, subverting its ideology, and wiping out its self-determination—all this while disregarding Cuba's national sovereignty and the relations of equality between neighboring countries, which should be the basis of all systems of collective regional security. Cubans cannot be accused of exaggeration when they assert that the United States and its policy have been, are, and will be a source of powerful and constant threats to Cuban national security.

U.S. Threats Against Cuba's Security

The worst threat to Cuba's national security in the past thirty years has been the possibility of a direct military aggression by the U.S. armed forces.[19] This danger has been considered in drawing up all of the Cuban state's security policies. For a country such as Cuba, armed confrontation with the United States represents a threat of enormous proportions. The United States possesses not only a much larger army, but also totally disproportionate naval and air resources. Moreover, U.S. strategic forces have weapons of mass extermination, including nuclear warheads. The possibility that they might be used against Cuba arose in October 1962, and it cannot be ruled out that they might be used in the case of a general nuclear war between the United States and the Soviet Union.[20]

A U.S. attack would take the form of surprise massive air strikes, an invasion by infantry troops, or a combination of the two (with the support of a naval bombardment). Moreover, the foreseeable theater of operations (the Cuban archipelago) is a long and narrow territory of small dimensions in which there will be no possibility of retreat because it is surrounded by the sea.[21]

These real, objective factors—plus the fighting experience of the Liberation Army (1868-98) and the Rebel Army (1957-59), and the country's Marxist-Leninist concepts of war and the armed forces—were taken into consideration in drawing up the Cuban military doctrine in order to prepare the Revolutionary Armed Forces and all the people to withstand and repulse any conventional military action that the United States may unleash.

Because of the conditions described above, this doctrine—that of the War by All the People[22]—is based, among other things, on the following main elements:

1. *To organize the country's defense, drawing on all the people, grouped around the Revolutionary Armed Forces, whose*

technical capacity, fighting spirit, and political preparation have been raised to the maximum. This idea of the people's participation took shape soon after the triumph of the revolution with the creation of the Revolutionary National Militia (MNR).[23] Now, following short training periods, more than 1.5 million Cubans have been incorporated in defense through membership in the Territorial Troop Militia, which complements the regular and reserve units of the Revolutionary Armed Forces and the Ministry of the Interior. The rest of the people are grouped in Production and Defense Brigades. This powerful force now constitutes the main guarantee of the nation's security from the military point of view.[24]

2. *To prepare the cadres, officers, and combatants politically and ideologically for a long struggle without quarter against an enemy that may even occupy a part of Cuba's national territory.* This aspect becomes important because of the likely type of combat engagements that will occur given the U.S. troops ostensible superiority in technical means. The Cuban leaders have stressed that *surrender* and *cease fire* are forbidden in the Cuban military lexicon. This is not a dogmatic or romantic decision.

3. *To continue to entrust Cuba's defense to the Cubans themselves.* This concept is based not on narrow criteria, but on an objective, realistic appraisal of Cuba's situation, its historic tradition, and a basic respect for those who have given Cuba help and solidarity. Since the War of Independence against Spain, José Martí emphasized that the Cubans themselves had to achieve their liberation. A U.S. citizen may better understand this position by comparing this Cuban position to that of the United States between 1776 and 1812, though with the difference that the asymmetry of power between Great Britain and the United States was much less than the asymmetry that exists between the United States and Cuba. Even though some authors, such as William LeoGrande, have speculated about this position of Cuba,[25] both President Fidel Castro and General Raúl Castro, Minister of the Revolutionary Armed Forces, have emphasized that this thesis in no way implies lack of confidence in the U.S.S.R.[26] Moreover, even though the fact that Cuba is an archipelago makes it harder for any aggressor to attack—since it has to come by air or sea and must first establish a beachhead—this factor also favors a

country such as the United States, which has many air and naval means close to Cuban territory at its disposal for imposing a military blockade, as it did in October 1962.

4. *To increase the costs of an eventual aggression so that the United States will abandon any plans to attack Cuba.* This element of the doctrine of War by All the People has been a constant in Cuban national security policy. It might also be affirmed that this is the doctrine's main goal: deterrence.[27] The adoption of the deterrent element underlines the defensive nature of Cuba's military build up, which has been so harshly criticized in works dealing with this topic.[28]

Cuba's security situation is further complicated by several complementary factors. First of all, there is the problem of the naval base that the United States occupies in Guantánamo Bay. This occupation, which is illegal under all circumstances and contrary to the wishes of the Cuban people and their government, constitutes an extremely delicate and irritating factor in the framework of the security relations between Cuba and the United States. It is clear that its maintenance is entirely irrelevant to U.S. strategic interests, even if we were to accept them as valid; the base is maintained, above all, as a bargaining chip.[29] Nevertheless, it should be emphasized that several U.S. administrations have used the base in fact as a means for provocation (the murder of Cuban border soldiers; the violation of Cuban airspace; military maneuvers; the instigation of illegal emigration, and, most recently, radio broadcasts by Miami Spanish-language stations from that territory). The only thing that has prevented a major incident thus far has been the serenity and realism with which the Cuban leaders have acted to avoid a clash over this imperial enclave. For Cuba, the base is not a minor matter; rather, it is a problem of central importance related to its national security.

The U.S. spy flights over Cuban territory are another direct threat to Cuba's national security. Ever since the 1960s, when Havana residents could easily see the outline of the electronic spy ship Oxford-Aga patrolling just over three miles north of the entrance to the port of Havana, the U.S. armed forces have claimed for themselves the right to inspect Cuban territory unilaterally and openly to assess the country's defense capability. It goes without saying that Cuba does not recognize and will never recognize such a "right," and that it will do everything in its power to eliminate that threat, as was shown during the 1962 missile crisis.[30] Thus, the cessation of the present spy flights—along with the return of the Guantánamo Naval Base and the lifting of the economic blockade—are among the main items on the Cuban agenda for normalizing relations.

If the United States is worried by the existence in the Caribbean of a powerful armed country such as Cuba, what do Cubans feel about the present U.S. deployment in the region?[31] The decade of the 1980s has witnessed a considerable increase in U.S. military resources in Central America and the Caribbean: the establishment of the Rapid Deployment Forces headquarters in Florida; land, naval, air, and combined maneuvers throughout the region; an increase in large-scale covert activities; and the application of the principles of low-intensity conflict in the area. The most important U.S. military operation since the Vietnam War—the invasion of Grenada—was carried out in this region in 1983. All these steps in the last few years show a substantial escalation of U.S. military policy in Central America and the Caribbean. The danger is evident, for the excuse that the U.S. authorities give for this tremendous deployment of forces is the supposed buttressing of Cuba's military capacity with Soviet assistance.[32] An analysis of the situation shows any impartial observer that the increase in Cuba's fighting capacity at the beginning of the 1980s was of a purely defensive nature, and was determined by the obvious dangers that threatened and still threaten the country's security.[33]

Cuba's geographic location and the fact that the United States is one of the two largest nuclear powers in the world pose a serious dilemma concerning problems of disarmament. Time and again, President Fidel Castro has emphasized that Cuba wants peace and general disarmament—especially of nuclear weapons. Moreover, Cuba has expressed its support for initiatives favoring the denuclearization of Latin America and the nonproliferation of nuclear arms. Nevertheless, for as long as the confrontation with the United States continues, Cuban leaders have had to remember that the United States is a nuclear power that occupies a part of Cuba's territory. Cuba cannot renounce the weapons it needs for its protection and security.[34] On this very sensitive subject, Cubans would be ready to agree with the noted Christian philosopher Reinhold Niebuhr that no imperiled nation is morally able to dispense with weapons that ensure its survival.[35]

It has been argued that, as a result of the cessation or substantial reduction of the CIA's covert operations and of the counterrevolution's working out of Miami, Cuba is no longer faced with a threat to its internal security.[36] This affirmation is not entirely objective. The activities against Cuba's internal stability have taken more subtle forms but, essentially, continue. It suffices to cite three examples. U.S. spokesmen say that there are no present plans for assassinating Cuban leaders, yet Cuban security agencies have found that the movements of Fidel Castro and other members of the leadership are reported to the CIA by its agents inside and outside Cuba. Moreover, in September 1987, a Cuban military traitor gave a press conference at the U.S. State Department in which he advocated assassinating both the president and the minister of the Revolutionary Armed Forces.

A second example: Not long ago, along with the campaign waged in international organizations against Cuba's record with regard to human rights, the deputy chief of the U.S. mission in Cuba stimulated the creation and activities of a small group of resentful elements to carry out campaigns inside the country against Cuba's prestige in this field. (The "report" that this small group presented to the foreign press in Cuba in February 1989 was almost a textual reproduction of the one that U.S. Ambassador Vernon Walters presented to the U.N. Human Rights Commission in Geneva in 1987.) The Cuban press reported on these facts on March 14 and 15, 1988.

A third example: In July 1987, Cuban television presented a series of programs showing the extremely broad espionage activities carried out by the permanent and temporary staff of the U.S. Interests Section in Havana.

The persistence of a serious threat to Cuba's internal security has forced Cuba to maintain a strong apparatus to repress counterrevolutionary activities. Its efficiency, acting with the support of the Committees for the Defense of the Revolution, has even been recognized by U.S. authorities. It is the height of irony that the United States, which has waged a secret and not-so-secret war against Cuba, is the main promoter of campaigns concerning the supposed violation of human rights in Cuba. As President Fidel Castro has recalled, the fact that Cuba has counterrevolutionary prisoners is due to the incentives the U.S. government has given to such activities.[37] Cubans can call attention to the serene way in which their government has reacted to even the worst acts of provocation in the U.S.-Cuban confrontation: the Bay of Pigs mercenaries were not mistreated; they were condemned after a trial following due process and were freed when the United States agreed to pay Cuba compensation for the damage caused. Many countries—including the United States—adopt policies of reprisals when what they consider terrorist attacks are made on their citizens; Cuba's response has always been political, even when a Cubana de Aviación passenger plane was blown up in flight in 1976, killing seventy-three people.[38]

Cuba's response to the establishment of Radio Martí in 1985 was another example of its serene, realistic attitude. The station went on the air as one of the measures that the Reagan administration applied against Cuban national security.[39] The Cuban broadcasting system has the capacity to respond to this unilateral U.S. measure but, aware of the harm that such a response may do to the normal development of private broadcasting in the United States, Cuba has preferred to follow the path of negotiation, by means of which it hopes to clear the way for Cuban radio broadcasts to U.S. territory.

The Cuban leadership considers Cuba's national security to be an economic matter as well, especially since Cuba has an open, vulnerable economy that has been subjected to an implacable economic blockade. Cubans have had to fight the blockade in various ways. Measures have been taken to substitute U.S. goods and markets and to redirect our exports (which has been done, especially with the help of the Soviet Union and the other socialist countries). Moreover, Cubans have subverted the blockade whenever they could.[40]

Both the Cuban president and the minister of the Revolutionary Armed Forces have emphasized the need to coordinate the two most important tasks: production and defense. Cuba is a small country that does not have any energy resources, is dependent on supplies from abroad, and has a still-narrow industrial base; the economic blockade to which the United States has subjected it has been an extremely harmful measure. The United States has not only tried to strangle Cuba's development, but has also used the blockade as a punitive measure, with the added purpose of weakening the country's readiness for war. The U.S. Senate has shown that the United States persists in this policy, for only recently it approved some new measures to beef up the blockade. Even though the U.S. government has not achieved the main goals it sought to reach with the blockade, this measure has been seriously prejudicial to Cuba, which has had to redirect its trade and get along without access to certain markets and without being able to purchase certain products. The Cuban leadership is entirely justified in making the lifting of the blockade a step that the United States should take in order to achieve a normalization of relations.

Cuba's Policies to Safeguard Its Security

The foreign policy of every state is an integral part of its system of national security. This is even more obvious in the case of Cuba because of the diplomatic isolation that the United States has tried to impose against it.[41] As a result, the Cuban leadership has had to apply an active, firm foreign policy that has sought, among other things, to counter U.S. activities and to broaden constantly its foreign policy ties.[42]

Cuba's foreign policy is based on two principles that are shared by the rest of the socialist countries: internationalism and the struggle for peace.[43] Nevertheless, in the case of Cuba, these are applied from its position as a Latin American state that is a member of the Movement of Nonaligned Countries. The Latin Americanist nature of Cuba's foreign policy is determined by historic and political ties that stem from the nineteenth century, when José Martí was its most eminent exponent. In addition, the Cuban revolution triumphed at a time when many African and Asian countries that had been under the colonial system obtained their freedom. Cuba's natural solidarity with those peoples and governments that struggled under the same conditions, plus Cuba's initial isolation from Latin America, were yet more incentives for Cubans' active incorporation in the Nonaligned Movement. Now, after thirty years, when relations have been reestablished with more than a dozen states in Latin America, it can be said—as Ricardo Alarcón, Cuban Deputy Minister of Foreign Affairs, has put in—that "the policy of isolating Cuba is utterly bankrupt."[44]

This combination of principles and legacies—internationalism, the struggle for peace, Latin Americanism, and nonalignment—is what gives Cuba's foreign policy its distinctive character. The United States questions these principled main guidelines and tries to include discussions of these topics on the U.S.-Cuban bilateral agenda. In fact, most U.S. authors of all persuasions agree in pointing out that the main threat to U.S. national security coming from Cuba lies in its active internationalist foreign policy in the Third World and, especially, its ties with the Soviet Union.[45] To these issues we turn.

Other chapters of this book analyze Cuba's relations with African and other Latin American countries, so I will not refer to this topic other than to bring out some characteristics of a general nature. Cuba's internationalism is solidly based on the two documents that guide its state and party policies: the Constitution of the Republic and the program of the Communist Party of Cuba. As President Fidel Castro has said, Cuba does not export revolution, for that would be impossible; rather, it gives its solidarity to those countries that, like it, are trying to overcome the colonial and neocolonial fetters of the past. A typical example is that of Grenada, a small Caribbean country to which Cuba gave effective, useful assistance, especially in the construction of an international airport. The U.S. government presented this project as a "textbook case" in which its national security was threatened by Cuban "adventurism"—when, in fact, that airfield, which Grenada needed, was built with British and Canadian participation. Now, many U.S. tourists benefit from its construction.[46] Some Cuban workers who shed their sweat to build it also shed their blood in 1983 when the Reagan administration sent in troops to invade the island.

Cuba's international policy is not necessarily aimed at undermining vital U.S. national security interests, but neither does the Cuban government have any special obligations with regard to what the United States claims are its security interests. With its aggressive policy, threatening Cuba's national security, and trying to isolate it, the United States stimulated Cuba to carry out an active policy in the Third World. It could also be argued that it was U.S. aggressiveness against Cuba that left Cuba no choice but to develop its defense capability to such a point that, when South Africa invaded Angola, Cuba was able to carry out Operation Carlota in support of the Angolan government in 1975. Vice President Carlos Rafael Rodríguez suggested in 1978, "If there are Cuban military equipment and soldiers outside our country now, . . . this is so not because the Cuban Revolution set this goal for itself. . . . That Cuban army of which some speak with unfounded fear was created when the people took up arms to defend their independence."[47]

Thus, to safeguard its security, Cuba was forced to develop powerful armed forces, which were later sent in response to the call of other peoples. The Cuban internationalist soldier's participation in other nations' struggles has had favorable effects on raising the moral and political education of the officers and soldiers, both in the regular forces and in the reserves of the Revolutionary Armed Forces—300,000 of whom, thus far, have gone on such missions. It is not a matter of Cuba's having sent its troops to gain fighting experience in other theaters of operations. The Cuban leadership would be incapable of training fighters at the cost of unnecessary sacrifice. What it does mean is that internationalist missions promote the spirit of combat in soldiers and their officers that is required for holding firm against and defeating an eventual U.S. attack. The Cuban leadership thinks that a combatant who has risked his life for the freedom of another people will be better prepared to defend his own country.[48]

Cuba's relations with the Soviet Union are a very important aspect of internationalist policy. Above all, those relations are based on their shared ideological principles and on their ties of friendship, based on mutual respect for the sovereign equality of both states, even though this is a relationship between a great power and small underdeveloped country. Many U.S. analysts—among them Dr. Treverton in this book—have emphasized that this is the aspect of Cuba's international position that is most dangerous for the United States, and is at the heart of Cuba's threat to its national security[49]—thus, Cuba's insertion in global problems of security. However, it must be said that U.S. arguments on the threat posed to the United States by Cuba's having close relations with the U.S.S.R. lack validity and are seen in Cuba as a means to undermine Cuba's sovereign right to conduct its international relations and to end the firmest guarantee for its security in the international sphere.

In his recent interview with Gianni Minà, Fidel Castro underlined the importance that Cuba gives to its relations with the U.S.S.R. by pointing out that they are enshrined in the Constitution of the Republic.[50] When an analysis is made of Soviet attitude toward Cuba throughout the years in the economic, political and military spheres, it is clear that these are strong ties for mutual benefit. It can also be argued that, even in the absence of ideological factors, Cubans had no alternative but to seek Soviet economic and military support to resist hostile U.S. attacks.

In the economic sphere, Cuban-Soviet relations go back to the U.S.S.R.'s position of giving Cuba assistance in the early years, when the United States first imposed its blockade. When the Eisenhower administration cut Cuba's share of its sugar imports, it was the Soviet Union that ensured Cuba a market for that product. When the U.S. government banned exports of machinery and spare parts to Cuba, it was the Soviet Union that extended credits and supplied Cuba with the material goods it needed for beginning its process of industrial development. Cuba's economic relations with the U.S.S.R. are excellent, extensive, and vitally different from the ones our country had had with the United States. With the Soviet Union, Cuba has ties of cooperation; with the United States, Cuba had been the victim of exploitation. It is precisely for this reason that Cuba is criticized so much in U.S. government and academic circles, which, falsifying reality, allege that Cuba receives a hefty subsidy from the U.S.S.R. Cubans do not consider this to be a gift; rather, it results from the two countries' establishment of the fair and equitable relations that should exist among all developed and underdeveloped countries, and should be the premise for a new international economic order not based on unequal exchange and the growing gap between rich and poor nations.[51]

Cuba feels that its political relations with the Soviet Union exemplify the kinds of ties that should exist between friendly countries. This aspect is also misinterpreted in U.S. circles. When Cuba and the Soviet Union agree on something, it is alleged that the former is a "satellite" of the latter; when they do not agree, then it is claimed that insuperable contradictions have arisen. Such analysts do not want to understand that, in addition to the close relations of friendship between Cubans and Soviets, their countries have similar domestic and foreign policies even though each set of policies has its own features because of their different historic and economic realities. Moreover, as Cuban leaders have brought out several times, the Soviet leadership would be incapable of approaching the Cuban leadership to impose a certain criterion or course of action in the international sphere.[52]

Soviet military assistance has been of decisive importance for Cuba in its struggle to preserve its national security against the U.S. threat.[53] The mercenary forces that the Central Intelligence Agency organized and sent to invade Cuba in April 1961 were defeated largely because the Soviet Union sent Cuba its first arms shipment in late 1960, after several western countries had bowed to U.S. pressure and refused to supply Cuba with arms. The U.S.S.R.'s assistance has extended to include advice and training for thousands of Cuban cadres in its military schools. Moreover, Cubans and Soviets share the mission of advising the armed forces of third countries in the defense of their national security. General Raúl Castro, Minister of the Revolutionary Armed Forces, recently described the relations between the Soviet and Cuban armed forces as indestructible.[54]

Cuba's close ties with the U.S.S.R. cannot pose a threat to U.S. national security, for these relations originated in the need to defend Cuba. It is ironic that the United States protests over these relations of friendship that its own aggressive policy helped to create, especially when, using the pretext of protecting U.S. security, the United States has deployed military forces in areas far from its territory but close to the U.S.S.R.—a policy that was reiterated recently in the report drawn up by a commission appointed by the Reagan administration to review U.S. military strategy in view of the security changes that will be effected in the coming decades.[55] President Fidel Castro has emphasized the unilateral way in which the United States approaches threats to its security, recalling that the Kennedy administration brought the world to the brink of nuclear war in 1962 because a few dozen medium-range missiles had been installed in Cuba, yet, in the 1980s, the Reagan administration installed several hundred intermediate-range missiles in Europe aimed against the Soviet Union.[56]

U.S. authorities have argued time and again that there can be no process of normalization of Cuban and U.S. relations without a prior change in Cuba's foreign policy—especially as regards its ties with the Soviet Union. It is completely irrational to attach such strings. To make an improvement in relations with a country the United States has threatened for nearly thirty years conditional on that country's renouncing its foreign policy—and especially its ties with its closest ally, the nation that came to its assistance at the most difficult time of it confrontation with the United States—implies either utter lack of realism or an entirely hypocritical attitude by setting conditions that are completely unacceptable for any country.[57] As the Cuban president said recently, "More than being a crime, it would be stupid for us to sacrifice our relations with our Soviet friends in order to improve our relations with our enemy, the United States."[58]

Nearly ten years ago, Cole Blasier argued convincingly that a solution for the Cuban-U.S. historic breach would not be against the interests of the U.S.S.R., and that the Soviet authorities would not look with suspicion on a process of normalization as long as it did not constitute a threat to the survival of an allied socialist state.[59] These arguments are even more valid today in view of the new thinking behind Soviet foreign policy since Mikhail Gorbachev became general secretary.

But, of course, although the Soviet position is important, it isn't the decisive thing in what is really a bilateral conflict. One of the conclusions that one can reach on the basis of experience in this breach between Cuba and the United States is that, in trying to use its coercive power against Cuba, claiming reasons of national security, the United States has fallen into the trap of which Arnold Wolfers warned thirty-seven years ago; as a result, its efforts have backfired. Therefore, we should ask if the time has come for the United States to accept Wolfers' recommendation that, "In most instances, efforts to satisfy the legitimate demands of others are likely to promise better results in terms of security."[60]

Prospects for U.S.-Cuban Agreements

The prospects for a solution of Cuba's serious national security problems in the context of the breach between it and the United States are not promising. Over the years, U.S. hostility has made agreement on almost all subjects impossible. Some topics of shared security of a secondary nature have been discussed by the two parties, but the results of such talks have been poor.

One example is the first Cuban-U.S. agreement signed after the triumph of the revolution—the one on the hijacking of vessels and airplanes. In 1959 and 1960, many Cuban vessels and planes were seized and taken to the United States. The U.S. government stimulated those actions. None of those responsible for those actions was ever tried; on the contrary, they were given a hero's welcome. None of the vessels or planes was ever returned. Early in the 1970s, the problem was reversed: airplanes belonging to U.S. companies began to be seized and taken to Cuba. The Cuban government enacted a law, returned the planes, offered guarantees to the passengers, and tried and convicted those responsible for those actions. The two countries negotiated and signed an agreement in 1973 to solve this problem—an agreement that mainly served the interests of the United States. In 1976, terrorists linked to the CIA blew up a Cuban passenger plane in flight near Barbados, killing seventy-three people. Cuba responded by annulling the agreement, yet continuing to abide by it. The number of skyjackings was not reduced until the early 1980s, but not because the Cuban authorities were tolerant of such activities. There were more cases of Cuban vessels being seized in this period, with none of the perpetrators tried or sentenced in the United States.

The agreement on the establishment of maritime boundaries between the two countries, which was signed in 1978, has not yet gone fully into effect. On that occasion, the two negotiating parties were praised for the serious, rapid, pragmatic way in which they reached an agreement. Even though Cuba has ratified that agreement year after year, the U.S. Senate has not yet approved it.

Several agreements of practical cooperation were signed in 1977 and 1978. They included a protocol of cooperation between Cuba's border patrol troops and the U.S. coast guard. At the insistence of the United States, this agreement included a provision on an exchange of information on the activities of drug traffickers.

Cuba, in turn, asked that an exchange of information on the activities of terrorist groups (seizures of Cuban fishing vessels on the high seas by armed launches from Florida were very common) be included, to which the United States agreed. This protocol became inoperative because the United States showed little interest in the aspects that harmed Cuba; by 1982, mutual cooperation had practically ended when Cuba annulled the agreement because of the false charges that were made against Cuban officials for supposed links with drug smuggling.

The important thing about the traffic in drugs is that Cuba has been a two-time victim: on one hand, it is located next to the smuggling routes between South and North America, which forces it to use resources and human efforts to catch smugglers; on the other, various U.S. authorities have repeatedly charged the highest-ranking Cuban leaders with responsibility for this illegal, vile traffic—a charge without the slightest grain of truth. President Fidel Castro has firmly rebutted these accusations. According to the *New York Times*, the traffic in drugs has already become a problem for the national security of the United States. If we accept that argument, it will be necessary to recognize that, by taking measures against the smugglers who come close to its coasts or who enter its airspace—as Cuba has done as a matter of principle—Cuba is indirectly helping to solve the problem, even though, as Fidel Castro has said, Cuba does not feel that it has any special obligation to the United States in this field.[61]

All of these cases show Cuba's constructive position on those matters of national security that are included in the bilateral dispute. This Cuban attitude has not been reciprocated by the United States, however, for it has either paid no attention to Cuba's legitimate security interests or has given priority to the U.S. policy of hostility instead of searching for coexistence based on mutual respect.

The two countries' positions on regional conflicts also contrast sharply. While the United States insists on helping the *contras*, preventing implementation of the Esquipulas agreements, and doing its utmost to overthrow General Noriega in Panama, intervening in the internal affairs of that country, the Cuban government—though it has given security assistance to Nicaragua and has expressed its solidarity with the popular movement in El Salvador—has called for negotiated solutions that will be acceptable to all. Repeatedly, the Cuban leadership has taken steps to contribute as much as it can to peace in Central America.[62]

The facts concerning the two countries' bilateral relations and the regional conflicts in which they have been involved as adversaries show that, when U.S. leaders do not perceive something to be in the interests of their country's national security, it is very difficult to reach an agreement—or, if an agreement is reached, it is a precarious one. In contrast, if the matter is viewed as serving the interests of U.S. national security, the ruling circles in the United States try to impose solutions by means of force, applying a criterion for their security that is unilateral, expansive, changing, and absolute.

This permanent hostility has forced the Cuban leadership to conclude that Cuba's national security cannot depend solely on an agreement with the United States—such as the one proposed by Jorge Domínguez and supported by Dr. Treverton[63]—unless this is complemented with specific steps. These steps must include lifting the economic blockade, cessation of U.S. spy flights, and return of the territory now occupied by the Guantánamo Naval Base. But, as Fidel has said since 1984, even if this is achieved, Cuba cannot neglect its defenses, for it would always be subject to the vicissitudes of the changes of administration in Washington and to the perception that the various power groups have of Cuban reality.[64]

This does not mean that the Cuban leadership opposes peaceful coexistence with the United States, considering it to be impossible. It is simply that, thus far, nothing in U.S. policy on Cuba makes it likely that the U.S. government will some day come to the conclusion that it will get more out of treating Cuba as an equal and respecting its security interests. Cubans, who are preparing for the worst and cannot exclude that possibility, must plan on the basis that the United States has been hostile, that the balance of power favors it, that the Soviet Union is thousands of miles away and, therefore, Cuba cannot wait for the first signs of danger to start mobilizing for its defense, because that may be too late. The Cuban leadership has repeatedly emphasized its willingness to solve the Cuban-U.S. historic breach by means of negotiation between sovereign states. Fidel Castro has said that Cuba will do everything it can to contribute to détente and peace, that Cuba has no interest at all in an armed conflict with the United States, and will be attentive to any signs from the United States that it is ready to treat Cuba with respect.[65]

In this context, an eventual solution for our problems of mutual security should be based on realistic considerations. Cuba, as its leaders have reiterated, has become accustomed to living under a constant U.S. threat; it is aware, therefore, that there can be no absolute guarantee for its security. There is a considerable asymmetry in terms of security: the United States is an incomparably greater threat to Cuba than Cuba could ever be to it under any circumstances.

A process of normalization of relations that includes the topic of security between Cuba and the United States should consider the interests of both countries on a basis of equality; the Cuban leaders' concerns about the security of their country are just as valid as are those of the U.S. leaders. U.S. analysts generally charge that Cuba has been turned into a gigantic Soviet aircraft carrier, ignoring the fact that Cubans have had to survive for thirty years with a hostile foreign military base inside their territory. One cannot call attention to one problem and ignore the other.

The earlier instances of détente between the United States and the Soviet Union were not accompanied by a more favorable attitude toward Havana on the part of Washington, in spite of U.S. insistence that the main threat coming from Cuba was due to its close relations with the U.S.S.R. Experience has taught the Cuban leadership that, when Soviet-U.S. relations get worse, Cuban-U.S. relations usually get worse, too, but the reverse is not the case; international détente does not necessarily imply an easing of tensions between Cuba and the United States.

We are now at the dawn of what may turn out to be a new period of détente—this time, a seemingly more thorough one than in the past. Steps have been taken to eliminate certain nuclear weapons, and both Soviet and U.S. leaders have spoken out in favor of continuing to advance along the path to disarmament and the easing of tensions. It is still to be seen if, on this occasion, U.S. leaders will allow themselves to be swayed by the earlier dialectical logic or if they take from Cuba the honor of considering it to be one of the United States' few adversaries in the world. Meanwhile, Cuba has no choice but to continue to guarantee its security and look to its defenses. The Cuban government should not be blamed for its attitude of healthy skepticism about the future of U.S. threats to its security.

108

Notes

1. See Arnold Wolfers, "National Security as an Ambiguous Symbol," *Political Science Quarterly*, Vol. 67, No. 4 (December 1952), pp. 481-502, and *Estudio sobre los conceptos de seguridad: Informe al Secretario General*, A/40/553 (New York, 1985).

2. In a speech given on the eve of Reagan's inauguration as president of the United States, Fidel Castro referred to the topic in these terms: ". ., The defense of the country is not an exclusively military phenomenon; it is, above all, a group of measures of a political and economic nature that are aimed at creating the conditions required for confronting all dangers and achieving victory." (Speech at ceremony creating the units of Territorial Troop Militias in Granma Province, January 20, 1981).

3. John Saxe-Fernández, *De la seguridad nacional* (Mexico City: Editorial Grijalbo, 1977). Other works referring to the same topic include *Proyecciones hemisféricas de la Pax Americana* (Buenos Aires: Amorrortu Editores, 1975), by the same author; Joseph Complin, *El poder militar en América Latina* (Salamanca: Ediciones Sígueme, 1978); and Manuel Medina Castro, *La doctrina y la ley de seguridad nacional* (Guayaquil: Departamento de Publicaciones de la Universidad de Guayaquil, 1979).

4. Raymond Aron, *Paix et guerre entre les nations* (Paris: Calmann Levy, 1962), pp. 82 and ff.

5. Walter Lippmann, *U.S. Foreign Policy: Shield of the Republic* (Boston: Little, Brown and Co., 1943), p. 51.

6. Andrzej Karkoszka, *Strategic Disarmament, Verification and National Security* (London: Stockholm International Peace and Research Institute, Taylor and Francis, 1977), p. 56.

7. Karl Deutsch, *The Analysis of International Relations* (Englewood Cliffs, New Jersey: Prentice-Hall, 1978), p. 101.

8. Henry Kissinger, *American Foreign Policy*, third edition (New York: W.W. Norton and Co., 1977), p. 35.

9. Mikhail S. Gorbachev, *La perestroika y la nueva mentalidad para nuestro país y para el mundo entero* (Havana: Editora Política, 1988), pp. 179-180.

10. Fidel Castro has explained this very clearly: ". . . Defense cannot be neglected. . . . It is a reality imposed on us by

our geographic location. The differences in political, economic and social systems that we have with our most powerful neighbor require that we always give maximum attention to defense." (Speech at the closing session of the Sixth Congress of the Federation of Senior High School Students [FEEM], Havana, December 8, 1984.)

11. See the works of Ramiro Guerra, *La expansión territorial de los Estados Unidos* (Havana: Editorial Cultura, 1935); *En el camino de la independencia* (Havana: Editorial Cultura, 1936); and Emilio Roig de Leuchsenring, *Cuba y los Estados Unidos, 1805-1898* (Havana: Sociedad Cubana de Estudios Históricos e Internacionales, 1949); *Los Estados Unidos contra Cuba Libre* (Havana: Oficina del Historiador de la Ciudad de La Habana, 1958), four volumes.

12. Excerpt from the unfinished letter that José Martí was writing to his Mexican friend Manuel Mercado just before his death in 1895, cited by Emilio Roig de Leuchsenring, *Tres estudios martianos* (Havana: Editorial Ciencias Sociales, 1983), p. 229.

13. The linking of the United States' economic and political penetration of Cuba with the dependent regime that atrophied its development and determined the root causes of the country's social backwardness and corruption are set forth in several excellent works by Cuban authors, including Oscar Pino Santos, *El imperialismo norteamericano en la economía de Cuba* (Havana: Editorial Lex, 1960); *El asalto a Cuba por la oligarquía financiera yanqui* (Havana: Casa de las Américas, 1973); and *Cuba: historia y economía* (Havana: Editorial de Ciencias Sociales, 1984). See also Julio LeRiverend, *La república: dependencia y revolución* (Havana: Editora Universitaria, 1966); *Historia económica de Cuba* (Havana: Editorial Pueblo y Educación, 1975). See, as well, Francisco López Segrera, *Cuba: capitalismo dependiente y subdesarrollado* (Havana: Editorial de Ciencias Sociales, 1981); *Raíces históricas de la revolución cubana* (Havana: UNEAC, 1980).

14. Carlos Rafael Rodríguez, "Cuba en el tránsito al socialismo (1959-1963)," in *Letra con filo*, Vol. 2 (Havana: Editorial de Ciencias Sociales, 1983), p. 336.

15. C.S.M. [sic], ed., *Resumen de un viaje* (Havana: Editorial Lex, 1960).

16. See Instituto de Historia del Movimiento Comunista y de la Revolución Socialista de Cuba, *El pensamiento de Fidel*

Castro: selección de temática, Vol. I, *Enero de 1959 a Abril de 1961* (2 volumes) (Havana: Editora Política, 1983). "The Cuban government does not want to be the enemy of the U.S. government or the enemy of any other government in the world." (Vol. I, p. 14). Taken from his appearance on *Ante la Prensa*, February 19, 1959, three days after being sworn in as Prime Minister.

17. Tad Szulc, *Fidel: A Critical Portrait* (New York: William Morrow and Co., 1968), pp. 480-481.

18. Instituto Superior de Relaciones Internacionales de Cuba, *De Eisenhower a Reagan* (Havana: Editorial de Ciencias Sociales, 1987). This is an analytical compendium of the main U.S. actions against Cuba.

19. Even though the word *aggression* may seem excessive to U.S. citizens, it is true that at least in 1961-62 and 1981-84, danger was imminent. It was latent in the rest of the period. Moreover, only a madman could conceive of a war caused by a Cuban attack.

20. The Committees for the Defense of the Revolution (CDRs) and the Civil Defense are responsible for protecting the noncombatant population in the case of nuclear war. However, the Cuban leaders believe that the possibility of surviving a nuclear exchange is very remote.

21. Speech by Comandante Raúl Castro, Minister of the Revolutionary Armed Forces, at the graduation ceremony at the General Máximo Gómez National War College, July 22, 1967, in *Documentos de política internacional de la revolución cubana*, Vol. 3 (Havana: Editorial de Ciencias Sociales, 1971), p. 305.

22. See *Programa del Partido Comunista de Cuba* (Havana: Editora Política, 1987), pp. 53-56; Fidel Castro, *Informe central al Tercer Congreso del PCC* (Havana: Editora Política, 1986), pp. 58-64; and Raúl Castro, "Discurso en el acto por el 70 aniversario de las Fuerzas Armadas soviéticas," *Granma* (February 22, 1988), p. 3.

23. The Revolutionary National Militia was created on October 30, 1960; it played a decisive role in the fight against bands of counterrevolutionaries and in the victory at the Bay of Pigs. In the 1960s, after the missile crisis, it was turned into wartime military reserve units. In 1981, in view of the growing threat posed by the Reagan administration, the Territorial Troop Militias were created.

24. Fidel Castro has observed that a U.S. invasion of Cuba would not succeed. See his interview with U.S. journalist Maria Shriver in *Juventud Rebelde* (February 28, 1988), p. 18.

25. William M. LeoGrande, "Foreign Policy: The Limits of Success" in Jorge I. Domínguez, ed., *Cuba: Internal and International Affairs* (Beverly Hills: Sage Publications, 1982), p. 168.

26. Comandante Raúl Castro gave the best explanation of this in the speech cited in note 21 (pp. 304-305): "support from abroad is good but nothing will ever be better than our own efforts." For his part, Fidel Castro said recently, ". . . . What we must learn and have as a philosophy is not to wait for anybody else to defend us but rather, first of all, be ready to defend ourselves." (Speech given at the closing session of the Second Congress of the Committees for the Defense of the Revolution, Havana, July 7, 1981.)

27. *Programa del Partido . . .*, p. 55.

28. Edward Gonzalez, "U.S. Policy: Objectives and Options," in Domínguez, ed., *Cuba*, pp. 194 ff.

29. Jorge I. Domínguez, "Cuban Military and National Security Policies," in Martin Weinstein, ed., *Revolutionary Cuba in the World Arena* (Philadelphia: Institute for the Study of Human Issues), 1979, p. 93.

30. Gianni Miná, *Un encuentro con Fidel* (Havana: Oficina de Publicaciones del Consejo de Estado, 1987), pp. 108 ff.

31. Francisco López Segrera of Cuba has made a detailed critical analysis of U.S. military strategy in the Caribbean: *La política de Estados Unidos hacia la cuenca del Caribe en los 80s: geopolítica y estrategia militar* (Havana: Instituto Superior de Relaciones Internacionales Raúl Roa García, 1986).

32. *Report of the National Bipartisan Commission on Central America* (New York: Macmillan Publishing Co., 1984), pp. 111-112.

33. Joseph Cirincione and Leslie Hunter, "Military Threats: Actual and Potential," in Robert S. Leiken, ed., *Central America: Anatomy of Conflict* (New York: Pergamon Press, 1984), pp. 175-176.

34. See Carlos Rafael Rodríguez's speech at the May 30, 1978, special session of the General Assembly of the United Nations. (Document of the General Assembly, p. 167.)

112

35. Reinhold Niebuhr, *The Irony of American History* (New York: Charles Scribner's & Sons, 1945), p. 39.
36. Domínguez, "Cuban Military and National Security Policies," p. 78.
37. Miná, *Un encuentro con Fidel*, p. 40.
38. *Ibid.*, p. 75.
39. For a Cuban approach to the topic, see José R. Cabañas, "Radio Martí, una nueva agresión," *Cuadernos de Nuestra América*, Vol. 1, No. 1 (January-July 1984), pp. 174-205.
40. In the interview mentioned above with U.S. journalist Maria Shriver, Fidel Castro recognized this. "We have the right to get around the blockade if we need medicine, medical equipment, or technological equipment, for we consider the blockade to be criminal and unfair. We always try and will always try to get around the blockade by any means." *Juventud Rebelde* (February 28, 1988), p. 14.
41. Domínguez, "Cuban Military and National Security Policies," p. 77.
42. LeoGrande, "Foreign Policy: The Limits of Success," p. 167.
43. A fuller explanation of this aspect is given in Carlos Rafael Rodríguez, "Fundamentos estratégicos de la política exterior cubana," *Cuba Socialista*, Vol. 1, No. 1 (December 1981), pp. 10-33.
44. Ricardo Alarcón, "Cuba. La política interior y exterior de una revolución: ¿qué ha logrado y cuáles son sus expectativas?" in *Balance y proyecciones de Cuba en los 80s*, a collection of papers presented by Cuban officials at the Friedrich Ebert Foundation Symposium, the Federal Republic of Germany, Centro de Estudios de Europa Occidental (CEEO) (Havana: 1983).
45. Central American and Caribbean Program, School of Advanced International Studies, Johns Hopkins University, *Report on Cuba: Findings of the Study Group on United States-Cuban Relations* (Boulder, Colorado: Westview Press, 1984), pp. 3-4.
46. Gregory Treverton, "U.S. Strategy in Central America," *Survival*, Vol. 28, No. 2 (March-April 1986).
47. He added, "Just as the arduous search for independence led Martí to proclaim war as a sad necessity—as he put it—the Revolution that sought to do away with the Army and fill the island with schools, rather than garrisons, has had to create the defensive instrument of the Cuban Armed Forces, which now not only serve Cuba's independence but also

make a modest contribution—as great as a small country can make—to protecting the independence of other peoples against imperialist aggression." United Nations General Assembly, Eighth Special Session, *Diario de sesiones* (May 30, 1978), p. 163.

48. Fidel Castro has emphasized that "Only a people that is capable of fighting for others is also capable of fighting for itself." (Speech given at the ceremony marking the fifteenth anniversary of the founding of the Ministry of the Interior, Havana, June 6, 1976, cited in *Ideología, conciencia y trabajo político*, p. 311.)

49. The most complete analysis in this regard is included in *A Strategy for Dealing with Cuba in the 1980s*, that Edward Gonzalez of the Rand Corporation prepared for the U.S. Department of State and for the U.S. Air Force (Santa Monica: September 1982). The conclusions reached by Gonzalez, who describes the Cuban danger as strategic, are not entirely shared by other specialists; see Treverton, "U.S. Strategy in Central America," p. 133, and *Report on Cuba*, of the Central American and Caribbean Program of the School of Advance International Studies at Johns Hopkins University. They agree with the thesis sustained in their respective works by Carla Anne Robbins, *The Cuban Threat* (New York: McGraw-Hill, 1983), and Wayne Smith, *The Closest of Enemies* (New York: W.W. Norton, 1987).

50. Miná, *Un encuentro con Fidel*, pp. 104-105.

51. *Ibid.*, p. 106.

52. "Our people are proud of their relations with this great country. They constitute a model of internationalist practice, of understanding, respect, and mutual trust. The Soviet Union, which has given our people such decisive help, has never come to us to demand that we do anything, to attach strings or to tell us what we ought to do." Excerpt from Fidel Castro's speech at the 25th Congress of the Communist Party of the Soviet Union, Moscow, February 25, 1976, in *Ideología . . .*, p. 321.

53. The best work on Cuban-Soviet military cooperation was published jointly by the Institute of Military History of the Ministry of Defense of the U.S.S.R., the Center of Military Studies of the Revolutionary Armed Forces of Cuba, and the Latin American Institute of the Academy of Sciences of the U.S.S.R.: *Valentía y solidaridad: el internacionalismo y*

114

la amistad combativa entre las Fuerzas Armadas de Cuba y la URSS (Havana: Editorial de Ciencias Sociales, 1983).

54. "Deep ties of brotherhood unite the Cuban people and the Revolutionary Armed Forces with the Soviet Armed Forces," Raúl pointed out in his closing address in the ceremony held to mark the seventieth anniversary of the founding of the Armed Forces of the U.S.S.R. *Granma* (February 22, 1988).

55. *Discriminate Deterrence: Report of the Commission on Integrated Long-Term Strategy* (Washington, January 1988), p. 5.

56. *Informe central ante el Il Congreso del Partido Comunista de Cuba* (Havana: Editora Política, 1983), p. 135.

57. Carlos Alzugaray, "La política exterior de la administration Reagan," paper presented at the "United States in the '80s International Round-Table Discussion," sponsored by Centro de Estudios sobre América (CEA) (Havana: March 1983).

58. Interview of Fidel Castro by Maria Shriver in *Juventud Rebelde* (February 28, 1988), p. 21.

59. Cole Blasier, "The Soviet Union and the Cuban-American Conflict," in Cole Blasier and Carmelo Mesa-Lago, eds., *Cuba in the World* (Pittsburgh: University of Pittsburgh Press, 1979), pp. 37-52.

60. Wolfers, "National Security as an Ambiguous Symbol," p. 497.

61. Interview of Fidel Castro by Maria Shriver, *Juventud Rebelde* (February 28, 1988), p. 14.

62. *Ibid.*, p. 15.

63. Domínguez, *Cuban Military and National Security Policies,* pp. 92 ff.

64. The Cuban president stated on December 8, 1984, in a speech during the closing session of the Fourth Congress of the Federation of Senior High School Students (FEEM), "Even though a situation of détente—which is what we want—may arise, defense cannot be neglected. This is very important, and we cannot forget what we have achieved. It is a reality that is imposed on us by our geographic location. The differences in the political, economic, and social system that we have with our most powerful neighbor require that we always give maximum attention of defense. Even if, someday, there were a socialist system in the United States, we could not neglect defense. Vietnam shares a border with China, and both are socialist countries, yet Vietnam cannot neglect its defenses." More recently, on April 7, 1987, in

his closing speech at the Fifth Congress of the Union of Young Communists (UJC), Fidel Castro reiterated that idea: "Therefore, we say that we do not postulate eternal hostility between the United States and Cuba; but, even when we live in peace—if that should happen—we would not neglect our defenses; we would not for a second forget what we owe to our determination to defend ourselves, to our readiness—the readiness of every man and woman in this country—to fight to the death to defend the Revolution and our homeland. . . . Therefore, even if we should live in peace one day, we would keep on digging trenches and making tunnels; we would keep on getting arms and training the people. We must not be deceived by the mirage of peace from a powerful neighbor, which any day may feel tempted to attack our country when it has one of its many changes of administration, which are capable of propounding the stupidest policies."

65. Fidel Castro. *Clausura del VI Congreso de la FEEM: nacimos para vencer y no para ser vencidos* (Havana: Editora Política, 1984), pp. 5-6.

5

The United States,
Cuba, and Southern Africa:
From Confrontation to Negotiation

Michael Clough

U.S. policy toward southern Africa has evolved considerably since the mid-1970s, when an unexpected coup in Lisbon led to the abrupt demise of Portuguese colonialism, sparking a civil war in Angola. Developments in the region, changes in the state of U.S.-Soviet relations, and domestic politics have altered the ways in which U.S. officials define U.S. interests and the strategies they have chosen to promote and protect those interests. Only by understanding the nature and significance of these changes will it be possible to assess the potential for a lasting cessation of conflict between Washington and Havana over southern Africa.

The Ford-Kissinger Era

Prior to 1975, the United States largely ignored southern Africa.[1] The low point came in 1970, when the Nixon administration adopted a strategy of calculated neglect based on the assumptions, then widely held, that southern Africa's white redoubt—consisting of the two Portuguese colonies (Angola and Mozambique), Rhodesia, Namibia and South Africa—was secure; that there was little prospect of significant Soviet involvement in the region; and, therefore, that the United States' relatively insignificant interests there were unlikely to be threatened.[2] These assumptions were shattered by the chain of events that followed Portugal's decision to grant independence to its African colonies following the April 16, 1974, coup.

The prospect of independence in Angola sparked a tripartite civil war, which quickly escalated into a regional conflict involving the United States, Zaire, and South Africa on one side, and Cuba and the Soviet Union on the other.[3] In Mozambique, the peaceful transfer of power to Frelimo (Frente de Libertação de Moçambique) changed the strategic balance in the eastern half of the region, intensifying pressure on Ian Smith's rebellious white regime in Rhodesia and causing South Africa's white rulers to reassess their strategies. The new realities created by these developments forced U.S. policy makers to redefine American interests and, for the first time, become deeply involved in the region.

On January 22, 1975, the Ford administration made a fateful decision to provide limited covert assistance ($300,000) to the FNLA (Frente Nacional de Libertação de Angola), one of three parties competing for power in Angola.[4] At the time, few of the officials involved expected conflict in this hitherto little-known African country to escalate into a major international crisis.

Not until two months later, when reports of substantial Soviet support for another Angolan group—the MPLA (Movimento Popular de Libertação de Angola)—had begun to reach Washington (and just as Saigon was falling to North Vietnamese forces) did Secretary of State Henry Kissinger start to reassess the significance of the situation in southern Africa. In the wake of the U.S. defeat in Southeast Asia, he decided to use the conflict in Angola to demonstrate to Moscow that the United States retained the resolve to act as a great power. Consequently, on July 17 the administration adopted a plan to provide $30 million in cash and arms to the FNLA and the third major Angolan group—UNITA (Union Nacional para a Independencia Total de Angola) led by Jonas Savimbi.

The Ford administration's intervention in Angola quickly became a debacle. On November 11, 1975, the Portuguese departed from Angola, leaving Luanda, the capital, in the hands of the MPLA, and the country engulfed in war. By this point, external intervention in the conflict had increased significantly. Military and financial assistance from the superpowers was supplemented by troops, first from Zaire, and later from South Africa and Cuba. After South Africa's intervention on behalf of the FNLA and UNITA became widely known, a majority of African states, led by Nigeria, recognized the MPLA as the government of Angola. In December, the U.S. Congress voted to halt continued CIA involvement in Angola.[5] Shortly thereafter, with its local allies—the FNLA and UNITA—in disarray, an isolated South Africa began to withdraw, leaving the MPLA, bolstered by more than 36,000 Cuban troops, in control of the country.

The MPLA's victory was widely hailed as a triumph for Cuba and the Soviet Union and a defeat for the United States. Fearing the possibility of further Soviet gains in the region, the Ford administration began to formulate a new regional strategy in early 1976. The Angolan experience taught Kissinger several important lessons, the most important of which was the need for an approach capable of winning broad-based support in Africa. Moreover, he now recognized that Congress was likely to oppose any strategy involving military action. The administration's only option, therefore, was preemptive diplomacy.

Kissinger first enunciated the new strategy in a historic speech on April 27, 1976, in Lusaka, Zambia. He outlined a set of policies to achieve a negotiated settlement in Rhodesia, an internationally supervised transition to independence in Namibia (South West Africa), and a peaceful end to "institutionalized inequality" in South Africa.[6] In all three cases the administration hoped to hasten and manage political change in order to prevent escalating violence, reduce the appeal and influence of "radicals," and hence eliminate opportunities for future Soviet successes. For Kissinger and his deputies, the goal in Rhodesia and Namibia was a reasonably rapid transfer of power to "moderate" black leaders. Priority was given to Rhodesia, where white rule was most immediately threatened, the risk of Soviet-Cuban intervention highest, and the prospect of a quick settlement greatest.

Kissinger believed the problem in South Africa was quite different from those in Rhodesia and Namibia. He regarded the Republic as an important, albeit politically problematical, regional ally. As he was aware, the South African government had already decided that a negotiated settlement was necessary in Rhodesia, and it was close to reaching a similar conclusion with regard to Namibia. Throughout 1976, Washington and Pretoria operated on a shared assumption that joint action to broker transitions in the two other white-ruled territories would give South Africa more time and political space to settle its own racial problems.

In mid-1976, after consultations with South Africa, Great Britain, and several African countries, Kissinger launched a concerted diplomatic effort to persuade Rhodesia's rebel government, led by Prime Minister Ian Smith, to accept majority rule.[7] By late September, thanks largely to behind-the-scenes pressure from South Africa, he had succeeded in convincing Smith to accept the principle of majority rule within two years and to agree to attend an all-parties conference to work out a plan for a transfer of power. However, the conference, held in Geneva in December, quickly stalemated.

The Carter Era

When President Jimmy Carter took office in January 1977, a decision was immediately made to continue the diplomatic initiative in Rhodesia. Toward this end, repeal of the so-called Byrd amendment, which had since 1971 allowed U.S. imports of "strategic materials" from Rhodesia in violation of United Nations sanctions, was made a major legislative priority. At the same time, an overall review of policy toward southern Africa was undertaken. The objectives—and priorities—identified by the Carter administration were the same as those of the Ford administration: negotiations leading to majority rule in Rhodesia and Namibia, and progress toward the same end in South Africa. But this similarity disguised several fundamental differences in the approaches of the two administrations.

Officials in the Carter administration emphasized human rights rather than geopolitics in explaining U.S. interests in southern Africa. For example, on May 19, 1977, in Maputo, in an appearance calculated to signal the shift in perspective, Andrew Young, the new U.S. permanent representative to the United Nations, told the delegates to an "international conference in support of the peoples of Zimbabwe and Namibia" that President Carter had "made it clear from the beginning that a renewed commitment to our responsibilities in the field of human rights required justice in southern Africa."[8]

The increased concern with human rights prompted a new view of the relationship between the Rhodesian, Namibian, and South African issues. A decision was made to push for progress on all three issues. In late May, Vice President Walter Mondale was dispatched to Vienna to meet with South African Prime Minister John Vorster to communicate the administration's approach: "We see all three issues [as being] of basic importance. We don't think progress on one issue excuses no progress on another. But any progress of significance will be appreciated, will be valuable, and will have to be recognized."[9]

This formula represented a compromise between those officials in the administration who believed the United States should go to the source of southern Africa's problems by focusing more directly on the apartheid issue, and those who believed more progress could be made by giving priority to the Rhodesian and Namibian initiatives. But no one in the administration, except possibly

National Security Adviser Zbigniew Brzezinski, shared Kissinger's view that Pretoria could be a strategic ally of the United States. Nor was there support for tempering criticism of apartheid in exchange for South African cooperation on the Rhodesian and Namibian issues. In practice, however, much more diplomatic energy was expended on the search for settlements in Rhodesia and Namibia than on the effort to end apartheid.

Initially, the Carter administration also viewed Cuba's role in southern Africa somewhat differently than had the Ford administration. In fact, Young stirred up a minor controversy at one point by making an off-hand remark that the Cubans might be playing a "stabilizing" role in Angola. While few in the administration would have endorsed Young's view on this point, most of the senior officials responsible for southern Africa policy were not particularly alarmed by the Cuban presence in Angola. If a settlement could be achieved in Namibia and relations with Luanda normalized, they believed the Cuban troop issue would, in all likelihood, resolve itself.

Finally, the Carter administration differed from its predecessor in showing greater regard for African opinion and multilateral institutions. ("We believe," Young declared in Maputo, "it is in our national interest to work cooperatively with African nations on mutual economic and political concerns.")[10] Whereas Kissinger preferred to operate through bilateral meetings, the new policy team, led by Secretary of State Cyrus Vance and Ambassador Young, favored joint initiatives involving other allied countries, international organizations, and multilateral groupings such as the Front Line States.

Because of the differing histories of the Rhodesian and Namibian conflicts, the diplomatic efforts undertaken to resolve them varied significantly. In the case of Rhodesia, bureaucratic responsibility was delegated to the State Department, which cooperated closely with its counterparts in Great Britain to develop the so-called Anglo-American plan. After nearly three years of on-again, off-again negotiations, a change of government in London, and several tactical adjustments, this effort produced a settlement. U.S. officials were not directly involved in the final negotiations at Lancaster House between September and December 1979. But without the Carter administration's diplomatic involvement and, most important, its refusal to bow to congressional pressure to lift sanctions and recognize the so-called internal settlement, the conflict would have dragged on much longer.[11]

In the case of Namibia, the U.S. delegation to the United Nations assumed the lead in developing a basis for an internationally supervised transition to independence.[12] This initiative resulted in the creation of a "contact group" consisting of the five Western powers then on the UN Security Council. In April 1978 this group unveiled a set of proposals for a settlement. Five months later, following extensive discussions with the Front Line states, South Africa, and SWAPO, the Security Council passed Resolution 435. Based on the contact group's proposals, this resolution soon became recognized as the only acceptable basis for an international settlement. However, the problem then, as it would ten years later, lay in gaining final South African agreement to the plan's implementation.

Following passage of Resolution 435, President Carter agreed to send Secretary Vance to South Africa with the other contact group foreign ministers. Prior to this trip, it was decided that the United States would consider supporting sanctions if Pretoria refused to move forward on Namibian independence. But when Prime Minister P.W. Botha offered only minor concessions, the Western leaders backed down. The negotiations continued to progress fitfully until November 1980, when Pretoria agreed to attend a "pre-implementation meeting" in Geneva in order to remove the remaining obstacles to a settlement. By this time, however, Ronald Reagan was about to replace Jimmy Carter. This prospect removed what little pressure South Africa might have felt to settle the issue at the time.

The Carter administration's efforts to promote political change in southern Africa achieved mixed but largely positive results. Administration officials deserve considerable credit for the settlement in Rhodesia, and for defining a basis for a settlement in Namibia. Their efforts in this area also made it possible to diminish the large reservoir of African distrust that had been created by the policies of previous administrations, thus establishing a groundwork for the development of a more productive relationship between the United States and Africa. At the same time, however, the Carter administration must be faulted for failing to develop a regional strategy that went beyond promoting an end to white rule. While they succeeded in developing relatively good working relationships with the governments in Angola and Mozambique, administration officials were unable to translate these personal relationships into more stable and sustainable society-to-society, state-to-state ties. The best evidence of this failure was the administration's inability to win congressional support for development aid to Mozambique and, more important, to normalize relations with Luanda.

Because of the circumstances in which the MPLA had come to power and the continuing presence in Angola of Cuban troops, the Ford administration had refused to recognize the Angolan government. Most Carter administration officials concerned with Africa regarded this posture as short-sighted and counterproductive, especially given the positive relationship that developed between the Angolan government and U.S. oil companies. In his memoirs, for example, Vance wrote: "The unwillingness to normalize relations never made sense in terms of our objective of getting the Cubans out of Angola and influencing Luanda toward moderate solutions to problems in which we had an important interest."[13] But Brzezinski, who otherwise had little influence over policy toward southern Africa, was able to veto several efforts by the State Department to recognize Angola.[14]

Had the Vance-Young contingent within the administration articulated a rationale for regional policy that went beyond promoting political change, they would have been better able to overcome Brzezinski's narrow globalism. By failing to do so, they set the stage for the seemingly abrupt reversal in the direction of U.S. regional policy that occurred following Ronald Reagan's election.

The Origins of Constructive Engagement

The foreign policy team that Ronald Reagan brought into office in January 1981 was deeply hostile to the Carter administration's policies toward human rights and political change in the Third World.[15] This outlook strongly influenced the formulation of policy toward southern Africa in the first months of the new administration. Convinced that their predecessor's approach to the region had been naive and overly moralistic, the Reagan team quickly set about shaping a more "realistic" posture. The strategy that emerged was largely the work of the Assistant Secretary of State for Africa designate, Chester Crocker.[16]

In many ways, the Reagan administration's policy toward southern Africa represented a return to the approach pursued by the Ford administration after the Angolan debacle. Geopolitical considerations once again became the driving force behind policy; the assumption that South Africa could be an important strategic ally resurfaced; and multilateralism fell into disfavor. The major difference was that, with Zimbabwe independent, ending white rule in Rhodesia was no longer on the agenda.

In his first televised interview, President Reagan referred to South Africa as "a country that has stood beside us in every war we've ever fought."[17]   Of more consequence, however, was a subtler formulation advanced by Crocker in a May 1981 memo to Secretary of State Alexander Haig:

> The political relationship between the United States and South Africa has now arrived at a crossroads of perhaps historic significance. After twenty years of generally increasing official U.S. Government coolness toward South Africa and concomitant South African intransigence, the possibility may exist for a more positive and reciprocal relationship between the two countries based upon shared strategic concerns in southern Africa, our recognition that the government of P.W. Botha represents a unique opportunity for domestic change, and a willingness of the Reagan Administration to deal realistically with South Africa.   The problem of Namibia, however, which complicates our relations with our European allies and with black Africa, is a primary obstacle to the development of a new relationship with South Africa. It also represents an opportunity to counter the Soviet threat in Africa. We thus need Pretoria's cooperation in working toward an internationally acceptable solution to Namibia which would, however, safeguard U.S. and South African essential interests and concerns.[18]

Proceeding from radically different assumptions than those of his predecessors, Crocker chose to continue the effort to broker a settlement in Namibia.   After a bruising confirmation battle in which he came under attack from Senator Jesse Helms for being too moderate, Crocker was given considerable latitude by President Reagan and Secretary Haig to chart a course in southern Africa.

The administration's Namibian strategy began to take shape shortly after Reagan's inauguration.   The new element in this strategy was the idea of linking final agreement on implementation of Resolution 435 to a withdrawal of Cuban troops from Angola. This idea first surfaced in a February 7, 1981, memo drafted by Crocker and approved by Haig. There were two main rationales for linkage. Crocker believed that linkage would make it possible to win final South African agreement to implement Resolution 435. In contrast to his predecessors, Crocker did not believe that Pretoria could be pressured into a settlement. Instead, he argued, they would have to be enticed to go along; linkage was to be one of the enticements. More important, however, linkage provided Crocker with a means of winning support for his Namibian initiative from senior administration officials. In contrast to the Carter administration, which had shown considerable ambivalence in its attitude toward Cuba, the Reagan administration—and Secretary of State Alexander Haig in particular—was strongly committed to reversing the gains Havana had made in the 1970s through its interventions in Africa and Central America. In fact, without the promise that a Namibian settlement would result in a reduction of Cuban and Soviet influence in Angola, Reagan and Haig would have had little interest in supporting Crocker's efforts.

If this strategy had succeeded relatively quickly, as Crocker evidently believed it would, the results would have been dramatic. A success would have legitimated constructive engagement, made it easier for the Reagan administration to cooperate openly with Pretoria, and possibly encouraged the Botha government to move ahead with internal reforms. It would have dealt a major blow to Soviet standing in the region, and significantly boosted U.S. credibility. However, Crocker's strategy had two problems. First, it assumed that South Africa was interested in a settlement; second, it failed to take into account the changing military situation inside Angola. As the negotiations proceeded, these problems became increasingly evident.

Crocker's initiative was set in motion on March 29, 1981, when he announced that the administration had completed its review of southern Africa policy. Over the next few months, he attempted to get an "unambiguous" statement from Pretoria that it was ready to negotiate in good faith. Once he was convinced that he had such a commitment, Crocker developed a three-phase negotiating plan. In phase one, agreement was to be reached on a set of constitutional principles to protect minority rights in Namibia after independence. Phase two negotiations would focus on remaining technical issues concerning elections, the mechanics of a ceasefire and troop withdrawals, and composition of the UN force that would supervise the transition. Finally, in phase three implementation of Resolution 435 would begin. Linkage was to be treated as a separate issue that would be addressed in bilateral talks between the United States and Angola once phase two was completed. On September 24 this plan was approved by the contact group. By this point, however, the contact group had become little more than a forum in which Washington unveiled its latest plans.

By mid-1982 phase one had been completed, and only minor issues remained in the phase two discussions. Attention thus turned to linkage. Following a series of talks between Crocker and Angolan Foreign Minister Paulo Jorge, President Reagan dispatched his special ambassador, Vernon Walters, to Luanda in June. In September the President sent a personal letter to African heads of state expressing his strong personal commitment to linkage. This letter was followed in November by a ten-stop trip to Africa by Vice President George Bush. Despite all of this activity—and a growing American willingness to confront the problem of security guarantees for Angola in the event of a Cuban troop withdrawal—a stalemate developed over linkage. The major problem was the growing strength inside Angola of UNITA's guerrilla forces, a development greatly facilitated by South Africa's decision in the late 1970s to increase aid to UNITA. UNITA's improving military fortunes made it increasingly difficult for Luanda to consider sending the Cuban troops home; at the same time, they gave South Africa an additional incentive to delay a settlement.

Throughout the Reagan administration's first term, U.S. policy toward UNITA was very ambiguous. Early in 1981, administration officials asked Congress to repeal the "Clark Amendment," which prohibited covert assistance to opposition groups in Angola. In his first major speech on regional policy, Crocker declared that UNITA was "a significant and legitimate factor in Angolan politics."[19] And, in December 1981, UNITA's President, Jonas Savimbi, made a highly publicized semi-official visit to Washington, where he met with Secretary of State Haig and other high-ranking officials. Six months later, a high State Department official told reporters that "we find it difficult to envisage the possibility of a regional solution that did not include some discussion leading eventually to some understanding between the key players in Angola."[20]

Any plans the administration might have had to resume aid to UNITA were stymied by the House of Representatives' refusal to go along with the Senate in repealing the Clark amendment in late 1981. Thereafter, UNITA received less and less attention in official U.S. statements; no effort was made to press the issue in Congress. Instead, the negotiations over linkage seemed to be moving Washington closer and closer to de facto recognition of the MPLA. In February 1983, Crocker told a congressional hearing that the administration was "fully prepared to respond to Angola's security concerns . . ." While reiterating the view that "UNITA was an important and legitimate nationalist movement inside Angola," he declared that resolution of Angola's internal problems was not an issue to be dealt with by the United States. "Whether the Angolan government and others will conclude that in order for these other issues to be resolved there will need to be some kind of an agreement on the issue of UNITA, that is for them to say. We have no conditions on that issue."[21]

While U.S. support for UNITA appeared to wane, however, South African and other assistance increased. This assistance, and repeated incursions by the South African Defense Forces (SADF) into southern Angola, contributed to a steady improvement in UNITA's military position, making it more and more difficult for the MPLA to meet U.S. demands for the withdrawal of Cuban troops. At the same time, the SADF grew increasingly confident of its ability to control the military situation in Namibia. As a result, by mid-1983 there appeared to be little prospect of a settlement.

Adapting Constructive Engagement

As hope for a settlement in Namibia began to dim, constructive engagement entered a new phase. While the administration concentrated on the diplomatic front in Namibia and Angola, Pretoria moved on the military front throughout the region. In 1980 and 1981, the South African Defense forces launched an aggressive destabilization effort designed to compel neighboring countries to accept a regional order supportive of Pretoria's interests—or, if this proved impossible, to so destabilize these countries that they could not threaten the Republic. Destabilization involved a series of cross-border raids by the SADF on Mozambique, Lesotho, and Botswana, support for antigovernment insurgents in Mozambique, Lesotho, and Zimbabwe, and efforts to manipulate the regional transport network.[22] As these actions began to engulf the entire region in a widening spiral of violence, Reagan administration officials became concerned. For the first time, they began to rethink their initial premise that the United States and South Africa had a common set of regional interests, and that their main task was to resolve the Namibian issue quickly in order to make open cooperation with Pretoria more politically acceptable.

The first indication of a change in thinking came in a little-noticed speech by Frank Wisner, Crocker's top deputy, in September 1982. "[W]e need to understand," Wisner said, "that Namibia is not the alpha and omega of U.S. policy interests in the region; there is a long agenda to which we need lend our efforts including working toward a more productive relationship with Mozambique and Angola, supporting the development of a strong, stable, and pro-Western Zambia and Zimbabwe, and assisting in the stable and democratic development of Botswana, Lesotho, and Swaziland."[23] Nine months later this reformulation of U.S. regional policy found its way into a speech by Undersecretary of State Lawrence Eagleburger that was billed as the most comprehensive and highest-level statement on southern Africa since the administration came into office. Eagleburger spelled out a vision of "a framework of regional security" in southern Africa based on respect for international boundaries, renunciation of violence, and political coexistence. Significantly, he also observed that, "A structure of regional stability is unlikely to take root in the absence of basic movement away from a system of legally entrenched rule by the white minority."[24]

The clearest manifestation of a shift in regional strategy was the new importance attached to relations with Mozambique. Relations between the United States and Mozambique had reached an all-time low shortly after Reagan's inauguration. Following an SADF attack on alleged ANC facilities just outside of Maputo, Mozambique's President Samora Machel expelled several U.S. officials on spying charges. In retaliation, Washington canceled all aid to Mozambique.

In early 1982, Machel quietly began to seek ways to reestablish a working relationship with the United States. The Crocker team was slow to respond. At first, few officials perceived the value of a rapprochement with Maputo. For example, one official wryly commented in private, "the problem is they haven't got any Cubans to send home." In fact, small numbers of Cuban advisers were in Mozambique, but their role was distinctly limited and their presence never assumed the importance, in practical or symbolic terms, that the Cuban troop presence in Angola did. As the issue began to be conceived in broader regional terms, however, the administration's view of Mozambique's importance changed; it became the centerpiece of the effort to stabilize the region and demonstrate the United States' unique abilities to serve as a regional power broker.

During 1983, Washington and Maputo engaged in an intense ongoing dialogue that led to the resumption of American food aid and the reestablishment of normal diplomatic relations. These discussions also played a major role in laying the groundwork for the signing of a nonaggression and mutual cooperation pact (the so-called "Nkomati accord") by South Africa and Mozambique on

March 16, 1984. The State Department was quick to portray this accord as a major U.S. success. Whatever the specifics of the U.S. role in the negotiations, it is clear that both Mozambique and South Africa were encouraged to enter into the agreement by expectations that doing so would win them favor in Washington and other Western capitals.

Progress in Mozambique was paralleled by apparent progress on the Angola-Namibia front. On February 16, 1984, South Africa and Angola signed a ceasefire agreement in Lusaka. Cuba did not participate in the negotiations leading to this agreement. In fact, many observers claim that Havana opposed the agreement. As in the case of the Nkomati accord, U.S. officials were quick to declare it a victory for constructive engagement. However, the State Department's optimism ebbed quickly.

Constructive Engagement Unravels

Between September 1984 and September 1986, constructive engagement came unraveled, and Assistant Secretary Crocker went from being hailed as a diplomatic genius to being everybody's favorite scapegoat.[25] An important factor in this rapid turn of events was the outbreak of sustained protest and violence in South Africa and the emergence of apartheid as a major political issue in the United States. These developments made it impossible for the administration to continue to give priority to regional issues. Moreover, by precipitating the adoption of increasingly tougher sanctions, internal developments in South Africa accelerated the transformation of Washington and Pretoria into regional adversaries. But internal developments in South Africa were not the only, or even the primary, cause of the collapse of Crocker's regional strategy.

Domestically, the most serious challenge to the regional strand of constructive engagement came from the right. In 1984 and 1985, support began to swell for the so-called Reagan doctrine endorsing U.S. aid to insurgents fighting to overthrow Marxist governments in the Third World. Although President Reagan's early rhetoric in support of "the heroic freedom fighters of Afghanistan" had encouraged conservative analysts to talk of a new approach, the President did not publicly endorse the doctrine that bears his name until his February 1985 State of the Union Address, when he declared that ". . . we must not break faith with those who are risking their lives—on every continent, from Afghanistan to Nicaragua—to defy Soviet-supported aggression and secure rights which have been ours from birth."[26] Ten days later, in his weekly radio broadcast, Reagan referred to "freedom fighters in Afghanistan, Ethiopia, Cambodia, and Angola," and pointed out, "Time and again in the course of our history, we've aided those around the world struggling for freedom, democracy, independence, and liberation from tyranny."[27] But these themes were given their most lengthy and detailed exposition in a speech by Secretary of State George Shultz on February 22, 1985, in which he declared that the United States had a "moral responsibility" to support "popular insurgencies against communist domination."[28] This rhetoric contrasted sharply with the policies the administration was pursuing in Angola and Mozambique.

The sudden upsurge of support for the "Reagan doctrine" manifested itself in July 1985 Congressional votes to repeal the Clark amendment.[29] If Congress had not repealed the Clark amendment, Crocker and his supporters might have been able to stave off the efforts of ideologically minded conservatives within the administration to provide aid to UNITA. Once the amendment was repealed, however, policy shifted quickly. By late November 1985, President Reagan was openly supporting aid to UNITA; early the next year, a $15 million package of covert aid was reportedly approved. This development had a chilling effect on negotiations between Washington and Luanda. The decision to aid UNITA encouraged conservatives to attempt to add anti-communist insurgents in Mozambique to the list of "freedom fighters."[30] Although this effort ultimately failed, it slowed the State Department's plans to provide greater support for Frelimo.

Between mid-1984 and early 1986, growing domestic opposition to white rule forced the Reagan administration to adopt a more hostile stance toward Pretoria, while conservative support for Savimbi and hostility toward the MPLA and Frelimo governments reduced the administration's options in the region. Gone forever were the days when Crocker was relatively free to chart his own course. Instead, he found himself caught between left and right in a tightening political vise.

Rethinking Constructive Engagement's Premises

Unrest in South Africa and political developments in the United States precipitated the collapse of constructive engagement. However, the root of the problem burrowed much deeper. Ultimately, the policy failed because it rested on a false set of assumptions about the underlying sources of regional conflict and the nature of South African regional interests and objectives. On March 22, 1982, Crocker succinctly outlined the administration's early views on these issues: "The Soviet Union alone has a vested interest in keeping the region in turmoil. It is to no one else's advantage, neither to that of the South Africans, the other southern Africans, nor certainly to the United States and the West."[31]

This position ultimately proved doubly wrong. By 1985-1986 it was clear that it was Pretoria, not Moscow, that believed regional turmoil was in its interest.

Initially, administration officials believed South African aggressiveness was a consequence rather than a cause of regional instability and external intervention. For example, in August 1981, Crocker rationalized Pretoria's large military buildup as a reaction to "large-scale foreign intervention, the pressure of African guerrilla groups, and strains in its relations with its traditional Western partners."[32] U.S. officials believed, moreover, that regional instability acted as a brake on the Botha government's efforts to carry out significant internal reforms.

Pretoria's destabilization campaign of 1980 to 1983 forced the administration to reassess its beliefs about the nature of South African policies. Out of this reassessment came a view of the Botha regime as a government divided into two factions: hard-liners who favored destabilization, and pragmatists, especially Foreign Minister Pik Botha, who shared the Reagan administration's understanding of the advantages of regional cooperation and stability. Influencing South Africa's internal debate over regional policy thus became one of the Crocker team's primary objectives. The Nkomati and Lusaka accords were viewed as examples of the effectiveness of this strategy. These successes, and the theory of a divided South African government, allowed Crocker and his aides to interpret Pretoria's aggressive actions between 1981 and 1983 as anomalies, and to retain confidence in their earlier assumption that South Africa's regional interests were fundamentally consistent with U.S. regional interests. This assessment proved to be as flawed as the administration's earlier belief that South Africa's regional aggressiveness was primarily defensive in character.

Two actions had a particularly dramatic effect on U.S. perceptions of South African regional policy. The first was Pretoria's failure to live up to the terms of the Nkomati agreement and completely end the flow of assistance to Renamo, the guerrilla movement opposed to the Frelimo government. As U.S. support for Maputo solidified, continued SADF support for Renamo increasingly placed the Reagan administration in direct conflict with South Africa. In June 1987, Crocker went so far as to challenge Pretoria's repeated denials by testifying at a congressional hearing that South Africa was still supplying Renamo.

A less understood but extremely important cause for growing U.S. hostility toward South African regional policy was Pretoria's efforts to coerce Botswana into signing a nonaggression pact similar to the Nkomati accord. Botswana has long enjoyed an extremely positive reputation in the United States as one of Africa's few multi-party democracies. It should have come as no surprise, therefore, when an SADF raid on an alleged ANC facility in Gaborone on June 13, 1985, provoked a strong reaction in Washington. Declaring that the raid "comes against a background that raises the most serious questions about [the South African] government's recent conduct and policy," the Reagan administration recalled its Ambassador to South Africa for consultation.

The conflict between the Reagan administration's regional policies and South Africa's destabilization campaign deepened just as shifts were beginning to occur in Soviet policy toward southern Africa.[33] These shifts occurred in several stages. In 1984-1985, mid-level Soviet officials and academics began to suggest that neither the Soviet Union nor the United States had vital interests in southern Africa. The implication was that this was a region where it might be possible for the two superpowers to work out a mutually advantageous modus vivendi. Moscow also appeared to recognize the growing tension in U.S.-South African policy. At the same time, Soviet analysts began to doubt the Angolan government's ability to win a military victory. These changes in Soviet thinking on southern Africa were communicated to the United States through a variety of channels, one of the most important being a series of bilateral meetings between Crocker and his Soviet counterparts, which began in 1983.

By late 1987, the State Department's view of southern Africa was quite different than it had been in 1981. Despite the ideological rhetoric surrounding the Reagan doctrine and the resumption of aid to UNITA, Crocker and his counterparts no longer believed that conflict in the region was a zero-sum competition between Washington and Moscow, or that South African regional policies benefited Western interests. These shifts set the stage for a serious attempt to break the diplomatic logjam that had developed over Namibia and Angola.

A Regional Breakthrough

In early 1987, the Angolan government decided to launch a major conventional offensive against UNITA.[34] After some initial successes, Angola's Forças Armadas Populares de Libertação de Angola (FAPLA) suffered a major defeat attempting to cross the Lomba River in southeastern Angola. As FAPLA retreated to Cuito Cuanavale, a key government staging base, they were pursued by UNITA and SADF units. By November these forces were threatening to overrun Cuito Cuanavale. This threat prompted an emergency meeting between Angola's President José Eduardo dos Santos and Cuba's Fidel Castro.

Cuba had opposed the decision to launch a conventional offensive. However, in November, Castro agreed to send more troops to Angola. The new units relieved Cuito Cuanavale and moved into position to directly threaten South African forces along the Namibian border. Had such a development occurred in the early years of the Reagan administration, alarm bells would have sounded in Washington. But in the winter of 1987-1988, the United States remained calm as thousands of Cuban troops arrived in Angola. Some U.S. officials even hinted that Cuba's moves served U.S. interests. This reaction was the result of Washington's growing frustration with Pretoria and its confidence that Havana and Moscow were interested in a negotiated settlement.

South Africa's crackdown on domestic opposition and its continued regional belligerence had embarrassed and frustrated Crocker. The failure of constructive engagement and the administration's refusal to consider economic sanctions left Washington with little leverage over the Botha government. In these circumstances, Cuba's military moves provided a timely warning to Pretoria that it was reaching the limits of its capabilities. With the Cubans now fully engaged in the fighting, the SADF for the first time faced a risk of high casualties. It is not clear that South Africa suffered a clear "defeat" in the battle of Cuito Cuanavale, as many have claimed, but it did experience heavier casualties than ever before, and, more important, would have risked a potentially devastating defeat had it not abandoned the effort to take Cuito Cuanavale. President Botha and his advisers reassessed their involvement in Angola, and increased their interest in exploring diplomatic options. The Cuban military threat thus ironically became Crocker's best source of leverage over Pretoria.

Equally important in explaining Washington's low-key response to the changing military situation in southern Angola was the fact that the Cuban buildup was accompanied by signals from Havana and Luanda of a willingness to return to the bargaining table and resolve the stalemate over linkage and timetables for Cuban troop withdrawal. In August 1987, Luanda had offered a compromise on the timetable for Cuban withdrawal from southern Angola, put forward in the "platform" presented to the United States in September 1984. Discussion of this offer was interrupted that fall by the rapidly changing military situation. In January, after the Cuban reinforcements had begun to arrive, the Angolan government informed Washington that it was ready to resume negotiations. These diplomatic gestures made it more difficult for U.S. conservatives to stir up fears that Cuba's moves signaled a commitment to a military resolution of regional conflicts.

A major breakthrough occurred in late January, when the United States accepted the presence of Cuban representatives in the discussions. This development was doubly significant. It provided formal U.S. recognition of Cuba's role in Angola and its right to be a party to the negotiations; and it signaled Havana's willingness to accept the United States' role as a mediator. This progress rested on an implicit understanding concerning the Angolan civil war and U.S. aid to UNITA: Angola and Cuba dropped their demand for an immediate end to U.S. support for Savimbi, and Crocker agreed to keep national reconciliation in Angola off the formal agenda. However, all parties recognized that these issues would have to be addressed eventually.

In early May, Crocker convened a meeting of negotiators from Angola, Cuba, and South Africa in London. Also present as an observer was a senior official from the Soviet Foreign Ministry. This meeting established the basic terms for subsequent negotiations. Significantly, all parties appeared to downplay differences on the UNITA issue in order to allow progress in discussions of South African and Cuban withdrawal and implementation of Resolution 435. After the London sessions, a period of intense maneuvering began. South Africa actively explored possibilities for a separate settlement with Angola that would not involve Namibian independence. When that gambit failed, it began to behave in ways, both diplomatic and military, that indicated it was having second thoughts about the negotiations. At the same time, both parties in Angola sent high-level delegations to the United States to test and influence U.S. opinion. All of the principals, prompted by fears about the potential costs of responsibility for the breakdown of the talks, remained engaged in the negotiations.

The negotiations began to move forward again in mid-July. During talks in New York, the parties agreed to a set of fourteen principles for a peaceful settlement in southwestern Africa. The agreement involved implementation of Resolution 435, South African and Cuban withdrawal from Angola, agreement on a number of rules of behavior (such as respect for territorial integrity and noninterference in the internal affairs of states), and formal acknowledgment of the mediating role of the United States. In early August, more concrete progress was made at a meeting in Geneva. On August 8, Angola, Cuba, and South Africa released a joint statement that set November 1 as the date for the beginning of implementation of Resolution 435; September 1 as a target date for agreement on a timetable for Cuban troop withdrawal; declared a de facto ceasefire; and announced approval of measures to reduce the risk of military confrontation.

By early November, considerable progress had been made in narrowing the gap between the troop withdrawal timetable offered by Luanda and Havana and that demanded by Pretoria and Washington. But both the September 1 and November 1 deadlines passed without a final agreement. The main issue blocking agreement was the most important item not on the formal agenda of the negotiations: the problem of UNITA. Two considerations—Angolan security and U.S. politics—made it impossible to keep the UNITA issue out of the negotiations. The Angolan government understandably feared that sending the Cuban troops home without a cut-off of aid to UNITA could threaten its security. But political pressure from the U.S. Congress made it impossible for U.S. negotiators to agree to cut off aid to UNITA unless Luanda negotiated directly with the Angolan rebels.

The domestic limits on Crocker's ability to maneuver were demonstrated in mid-October, when the Senate voted to block the use of U.S. funds to support UN-supervised elections in Namibia until and unless the Angolan government agreed to national reconciliation with UNITA. Senate concerns were spelled out in a letter to President Reagan, signed by fifty-one Senators, urging that UNITA be brought into the negotiations; settlement of the international issues—Namibian independence and Cuban troop withdrawal—be linked to national reconciliation in Angola; and U.S. aid to UNITA not be halted until all Cuban troops were withdrawn and the MPLA agreed to a government of national reconciliation.

In mid-November, the negotiators announced that an agreement had been reached. The agreement, which was formally signed in

New York on December 22, 1989, provided for implementation of Resolution 435 and a phased withdrawal of Cuban troops over a twenty-seven-month period. No mention was made of UNITA and national reconciliation in Angola. The MPLA was coming under intense pressure to reach some sort of an accommodation, and most observers expected that a deal would eventually be worked out, but only after the MPLA leadership had time to recognize that only a negotiated settlement involving UNITA would end the war.

Conclusions

A settlement in Angola will remove a major source of tension in U.S.-Cuban relations. Once Cuban troops are withdrawn from Angola, southern Africa will in all probability drop off the U.S.-Cuban agenda. There will be continuing disagreements over apartheid and other regional issues, but these will be of relatively minor importance in terms of the overall bilateral relationship. Nothing short of a reintroduction of Cuban military forces into the region would be likely to change this relationship.

The more important question is whether the productive diplomatic relationship that has been built up in dealing with the Angolan issue will spill over into other areas. The answer will depend on the lessons that leaders in each country draw from the negotiations. If U.S. officials conclude that the primary reason a settlement occurred was because of U.S. resolve as manifested in the decision to aid UNITA, or if Cuban officials conclude that it was their show of force in the winter of 1987-1988 that forced a settlement, the success of the Angolan negotiations will not create opportunities for progress on other issues. If, instead, officials in both countries realize that a settlement was made possible by each side's willingness to abandon ideological posturing and recognize the legitimacy of the other's interests and concerns, then a basis will be laid for productive negotiations on other issues.

Notes

1. See Anthony Lake, "Caution and concern: The Making of American Policy toward South Africa," Ph.D. dissertation, Princeton University, 1974.
2. See Mohamed El-Khawas and Barry Cohen, eds., *The Kissinger Study of Southern Africa* (Westport, Conn.:

Lawrence Hill, 1976); Anthony Lake, *The "Tar Baby" Option: American Policy Toward Southern Rhodesia* (New York: Columbia University Press, 1976), pp. 123-157; Roger Morris, *Uncertain Greatness: Henry Kissinger and American Foreign Policy* (New York: Harper and Row, 1977), pp. 107-120.

3. See John Marcum, *The Angolan Revolution, Volume II: Exile Politics and Guerrilla Warfare* (Cambridge: MIT Press, 1978); and Arthur Klinghoffer, *The Angolan War* (Boulder: Westview Press, 1980).

4. See Roger Morris, "The Proxy War in Angola," *The New Republic* (January 31, 1976); Nathaniel Davis, "The Angola Decision of 1975," *Foreign Affairs* (Fall 1978); Gerald Bender, "Kissinger in Angola: Anatomy of a Failure," in René Lemarchand, *American Policy in Southern Africa* (Washington: University Press of America, 1978); Alexander George, "Missing Opportunities for Crisis Prevention: The War of Attrition and Angola," in George, ed., *Managing U.S.-Soviet Rivalry* (Boulder: Westview Press, 1983).

5. On the congressional debate over Angola, see Neil Livingstone and Manfred von Nordheim, "The United States Congress and the Angola Crisis," *Strategic Review* (Spring 1977).

6. *U.S. Department of State Bulletin* (May 31, 1976).

7. On Kissinger and the Rhodesian negotiations, see Steven Low, "The Rhodesian Negotiations," (unpublished ms.); and Michael Clough, "From Rhodesia to Zimbabwe," in Clough, ed., *Changing Realities in Southern Africa: Implications for American Policy* (Berkeley: Institute of International Studies, University of California, 1982).

8. Office of the Historian, Bureau of Public Affairs, U.S. Department of State, *The United States and South Africa: U.S. Public Statements and Related Documents, 1977-1985* (hereinafter cited as *The United States and South Africa*), Research Project #1467 (Washington D.C.: September 1985), p. 8.

9. *The United States and South Africa*, p. 13.

10. *The United States and South Africa*, p. 8.

11. On the Carter administration's role in the Rhodesian negotiations, see Clough, "From Rhodesia to Zimbabwe;" and Jeffrey Davidow, *A Peace in Southern Africa* (Boulder: Westview Press, 1984).

12. On the Namibian negotiations, see André du Pisani, *SWA/Namibia: The Politics of Continuity and Change* (Johannesburg: Jonathan Ball Publishers, 1986); and Michael Clough, "From South West Africa to Namibia," in Clough, ed., *Changing Realities in Southern Africa.*

13. Cyrus Vance, *Hard Choices: Critical Years in America's Foreign Policy* (New York: Simon and Schuster, 1983), p. 275.

14. See Zbigniew Brzezinski, *Power and Principle* (New York: Farrar, Straus, Giroux, 1983), p. 143.

15. See Jeanne Kirkpatrick, "Dictatorships and Double Standards," *Commentary* (September 1979).

16. See Chester Crocker, "South Africa: A Strategy for Change," *Foreign Affairs* (Winter 1980-81).

17. *The United States and South Africa*, p. 58.

18. This document was published in *Counterspy* (August-October 1981), p. 54.

19. *The United States and South Africa*, p. 83.

20. *The United States and South Africa*, p. 118.

21. *The United States and South Africa*, p. 172.

22. See Joseph Hanlon, *Beggar Your Neighbors: Apartheid Power in Southern Africa* (Bloomington: Indiana University Press, 1986); Phyllis Johnson and David Martin, eds., *Destructive Engagement: Southern Africa at War* (Harare: Zimbabwe Publishing House, 1986).

23. *The United States and South Africa*, p. 122.

24. *The United States and South Africa*, p. 192.

25. See Clough, "Beyond Constructive Engagement."

26. *U.S. Department of State Bulletin* (April 1985), p. 9.

27. Ibid., p. 9.

28. Ibid., p. 18.

29. See Michael Clough, "Coming to Terms With Radical Socialism," in Clough, ed., *Reassessing the Soviet Challenge in Africa* (Berkeley: Institute of International Studies, 1986).

30. For example, see Republican Study Committee, "Missing Opportunities in Angola and Mozambique: The Failure of Constructive Engagement," October 18, 1985.

31. *The United States and South Africa*, p. 106.

32. *The United States and South Africa*, p. 81.

33. On recent shifts in Soviet policy toward southern Africa, see Winrich Kuhne, "What does the case of Mozambique tell us about Soviet ambivalence toward Africa?" *CSIS Africa Notes*, no. 46 (August 1985); and Kuhne, "A 1988 update on

Soviet relations with Pretoria, the ANC, and the SACP,"
CSIS Africa Notes (September 1, 1988).

34. The most comprehensive account of the developments
leading up to the breakthrough in the Namibian negotiations
is Gillian Gunn, "A guide to the intricacies of the Angola-
Namibia negotiations," *CSIS Africa Notes* (September 8,
1988).

6

Cuban Policy for Africa

Armando Entralgo and David González López

Cuban revolutionary praxis with respect to Africa has often been perceived by successive U.S. administrations as running counter to its interests and those of its allies. Therefore, many Western views of the subject have tended to distort Cuba's objectives, dramatize its impact, and misrepresent the essence of its actions, especially over the past twelve years. It has now become standard for any meeting of U.S. and Cuban scholars on the general subject of relations between the two countries to include the question of these links (which Cuba and a good number of African countries have been establishing, exercising their respective sovereignty) as an "issue of conflict" between these two countries of the American continent.

However, a quick review of a comparison of declarations and deeds over thirty years of revolutionary policy allows us to formulate the hypothesis that the execution of Cuba's Africa policy has been coherent with respect to the principles stated, and continuous on the basis of postulates that have been maintained throughout the period in question, beginning in 1959. This, of course, does not exclude adjustments, appropriate clarifications, adaptations to particular circumstances, or even changes of perspective or assessment of a concrete situation.

That is, while preserving its essential principles, easily identified throughout these three decades, Cuba's policy, far from immobile, has adopted nuances under the effect or the circumstances of the historical moment. Based on this adaptation, its relations with a given country might have changed. The most frequent cases can be generally classified in two kinds of circumstances. The first includes some African governments that at a given moment and notwithstanding a platform of progressive policies, made certain concessions that were inappropriate from the viewpoint of Cuba's policy towards Africa. In most of these cases, these governments' actions brought them nearer to their own extinction or isolation. The case of the Somali regime is the paradigm of this first category (particularly after its opportunist aggression in 1977 against the nascent revolutionary process in Ethiopia). Also in the first category are Morocco and post-Nasser Egypt, whose policy turnabout stifled relations with more than one Third World country.

The second category groups the African countries perceived by Cuba as extremely dependent on capitalist countries but that, at a given moment, began to take—or actually took—clear nationalist and anti-imperialist stands. Thus, they received the support of socialist countries, notably Cuba. This category includes Cuba's good relations with successive Nigerian military governments, or the gradual establishment of diplomatic and other normal relations with governments that are ideologically different from that of Cuba (such as Zaire and the Ivory Coast) as well as the slow but steady renewal of contacts with Hosni Mubarak's Egypt that appears to have—according to Cuban perspectives—more pragmatism in foreign policy than its predecessor, in spite of persisting profound differences.

The Bases of Cuban Policies

There is an old history of the human links between Cuba and Africa and, as a result, there has been a significant impact of African culture on Cuban culture. Nonetheless, relations between Cuba and Africa were quite limited until the Cuban revolutionalry government expanded them after 1959. This happened only to a small degree as a result of this cultural background or as a consequence of the fact that only after 1960 did the massive decolonization of African begin: Latin America—including that part of Latin America with a heavy black influence—barely had relations with Africa in the 1960s and the 1970s, due fundamentally to an orientation similar to that of Cuban governments before 1959. This factor also delayed the incorporation of the official Latin American world into the Nonaligned Movement. What mainly motivated the development of Cuba's relations with African countries after 1959 was the nature of Cuban foreign policy, the principles that sustain it, and its evident acceptance on a continent recently liberated from colonial occupation and that is still the victim of colonialism's effects.

The principles of Cuba's policy toward Africa are clearly put forward in many fundamental documents of the Cuban revolution. They can be summarized as follows:

1. *Denunciation of colonialism and support for national liberation struggles.* From the first statement by the new representative of the Cuban revolutionary government to the United Nations in 1959, Cuba's solidarity with the cause of the Algerian patriots was made evident. Beginning thereafter, Cuba repeatedly condemned the Portuguese colonial presence during the entire period of its existence.

2. *Denunciation of institutionalized racism in southern Africa in the form of apartheid in South Africa, its extension to Namibia, and its expression in the Rhodesian regime.* Hence, Cuba's support for the nationalist movements in the three countries was made known early on.

3. *Denunciation of the neocolonial policy of the leading capitalist powers in Africa.* This principle encompasses the firm solidarity with the cause of Patrice Lumumba and with the countries of the "Casablanca Group" since its inception in 1961. The Cuban revolutionary government identified this group of countries as the most committed to the struggle for real decolonization and for positive nonalignment, in the founding of which they were co-participants.

4. *Support for the cause of anti-imperialist unity among African states, culminating in 1963 with the creation of the Organization of African Unity (OAU) with the essential aim of eradicating the powerful colonial-racist remnants and neocolonial interference.* These aims were consistent with those of the Cuban revolutionary government. Therefore, Cuba offered active and unlimited support for African unity, regardless of the OAU's limitations, particularly in its first years of existence.

5. *Establishment of diplomatic relations and mutually beneficial collaboration with any member of the OAU, irrespective of its political regime.* Relations were first established with the governments of the "Casablanca Group" and later with Congo-Brazzaville and Tanzania. By the late 1960s and early 1970s, diplomatic ties and collaborative links were developed with a considerable number of countries that were very active in the UN and in the Nonaligned Movement in the search for converging interests worldwide.

It must be remembered that during all these years Cuba lacked, and still lacks, the capacity that would allow it great volumes of commercial exchange or financing for large-scale projects with its African counterparts. However, in connection with the principles previously stated, the revolutionary government developed an increasingly strong policy of collaboration.

While the military aspect of Cuba's collaboration with the African countries—and particularly the presence of its troops—monopolized the attention of western mass media from 1975 on, Cuba's civilian collaboration has been more continuous and extensive than its military counterpart in terms of its economic worth, the variety of its forms, and the growing number of beneficiary countries. The main characteristics of Cuban civilian collaboration are:

1. *Concentration in spheres of social impact in which Cuba has achieved notable progress, essentially those of health and education.* Cuba sent its first group of doctors and other health personnel to Africa (specifically, to Algeria) in 1963. Since then, Cuba's civilian collaboration has expanded and diversified. But health and education continue to be the two favored spheres. In the 1980s, the number of African scholarship students in Cuba exceeded 13,000, a substantial number in absolute terms and even more so relative to Cuba's total population.

2. *Grants without profit motive or conditionality.* The departure of the first Cuban doctors for Algeria—just when the exodus of this professional group from Cuba forced the new revolutionary government to stretch its resources while launching its domestic projects to increase access to these services at home—set a precedent in the nature of Cuban technical collaboration: it was intended as an act of solidarity having a local, positive impact. It would not be a lucrative arrangement nor an attempt to place excess personnel abroad. Cuba's civilian collaboration was generally offered free of charge until 1977. In 1978, Cuba began to charge modest sums for some of the services offered mainly to oil-exporting countries whose incomes gave them the ability to pay. But the essential principle was not altered. Most African countries, which suffer from serious economic problems, continued to receive the assistance free of charge.

In general, the host government covers the Cuban technicians' lodging and food expenses and gives them a modest per diem fee. The living conditions of these Cubans are much more austere than those of the typical foreign technicians; therefore, the host country can afford them more easily. Afterwards, at the beginning of the 1980s, when the economic crisis struck Africa hardest, most of the countries that were being charged modest sums were exempted from payment, given the financial adversities that they were facing. Suffice it to mention the most important case in terms of the amount of the aid offered: from 1983 onward, Angola was again exempted from payment. Cuba's main gain from this type of collaboration lies essentially in the ideological and professional development of its specialists because they face particularly difficult working conditions, which they must overcome.

3. *Ability to respond and to adapt to local conditions.* On occasion, Cuba's granting of civilian assistance—in rapid response to urgent needs—even preceded the formal establishment of cooperation agreements, as was the case of Algeria (1963), Guinea-Conakry (1965), Congo-Brazzaville (second half of the 1960s), and Angola (1976), among others. Furthermore, aspects such as the austere lifestyle of the Cuban collaborators and the special programs adapted to the needs of the African students on Cuba's Isle of Youth point to the serious Cuban effort to adjust its collaboration to the requirement of the recipients.

4. *Good local acceptance and compatibility in the spirit of South-South cooperation.* The above-mentioned peculiarities have made Cuban cooperation very popular in Africa; local sources have often described it as an example of collaboration among developing countries.

Nevertheless, much of western attention focused on the military aspect of the collaboration. But here, too, it would be fitting to recall its origins and patterns of occurrence. The most common manifestation of this type of collaboration consisted in the training of African cadres; sometimes, this type of cooperation led to small numbers of Cuban advisors being posted on African soil. In truly exceptional circumstances, military collaboration has led to the dispatch of combat forces. Although their appearance in Algeria in 1963 to assist that country in its war with Morocco—the first example of this exceptional situation—did not give rise to much controversy, more than a decade later the provision of a similar kind of assistance, albeit of larger proportions, to the governments of Angola and Ethiopia has remained in the headlines for several years.

In the case of Angola, the nature and extent of Cuba's commitment have been thoroughly explained from the Cuban perspective. Solidarity with the cause of the Angolan revolution was built on the basis of a shared history of oppression, rebellion, and heroism. But an outstanding factor was the way in which African governments, as well as African public opinion, accepted both the amount and the nature of Cuban assistance. In general, this Cuban military support for Angola was perceived in Africa as an active example of the defense of the juridical principles contained in the UN Charter and reaffirmed in that of the OAU, especially the exercise of the right to self-determination and the protection of national sovereignty in the face of an act of aggression by the South African racist regime against Angola.

In the case of Cuban military support for Ethiopia, which faced an invasion from Somalia in 1977-78, some of the factors of the Angolan scenario were not present, but African objections were not raised in this case either, owing to the fact that here another fundamental, very sensitive principle, peculiar to the OAU, was involved: that which precluded the use of force to change the borders inherited from colonialism. Of course, this does not exclude that governments such as that of Somalia (feeling directly affected by Cuban actions in Ethiopia) and others would have encouraged or promoted some of the actions that caused Cuba's military presence in Angola or Ethiopia. But the truth is that no significant objections were made, and Pan-African policy readily and clearly accepted Cuba's actions. These Cuban actions received important support, publicly stated, from governments ideologically quite distant from Cuba.

The arrival of Cuban military contingents on African territory and their permanence in Angola and Ethiopia over more than a decade allows for specific conclusions to be drawn concerning the circumstances in which these actions take place and the principles governing them:

1. *The action takes place following the breaking off of negotiations, of a pledge, or of an agreement by one of the parties, which decides to opt for a quick military victory through foreign intervention, unlawfully crossing internationally recognized boundaries.* Often Cuba's

initiatives—initiatives that make clear its persistent effort to encourage peaceful solutions—have been ignored, even when these inititiatives may necessarily imply concessions on the part of friendly forces.

2. *Cuba's favorable reply to the African request for aid has had generalized support among the governments of the continent and has been accepted by the OAU.* Respect for—and defense of—the objectives and principles of the OAU have been at the heart of Cuban concerns.

3. *The Cuban presence responds exclusively to situations of concrete aggressions or threats of aggression originating in other countries.* Both the continued behavior patterns of Cuba's troops within the borders of the host countries and the circumstantial fluctuations of the number of its forces according to the situation prove the point.

4. *The permanence of Cuban troops depends on the sovereign decision of the host government and does not in any way hinder continued negotiations between the conflicting parties, who seek a lasting solution that would make said presence unnecessary.* In all the cases of conflict in which the military presence has been maintained, the host government has entered into negotiations of its choice—bilateral or multilateral, with or without Cuban participation—with a view to a definitive and honorable settlement for all parties involved. The recent evolution of the conflict in southern Africa, given its particular complexity, is probably the best example of this modus operandi.

The Negotiated Settlement in Southern Africa

In the early 1980s, the prospects for just solutions to the problem of Namibia and for the generalized crisis in southern Africa receded. From the perception of Cuba and of the black-majority governments of southern Africa—supported by the OAU—the paralysis stemmed in good measure from the attempts to establish a link between the independence of Namibia and the presence of Cuban military forces in Angola, the first being conditioned on the prior unilateral cessation of the second. According to the point of view of Cuba and the African governments, the paralysis was further complicated by the renewed and strong western support for the South African regime and the considerable overt assistance granted to the Angolan counterrevolution after 1985, two matters in which the U.S. government has played a leading role.

Taking stock of the most recent years, the crucial element to be considered when analyzing future prospects is the fact that, contrary to many western predictions, the African "Front Line" states facing South Africa have resisted pressures and acts of aggression of exceptional dimensions. Cuba's positions in the region, instead of being eroded, have enjoyed a growing endorsement in Africa and in other parts of the world. Even western sources that earlier criticized the "intransigence" of the Angolan and Cuban positions now consider that the joint communiques and common actions show signs of "realism" and "flexibility," despite the fact that the underlying principles have remained unchanged.

Some of the milestones on the road to the definition of common Angolan-Cuban positions bear this point out. After the signing of the Lusaka Accords between Angola and South Africa with the mediation of the United States—accords that were violated repeatedly by South Africa—a Cuban-Angolan Joint Communiqué was issued in March 1984. It stated the principles that could have served as a basis, at that stage, for a "negotiated, fair, and honorable" agreement for all the parties. "Negotiated, fair, and honorable" are three key words to be taken into account to understand all the public positions taken by Cuba before and after this date. However, shortly afterwards, the resumption of the arms supply to UNITA by the United States stopped the talks, which had been going on for many months, between that country and Angola.

More recently, and just when Angola and Cuba were compelled to reinforce their military defenses due to the increase in South Africa's acts of aggression, Cuba and Angola formed a joint delegation, which participated in talks in Luanda with a U.S. delegation on January 28 and 29, 1988. According to the editorial published in Cuba's daily newspaper *Granma*,[1] at the meeting Angola and Cuba maintained that the indispensable conditions for a settlement were:

- the cessation of foreign intervention in the internal affairs of Angola (which was expressed in U.S. and South African logistical aid to UNITA);
- the withdrawal of South African forces, which have systematically raided Angola;
- implementation of Resolution 435 of the UN Security Council that leads to Namibia's independence; and

- international guarantees that there will be no more attacks on Angola.

The editorial added that, upon reaching an agreement on these bases, Cuba and Angola would be prepared to implement a "time table for a gradual withdrawal of the Cuban internationalist contingent until all our combatants are repatriated." As in other statements that elaborate on the Cuban positions, the editorial adds that these are based on international law, on the UN Charter, and on successive UN Security Council resolutions. However, at that time the clear and precise Angolan-Cuban position referred to a scenario in which numerous elements of ambiguity still remained with regard to the positions of the other actors involved in the regional conflict, and which gave rise to a good number of doubts.

In the first place, toward late 1986 and early 1987, there were indications that some type of revision of U.S. policy for Africa was under way that might later facilitate the resumption of talks in the search for a settlement. It remained to be seen, however, whether this change of attitude was sufficiently comprehensive in the U.S. policy-making circles, and (even assuming that the shift reflected something more than a characteristic posture of a government nearing its end, and with that perspective alone in mind) whether U.S. diplomacy could at this time maintain its momentum and its ability to take the initiative, to make decisive progress along the difficult road to a settlement in the few months remaining in Ronald Reagan's presidency.

Other factors that fostered doubt were those introduced by the South African regime. At a time when preparations were being made for the dialogue between the joint Angolan-Cuban delegation and the U.S. delegation, toward the end of 1987, the South African army launched an attack deep into Angolan territory. It was the most important act of aggression since 1976. In addition, in an unprecedented action, high officials of the apartheid regime for the first time confirmed that their intention was to block an imminent UNITA military defeat.

These elements seriously threatened progress in the negotiations that seemed about to begin. In the military sphere, the unprecedented South African action forced Angola and Cuba to proceed with a major military reinforcement, which increased the number of Cuban troops in Angola to approximately 50,000. It also meant the urgent deployment of advanced military technology to Angola. In the diplomatic field, South Africa also jeopardized what remained of the U.S. project of so-called "constructive engagement," since its actions also cast doubt on the presumed U.S. mediation ability to exercise a "moderating influence" on South Africa.

The above-mentioned *Granma* editorial foresaw alternative scenarios, in each of which the positions of South Africa and the United States would be decisive. It observed that "the solution now depends, fundamentally, on the position adopted by the government of the United States" regarding noninterference in the internal affairs of Angola and the firmness with which it commits itself to a political solution. This proposition was based on the conviction that "South Africa could not defy the entire world community if the United States were to join in the unanimous demand for implementation of Resolution 435."

The editorial does not rule out the alternative scenario of South Africa seeking a military solution. This option would be extremely dangerous, but it posed a real, though latent, threat to be taken into account. In such a scenario, the editorial anticipated that the final outcome could very well be "the swan song of the odious apartheid regime," and for that reason it represented a much costlier risk for South Africa, "much more than what it would have to grant in order to find a negotiated solution as has been urged upon" all the parties.

The second scenario, according to the editorial, would foresee a negotiating process that would make unlikely the occurrence of the first scenario. In line with the principles that have characterized nearly a quarter of a century of the Cuban revolution's policy with respect to Africa, in good faith Cuba proposed the only course of action that could lead to a satisfactory settlement for all the parties. With Cuba's many years of experience based on excellent links with the African continent, and with complete confidence in the future, the editorial concluded "a solution in a relatively short time is, in reality, objectively possible."

During the first months of 1988, the South African offensive against Cuito Cuanavale was stopped. Angolan, Cuban, and SWAPO troops carried out a counteroffensive that took their forces well to the south near the Namibian border. The reaction to these developments unleashed within South Africa itself was among the main reasons why South Africa decided, for the first time, to try to negotiate a just and lasting agreement that would encompass all of southwestern Africa. The four-party meetings, begun in London in May 1988, ended with the signing of the peace agreements for southwestern Africa on December 22, 1988, at UN headquarters in New York. These meetings were proof of the joint

Cuban-Angolan delegation's will to negotiate in spite of "the deliberate hesitations and arrogant stands of the South Africans, and, at times, of the inconsistencies of the mediator [the U.S. government], an unmistakable ally of South Africa."[2]

The speech of Isidoro Malmierca, Cuba's minister of foreign relations, at the signing of the Tripartite Agreement was especially clear when he referred to Cuba's assessment of the importance of and the circumstances that made possible this agreement. He stated that "at long last it may be possible that the illegal occupation of Namibia may end and that this land may cease to be a South African colonial dependency and become instead a sovereign and independent country." Together with the withdrawal of South African forces from Angola, this creates "some of the fundamental bases to guarantee the security of the People's Republic of Angola and to permit the Angolan people to find the means and the ways to solve the conflicts that have led to a fratricidal war."[3]

Days later, Cuba's President Fidel Castro expressed his views on the talks and on the agreements reached: "The most wonderful outcome is to have reached all the goals that we set for ourselves without shedding even one drop of blood beyond what was necessary in order to solve the difficult military situation that appeared at the end of the past year. Though great were the accomplishments of the Cuban internationalist troops and of the courageous Angolan fighters on the battle fields, great, too, were the accomplishments in the diplomatic realm." He went on: "We have negotiated seriously and we have reached a serious accord."[4] From Cuba's point of view, the signing of the Tripartite Agreement "successfully ends one of the most glorious pages" of Cuban history.[5]

In summary, for the Cubans, the return of their 50,000 troops from Angola represents the successful culmination of what has been the most important page in the history of these last thirty years of relations between Cuba and Africa. At the same time, it is a good opportunity to reaffirm the principles, objectives, and actions of Cuba's policy toward Africa. Cuban leaders have underlined that, once all the soldiers are back, "humanity will have witnessed the loyalty to principles that explain and encourage the policy of solidarity of the Cuban Revolution."[6] For Cubans, this aid "represented a modest but certain contribution to the struggle of the African peoples against colonialism, racism, and apartheid,"[7] and, at the same time, the "opportunity to honor our debt with Black Africa, one of the roots of the Cuban nation."[8] Our loyalty to these principles determined the firm decision to remain on

African soil for as long as was needed, actively helping to strengthen the sovereignty of a sister nation against foreign aggression. The same commitment to principle was evident in our unwavering readiness to search for lasting solutions to the complex conflicts by means of negotiations "in close and creative brotherhood with the government of Angola, both acting fully independently and with the resolute will to favor a negotiated solution."[9]

This sustained, firm position eventually affected the "will of all parties" to the conflict—mainly South Africa and the United States—to contribute to, and it was the indispensable element to facilitate, an agreement acceptable to all interested parties participating in the negotiations. The Cuban government in particular rejects the versions that "grossly simplify what has happened, trying to present it as a simple understanding between the great powers, as if the rest of us were only the obedient implementors of their plans."[10] In response to the analysis that attributed to Cuba the wish to perpetuate its presence in Angola—and that, therefore, considered the withdrawal of Cuban troops a "failure" of Cuba's alleged aspirations—Cuba's leaders have reiterated what they have invariably stated since 1975:

> We did not go the People's Republic of Angola in search of economic benefits, nor to defend strategic interests to which, as a small Third World country, we cannot aspire. Cuba does not leave behind in that sister nation military bases, or properties of any kind, or rights over Angola's riches. As we said twelve years ago, from Angola we will take only the love and the respect of its long-suffering and heroic people and the remains of the sons of the people of Cuba, who fell defending Angola's sovereignty and integrity against external aggression and apartheid.[11]

The Front Line states, the OAU, the Nonaligned Movement, and other important international actors have understood and welcomed not only the actions carried out by Cuba in 1975, but also Cuba's policy towards Africa in general. Thus, a growing number of countries are willing to accept Cuba's offer, presented by its Minister of Foreign Relations, Isidoro Malmierca, in the following terms:

> We will work without fail to achieve peace and security in southwestern Africa and in any other part of the world where we may make a

contribution to the opening and the consolidation of a potential of independence and development for all peoples without exception. Toward those ends, we will be ready to work with all those prepared to undertake real and specific actions, in the absence of a search for hegemony and of the ambition to profit.[12]

Notes

1. "¿Cuál sería la esencia de una solución negociada a los problemas de Angola y Namibia?" *Granma* (February 4, 1988), p. 1.
2. "La historia de Africa será diferente antes y después de Cuito Cuanavale," *Granma* (December 23, 1988), Editorial on p. 2.
3. "Cuando el último combatiente internacionalista retorne a su patria, la humanidad habrá sido testigo de la lealtad a los principios que explican la política solidaria de la revolución cubana." Speech by Isidoro Malmierca, Minister of Foreign Relations, in *Granma* (December 23, 1988), p. 7.
4. "Efectuado el VIII pleno del Comité Central," *Granma* (December 16, 1988), p. 1.
5. *Ibid.*
6. "Cuando el último," p. 7.
7. "La historia de Africa," p. 2.
8. "Cuando el último," p. 7.
9. *Ibid.*
10. *Ibid.*
11. *Ibid.*
12. *Ibid.*

7

Cuba and U.S. Foreign Policy in Latin America: The Changing Realities

Howard J. Wiarda

Introduction

Since 1959, Cuba has been the dominant preoccupation of U.S. foreign policy in Latin America. The Cuban Revolution and its conversion to Marxism-Leninism, the realignment of Cuban foreign policy in accord with that of the Soviet Union, the use of Cuba as a Soviet military base, and the Cuban/Soviet efforts at subversion and destabilization of existing governments in Latin America and elsewhere were the main precipitating factors. These events have forced the United States to pay serious attention to Latin America for the first time and to devise, in reaction, a variety of programs for the area.[1]

The Cuba/Soviet/Cold War preoccupation of U.S. policy in Latin America is well illustrated by a personal anecdote. Once, on a speaking tour of Central America, a young student came up to the author and said, "Oh, you Americans; the only reason you're interested in us is because of the Cold War." Perhaps because it was the end of the day and I was tired and needed some refreshment, or perhaps out of pique or sheer honesty, my response was a cynical one. I replied, "You're absolutely right and, therefore, you should be thankful for the Cold War because without it the United States would not be interested in you at all!" This story indicates the lack of U.S. interest in Latin America in the past and the preeminently strategic motivations underlying our more recent interest in the area.

Historic U.S. Policy Toward Latin America

Historically, the United States has not often paid serious attention to Latin America. The main foreign policy preoccupations of the

United States have been Soviet relations, Europe, the Middle East, and more recently, Asia—but not Latin America. We have tended to ignore Latin America and not think of it as important for complex reasons involving social and psychological factors as well as strategic ones. Strategically, the United States had never thought that a serious threat to its interests could or would come from Latin America. Latin America, especially Central America and the Caribbean, consisted of small and/or weak states that were chronically unstable; no strategic danger could, it was presumed, come from this quarter—unless it took the form of an outside and larger power (Spain, France, Great Britain, Germany, and now the Soviet Union) taking advantage of Latin American instability to establish a base of operations there; hence, the Monroe Doctrine, and the continued U.S. concern since then that revolutionary upheavals in Latin America might enable a foreign power to take advantage of local instability to embarrass, build bases against, and to prey upon the United States.[2]

The socio-psychological factors regarding the historic U.S. disinterest in Latin America were at least as important. The United States has long considered itself—and by objective economic, social, and political indexes been so considered—a successful society, while Latin America has been considered unsuccessful. Doubtlessly, racial and religious considerations are also involved. By comparison with those of the United States, Latin American economic, social, cultural, and scientific accomplishments have been meager. In the grand tradition of European and North American thinking, little of significance has ever emanated from Latin America, as exemplified in Hegel's comment that the area had "no history" and in Marx's similarly disparaging remarks about the region. On the foreign policy front, one recalls the quip of Henry Kissinger that the axis of the world flows through Moscow, Bonn, Paris, London, Washington/New York, and Tokyo, thus minimizing Latin America's importance, or excluding it from the world's stage altogether.

These attitudes, widespread historically (and to some extent even today) in both North America and western Europe, have helped breed in Latin America enormous frustrations and a gigantic inferiority complex. Such attitudes were and are particularly strong in Cuba, which lived so close to and was so much under the shadow of the United States.[3] Even though Cuba before the revolution was relatively well off by Latin American standards (fourth in per capita income, fifth in manufacturing, first in transportation and communication, 60 percent urban, 75 percent literate), that did not solve the Cuban inferiority complex because, for Cubans, the standard was the United States and western Europe, not Latin America. By those criteria, Cuba came off very badly indeed. When this national inferiority complex was combined with Cuba's history of frustrated nationalism (due to Spanish colonialism, then the Platt amendment and U.S. interventions, and finally Cuba's own corrupt and inefficient regimes), one has a powerful explanation both for the Cuban revolution and the particular direction it took (Marxist-Leninist, anti-U.S., nationalist, and pro-Soviet Union) that rivals the class- and economics-based explanations usually offered.

Cuba and the Cuban revolution were particularly damaging from the U.S. strategic perspective for the three following reasons: First, Cuba represented a new and alternative (Marxist-Leninist) model for Latin American development, thereby introducing not only a formula with which the United States could, with difficulty, live, but making the path of the U.S.-favored democrats and centrists far more difficult. Instead of the old struggle between the defenders of the status quo and the forces for democratic reform, a new and third force (Marxist-Leninist and allied with the Soviet Union) was introduced that made far more complicated both the domestic politics of Latin America and U.S. relations with the area. Second, particularly in the 1960s, Cuba sought to subvert and destabilize a variety of Latin American regimes that the United States had an interest in keeping stable. Third, Cuba allied itself with the Soviet Union and allowed the Soviets, as in the 1962 missile crisis, to use Cuba as a military base for further forays into the western hemisphere and as a direct threat to the United States itself.

The Cuban/Communist threat was taken very seriously by a succession of U.S. administrations, Republican and Democratic alike, and forced the United States not only to begin examining Latin America in a serious vein but also to revamp its political and strategic policy towards the area.

The United States, by generally ignoring Latin America, had devolved a minimalist foreign policy strategy for the region. The main components of the U.S. strategy traditionally were, first, to keep out hostile foreign powers and prevent them from establishing bases in the region; second, to do what it could to help maintain stability in a region seemingly characterized by endemic instability, a tack that implied accommodation to peaceful change and not some static defense of the status quo; and third, to maintain a string of bases, stations, and posts throughout the Caribbean and

Central American region to protect its interests. The United States encouraged economic investment in the region although by comparison the volume was not large and the main purpose was again strategic. Investment would give the United States an added lever of influence in the region and might help promote stability in a region not known to be strong on that feature. Similarly with democracy and human rights: The United States often, albeit sporadically, favored these goals, both for their own sake but also (and mainly) because it was thought democracy and human rights would serve the even more bedrock strategic goals of maintaining stability and keeping out hostile foreign powers.

These basic assumptions of U.S. foreign policy carried a number of implications, among them that the United States paid far greater attention to the countries of Central America and the Caribbean that were "close to home" than to the larger countries of South America. It also meant that U.S. policy was generally reactive and crisis-oriented rather than forward-looking and positive, neglecting the region until some new crisis forced its way onto U.S. television screens. A third implication was the development of the doctrine of "economy of force"—that Latin America was unlikely ever to be the main theater of conflict. It should, therefore, be dealt with on the basis of an economy of resources (military as well as economic) so that the main U.S. forces could be concentrated where, presumably, the main conflict would be (Central Europe, perhaps the Middle East) and not be tied down by having to deal first with some second-order conflict in some second-order area (Latin America). A fourth implication was the secondary place accorded democracy and human rights in U.S. policy.

These factors, although summarized here in too-brief form, help explain a great deal about U.S. foreign policy, historically, in Latin America. The policy has generally been based on inattention to the region except in times of crisis; on ignorance, condescension, and a general disparagement of Latin America's culture, institutions, and importance. These factors also help explain the Latin American reaction to this policy, derived from a history of frustrated nationalism and inferiority complexes, including xenophobic nationalism, a desire to lash out at the United States, and—rather like the cartoon strip character "Plucky Pierre"—a willingness to "go down in flames" for some supposedly "glorious" cause rather than make a patient and gradual resolution, over the long term, of the nations' problems and differences. That, unfortunately, has been the history of the Cuban Revolution for a good part of the period since 1959.

What we have described above is *historic* U.S. attitudes toward Latin America and the *historic* U.S. policy response derived, in part, from those attitudes. However, the fact is that both Latin America and the United States have changed significantly in the intervening thirty years since the Cuban revolution.[4] The changes have been profound and deep-rooted. They offer the hope and promise that the United States and Latin America may be at the point of putting their relations on a better, more stable, more mature, even normal basis that has long been called for. The great tragedy for Cuba in all of this is that it is likely to remain the odd country out, diminished in influence and—because of past misdirections— unable to take advantage of the new climate of relations, the new opportunities, and the more mature future relations likely to prevail in U.S.-Latin American relations.

New Realities in U.S.-Latin American Relations

Latin America has changed enormously in the last twenty-five years. With only a few exceptions, the countries of the area are far more developed, industrialized, modern, and sophisticated than before. Per capita income in many countries, despite their recent economic troubles, has quadrupled since the 1950s; the rates of social modernization (literacy, urbanization, life expectancy) have been similarly impressive. In this same interval, Latin America has become much more assertive, nationalistic, and independent, with a greater diversity of international connections and relations. This new assertiveness, however, has not prevented prudent Latin American leaders from working out realistic, new, and at the same time necessary relationships with the United States.

While these and other vast changes have been under way in Latin America,[5] the United States has changed a great deal. These changes also provide a basis for significantly improved and more mature U.S.-Latin American relations. Here we list only some of the major "sea changes" in the United States and its policy that have contributed to the new relationship with Latin America.

1. *The United States has itself become something of a Caribbean country.*[6] In this regard, one need only look at the demographics and ethnic makeup of Florida, Louisiana, or the Southwest (Texas, Arizona, New Mexico, Nevada, and California), or the fact that New York City is the second largest Puerto Rican city in the world, the second

largest Haitian city, and so on. The Latin American immigrant communities are now spilling out of these historic enclaves to other states and cities as well. In the 1990s, Hispanics will replace blacks as the largest ethnic minority in the United States.

Not only are Hispanics growing in numbers, but the cultural influence of the Hispanic communities are now—for the first time—reaching out to influence the broader American culture as well, in the form of music, theater, restaurants, arts—even language. Moreover, the political power of the Hispanic communities is also growing as more and more Hispanics vote, become organized, and mobilize to influence the political process. It is no coincidence that in 1988, several of the presidential candidates sought to showcase their Spanish-speaking abilities and their knowledge of Latin America, thus courting the Latin vote. The Hispanic community is not of one mind in terms of its political goals, but its members do maintain an intense interest in the countries of their birth, and want to promote democracy, human rights, and national dignity and respect for their own native lands. These changes have profound implications in the long term for U.S.-Latin American relations and for U.S. policy in the region.

2. *United States interdependence with Latin America has grown enormously.* During the 1970s, what was called "dependency theory" gained a considerable measure of credence in U.S. universities[7] and one must say that, of course, Latin America is dependent on the United States in various ways. Such dependence will doubtless continue long into the future because that is the inevitable nature of relationships borne of asymmetry between large, powerful nations and small, weaker ones.[8] Realistic and prudent Latin American presidents have adjusted and accommodated to these realities, while, at the same time, seeking constantly to readjust the imbalance in their favor.

But along with the old dependency has grown a new and complex *interdependence* in U.S.-Latin American relations. The flow of trade, investment, tourists, immigrants, labor supplies, capital, government officials, and bankers, to say nothing of ubiquitous drugs, has reached mammoth proportions—and the flow is not all one way. Latin America is still dependent on the United States in a variety of particulars; but in terms of the United States' relations with Mexico, Brazil, Argentina, Chile, and Venezuela—even Central America and the Caribbean—a much more interesting and complex set of *interrelations* has come into existence. The U.S. and the Mexican economies are so interdependent, for example, that a *de facto* North American common market has come into existence, even if that fact cannot be formally admitted as yet by politicians. The same kind of new and complex interdependence, although to a somewhat lesser degree, characterizes the relations of the hemisphere's other countries and regions with the United States. This ongoing process has not only brought the hemisphere far closer together in all kinds of ways, but it has also worked to the mutual advantage of both partners, or sets of partners, in the relationship. The United States' hegemonic presumption is not entirely gone, but it must now coexist in often uneasy relationship with this newer cluster of issues that has grown up alongside it and that serve to attenuate the older domination.

3.   *There is a growing consciousness of Latin America in the United States.* Latin America has begun to intrude itself, not just onto our television screens, but also into our consciousness.   Latin American problems—the debt issue, migration, drugs, trade, commerce, political stability—have become U.S. problems.   Once again, the theme is complex interdependence.   Wherever one looks, the awareness of Latin America in the United States is far greater at present than it was earlier.   Because of television and media coverage of Central America, the U.S. public is now far more aware of Latin American issues and problems.   Quite a number of Latin American-made movies have become popular, and some Latin American authors have become household names.   The number of seminars and briefing sessions on Latin America for congressional assistants, journalists, church persons, and other officials and opinion leaders now runs into the thousands yearly.   Latin American studies are booming, not only in our universities, but also on Capitol Hill, in the executive departments, and in the Washington-based Think Tanks.[9]

All this attention has enormously increased U.S. consciousness about Latin America, serving gradually not only to increase our awareness about the area, but to make it virtually inconceivable that the United States can ever return to a policy based on benign neglect.

4. *The human rights/democracy agenda has become dominant.*
    Often honored chiefly in the breach, the United States has
    long had a somewhat missionary-like zeal to export
    democracy and human rights in Latin America. But in the
    1960s, when occasionally faced with the choice between
    wobbly democrats who, it was feared, could not control
    their local Castro-Communist forces, and the authoritarian
    militaries who could, the United States at times regretfully
    sided with the "lesser evil" of military rule.[10]
    A variety of new forces and influences now make a
    greater emphasis on democracy and human rights in U.S.
    policy all but inevitable. For one thing, Latin America is
    more strongly committed to democracy than ever before,
    and not to extremisms of either right or left. Moreover, it
    has the infrastructure and socioeconomic base to sustain
    democracy in ways not possible before. Second, U.S.
    administrations have discovered that standing for democracy
    and human rights is the best way to get Congress, the
    media, public opinion, and U.S. allies to back U.S. policy.
    Third, there is widespread bipartisan support for this
    agenda, meaning it will be at the heart of U.S. policy
    regardless of which party or individual heads the future
    administrations. The U.S. government and politicians of all
    stripes have discovered that democratic regimes seldom try
    to subvert their neighbors or begin wars, are more
    reasonable to deal with, and generally cause less grief for
    U.S. policy than regimes of either the extreme right or left.
    Fourth, the democracy/human rights agenda enables the
    United States to isolate its foes in Latin America (on both
    the left and right) who emphatically do not stand for
    democracy and human rights, and gives it a weapon to use
    in the propaganda war with the Soviet Union. Fifth, U.S.
    strategic policy has now moved beyond its earlier orientation
    toward finding military solutions to Latin American
    problems to encompass a far broader conception that also
    includes a strong commitment to democracy and human
    rights.[11] Sixth, the democracy/human rights agenda
    provides a powerful moral base to U.S. policy and serves as
    a means of wedding a strong strategic and national interest
    component with the historic missionary orientation of U.S.
    policy. For all these reasons, a more enlightened U.S. policy
    that includes a strong democracy/human rights component is

likely to continue as an attractive, bipartisan, and popular policy.

5. *The United States has devised a broad, multi-pronged policy toward Latin America.* Such a strategy was set forth in the Kissinger Commission five years ago, and in the Alliance for Progress over twenty-five years ago. Despite the flaws in these programs[12] and the fact not all their recommendations have been implemented completely, all agree that the Alliance and the Kissinger Commission program are infinitely preferable to their alternatives: benign neglect on one hand, narrowly defined military solutions on the other. It is clear that a diverse and broad-based program like the Alliance, and as recommended in the Kissinger Commission Report, will continue to be U.S. policy toward Latin America.

Both the Alliance and the Kissinger Commission recommended a policy that combines socio-economic assistance for Latin America with some limited military aid, a strong pro-democracy and pro-human rights agenda along with, and at the base of, critical strategic considerations, and generous amounts of public assistance as well as the stimulus of private investment. As the debt crisis has continued, the United States has added to this agenda by pushing for internal reform in the Latin American countries as well as debt relief by providing short-term budgetary support as well urging the need for growth as the only long-term solution. It is a complex and multi-faceted policy that offers the best hope for securing domestic support in the United States, for assisting Latin America, and for securing the interests of all the parties involved.

6. *The U.S. foreign policy community now takes Latin America seriously for the first time.* Not all that long ago, Latin America was considered by the U.S. foreign policy and academic communities as a "second-rate area for second-rate minds." That condition, and the attitudes underlying it are changing very rapidly. Latin America is now "on the front burner,"[13] the subject of seemingly endless conferences and seminars. Foreign policy generalists who previously denigrated the area are now trying busily to catch up with their research and to write intelligently about it. Their efforts are not always successful, but there can nevertheless be no doubt of the effervescence of interest in Latin America. Over the long haul, the fact that the U.S. foreign

policy-making community is now, for the first time, paying serious attention to Latin America is bound to produce greater public consciousness about the area, as well as more sophisticated policy towards it.

7. *U.S. strategic policy has come to view Latin America as central.* U.S. strategists used to consider Latin America as peripheral, far removed from the main theaters of potential conflict, which were assumed to be the NATO region or the Middle East. But now that view is changed. A nuclear exchange with the Soviet Union is presently viewed as very unlikely (and probably has been unlikely since 1945, when the first atomic weapons were used), nor do U.S. strategic planners see much likelihood of a largely conventional war on the plains of Central Europe. Far more likely are the kind of murky, political-psychological-military conflicts that we saw earlier in Southeast Asia and that we now have to deal with in southern Africa and Central America. From the point of view of U.S. strategic thinkers, therefore, Latin America is no longer considered on the periphery; it is the main theater. Particularly when this interest on the part of strategists—whose current concept of security, recall, is much broader than the older, strictly military one—is combined with the resurgence (or perhaps initiation) of interest in Latin America from the academic, foreign policy, and other communities, it suggests a much stronger, long-term, enlightened, and continuing preoccupation with Latin America than ever before. There is widespread agreement that the approach to solving U.S. security problems must be multi-pronged, involving broad development efforts as well as military assistance, encompassing North-South dimensions as well as East-West ones.[14]

8. *U.S. policy has matured.* The Reagan Administration got off to a very shaky start in terms of its foreign policy toward Latin America. But there was a gradual learning process within the administration; a bureaucratic process, by which the regular foreign policy bureaucracies (the State Department, for example) recaptured policy making from the more ideological officials who sometimes dominated the discussion in the early months; and a political process through which the United States has come to understand what it can do and what it cannot do in Latin America.[15]

The result is a more sophisticated, more mature, multi-faceted policy toward Latin America. Despite international and media preoccupation with, first, El Salvador, and more recently, Nicaragua, the fact is that—in recent years and rather quietly—the U.S. has put its bilateral relations with most of Latin America on a more regular and normalized basis. U.S. relations with most individual countries and with the region as a whole are actually quite good—even "boring" in some respects, one would have to say. Differences will continue, regardless of who is in power in the White House or in the Latin American capitals, because our interests will sometimes be divergent; but such differences are most often resolved through negotiations, not force. The United States has begun to put its relations with Latin America—an area to which it had not previously paid serious attention—on the same regular, normal basis that it had long maintained with the countries of Western Europe. As compared with the inattention alternating with crisis-response of the past, the fact that a regular, almost routine pattern of relations has begun to emerge would seem to represent an enormous set of strides in the right direction.

9. *The U.S. may well recover the capacity to carry out rational, coherent, long-term foreign policy.* I want to suggest, without being Pollyanna-ish, that in the future, there may be less paralysis and more consensus in U.S. policy, and therefore some greater capacity to act internationally with some coherence and consensus. The legacy of Vietnam is fading; we have witnessed the termination of a period of two quite ideological presidencies (those of Carter and Reagan); we have a more centrist administration; and therefore the severe polarization and fragmentation of policy that we have seen in the last twenty years may be somewhat attenuated, as well. This is not to say that all the elements of incoherence and disarray that we have seen recently in foreign policy will somehow magically end,[16] but the divisions may be less sharp. There are, in fact, many elements of consensus, even on such a charged issue as U.S. policy toward Central America,[17] and one should therefore not be too surprised to see a new centrism and some greater coherence on foreign policy arise.

These new enthusiasms for Latin America must, of course, be balanced by recognition of the still-existing ethnocentrism and paternalism of the past, the continuing pursuit sometimes of stupid and self-defeating policies toward the area, the reluctance of many

U.S. policy makers to expend much foreign aid on Latin America, and the United States' changed global position economically (which can easily be overstated; to paraphrase Mark Twain about his death, news about the overextension and demise of nations can easily be exaggerated) that imposes limits on what the United States can and will do for Latin America. We will, of course, have to wait and see how these current trends crystallize; the United States must overcome a long history of distrust in Latin America. Nevertheless, when all the factors listed above are assessed cumulatively as well as considered individually—the "Latin Americanization" of the United States, the new interdependence, the greater knowledge and understanding of Latin America, the more sophisticated and realistic policies—they all add up to a quite fundamental transformation both in inter-American interrelations and in U.S. policy. In all of these changes, Cuba appears to be the country at odds, not only with the U.S., but also with the new realities of Latin America and of Hemispheric relations, and to have made some major—and ultimately self-defeating—miscalculations.

Cuba in the Inter-American System

In the early to mid 1960s, Cuba engaged in a variety of actions to try to spread its revolution throughout Latin America. These actions included assistance and advice to a number of like-minded groups in Latin America, efforts to subvert both authoritarian and democratic regimes, aid to other Marxist-Leninist guerrilla groups, and attempts, as the slogans of the times proclaimed, to "spread the fire throughout the Andes." For quite a number of small and weak Latin American countries, to say nothing of the United States, the Cuban threat seemed very real indeed, and had to be resisted.

In retrospect, it seems clear that the threat was vastly overstated. Cuba was—and is—a small, weak, dependent, underdeveloped country, incapable of destabilizing Latin America. Since the 1960s, Cuba has developed into something of a Third World military juggernaut (the advance troops of the Soviet Union, as Senator and then-UN Ambassador Daniel Patrick Moynahan called them), but two decades ago Cuba's force capacity was still limited. The larger (and even some smaller) Latin American countries recognized that Cuba posed no threat to them; they thought of Cuba as just a small island in the Caribbean whose revolution had little relevance for their realities. But, of course, that did not stop these countries from sometimes exaggerating their own internal "Cuban threat" so as to pry more Alliance for Progress funds and other favors out of the U.S. government.[18]

Not only was the Cuban threat exaggerated, but so was the attractiveness of the Cuban model. Few Latin Americans are eager to go in a Marxist-Leninist direction. Survey after survey has shown that the overwhelming majority of Latin Americans (at least 90 percent in most countries) do not wish to live under a communist regime—even if they are sometimes also critical of their own democratic and capitalistic institutions. The communist model is to them too violent, rigid, authoritarian, closed, gray, and dismal to be attractive. Moreover, as the limited accomplishments, especially economically, of the Cuban revolution have become better known throughout the hemisphere, Cuba's attractiveness as a developmental model and alternative has diminished still further.

The new literature, in fact, has begun to talk not of Cuba's strength and attractiveness, but of its weaknesses and vulnerabilities.[19] Here we cannot analyze in detail all the factors involved in the "vulnerability" thesis, but it may be appropriate to list them briefly:

1. *Economy.* The Cuban economy is widely thought of as deeply troubled, to have shown little growth since the 1950s, and to have failed to keep pace not only with neighboring, more open-market economies, but also with other socialist countries. Determined Cuban efforts to diversity the economy have not been notably successful. There is little fuel or traffic, little to buy, only limited industrialization, and no future whatsoever in sugar. The sense is growing among expert, less ideologically committed observers that all the sacrifices of the earlier years of the revolution (and still today) may *not* pay off in future economic growth. Eventually, the revolution must produce in terms of economic growth, consumer goods, and a higher standard of living, or the regime will be in trouble.

2. *Leadership.* The Cuban leaders are aging, becoming elder statesmen. That is, they are listened to politely, even reverently at times, but are not always taken seriously. There is a generation gap, and some say the leadership is not fully informed of the new realities. There are crude jokes about the leadership's apparent desire to surpass Stroessner of Paraguay (35 years) as the longest-lived regime in the history of the western hemisphere; as a rule of thumb, it seems fair to say that when a leadership is joked

about in this way, it may have to start thinking about retirement.

3. *Social programs.* The revolution's early social programs (health, education, housing) were viewed as successful; but now there is evidence that some of these claims may have been exaggerated, and even of slippage backwards in areas such as housing. The vaunted social programs of the Revolution, in the absence of much economic accomplishment, may not represent the great success stories that the regime has trumpeted.[20]

4. *Élan.* In many respects, a good deal of the spirit seems to have gone out of the Cuban revolution. The *élan* is fading. Many Cubans appear to go through the motions of waxing enthusiastic for the revolution, but genuine emotion seems to be lacking. What was sensed as an intoxicating explosion and surge of liberation and optimism in the early days of the revolution are no longer there. By the same token, the liberating appeal for the revolution felt by Latin America in 1959 is currently (except in some limited ideological and intellectual circles) wholly lacking.

5. *Generational differences.* The generation of Cubans that was personally acquainted with and repelled by the preceding Batista regime is now mostly gone; for the newer generations, the dark days of corruption and dictatorship are little more than revolutionary myths and slogans. A new class of Cuban leaders has grown up. They only dimly (if at all) remember the revolution; they are bureaucrats and apparachniks who know how to mouth slogans and catchphrases, but whose Marxism-Leninism seems less than enthusiastic. By now, a second generation is growing up, as in eastern Europe, that will soon demand the freedoms and liberties enjoyed by the West. There is a crisis of ideology and of generational change in all the communist systems, including Cuba.

6. *Public attitudes.* Many observers have sensed a considerable amount of sullenness and cynicism in Cuba. People do not like but cannot change the system, so they have resigned and accommodated themselves to it. But as in eastern Europe, there is in Cuba an underlying bitterness and resentment; some estimates are that one-third of the population would leave if, à la Mariel, the boats were made available.

7. *Distance.* Cuba is far from Soviet shores; one senses little genuine affection for the Soviet Union on the island; and, unlike eastern Europe, there is no Soviet occupation army. A growing literature suggests Cuba since the revolution has only changed one form of dependency (with the United States) for one (with the Soviet Union) that is even less advantageous to Cuba.[21] Not only is the physical distance between Cuba and the Soviet Union great, but a testing of attitudes and the Soviet/eastern European isolation in their compounds suggest that the psychological distance is great, as well.

8. *Pull of the United States.* While the Soviet logistics and affinities are difficult and strained, the pull and attractiveness of the United States in Cuba is great. Even now, almost thirty years after the revolution, the United States—its styles, music, dress, jeans, political and economic system, as well as its foreign policy—remains the chief outside preoccupation of Cubans. It is doubtful, after three decades and strenuous efforts on the part of the regime, whether Cuba can actually escape the U.S. orbit.

9. *Depression.* Cuba seems to visitors an unhappy country. There seems little spontaneity, enthusiasm, or *joie de vivre.* Its vitality seems to have been sapped. There is little money, and little in the way of consumer goods on which to spend it. The system seems to be a burden that people bear, and no longer one to become enthusiastic over.

10. *Divisiveness.* A great division exists in Cuba between the generations, between the leadership and the medium- and lower-level bureaucracy, between the leadership and its increasingly discontented population, and over the future course of the revolution. Only thinly disguised from the outside world, these divisions threaten Cuba with future fragmentation and perhaps a certain unraveling.

11. *Isolation.* Despite its recent diplomatic successes in establishing better relations with quite a number of Latin American countries, Cuba remains terribly isolated from the outside world, not just from North America but from Latin America, western Europe, and Asia, as well. The number of flights landing per week at José Martí International Airport, for instance, is less than one-twentieth the number landing in Puerto Rico. But I would argue that Cuba is not only isolated physically; it is also isolated politically from the main currents—democracy, human rights, and

development—that are profoundly stirring her neighbors. It is very dangerous, especially for a socialist regime, to be seen as out of step with history.

12. *Glasnost and perestroika.* Cuba's mentor and *patrón*, the Soviet Union, is going through a period of reform and self-examination. It needs to restructure its economy and reform its system, and both domestic and international pressures are forcing it to provide greater freedoms and human rights to its citizens. Although the internal debate continues in Cuba as to how and whether it should follow the Soviet lead, thus far Cuba has shown few signs of opening its system, even partially, as the Soviets, and has been quite critical of the Soviet initiatives. It is hard not to conclude that this stance on Cuba's part will not only produce friction between it and its sponsor, but will remove Cuba even further from the world's main, driving currents toward democracy, human rights, and freedom in both the West (including the rest of Latin America) and, now, the East.[22]

If one puts together these several factors, they add up to a somewhat inpropitious prognosis for the Cuban socialist regime. But since domestic situations and foreign policies are intimately related, perhaps no less so in socialist countries over the long term than in other kinds, the factors discussed above carry important implications for Cuban foreign policy, as well.

First, it seems quite possible that future Cuban foreign policy may not be dealing from a position of strength, but of considerable debility. Of course, in the short run, a small nation—especially if supplied massively from the outside—can continue for a time to play the role of a large power in ways that reach beyond its capabilities. But eventually, in all states, a weaker or fragile domestic situation is certain to be translated into a more circumscribed foreign policy.

Second, we need to consider more deeply the new openings of Cuba with other Latin American countries. In the 1970s and 1980s, Cuba in fact expanded its diplomatic, cultural, economic, and political relations with a variety of Latin American regimes from which it had been cut off in the early 1960s. It is also following a far more complex and sophisticated foreign policy than was the case in the 1960s.[23] While the opening to Latin America has been heralded as a major victory for Cuban foreign policy, it may actually be less than that. Whereas in the early 1960s, quite a number of Latin American countries felt potentially threatened by the Cuban regime, now that is seldom the case. Of course, this statement applies more to the larger and better institutionalized countries of South America than to the smaller, weaker countries of Central America. But overall, the position of Cuba vis-à-vis Latin America has, in fact, been reversed in the intervening two decades, relating to the relative vitality and strength of the Latin American countries' economies, societies, and political systems.

Most of the Latin American countries are now dealing from a position of strength compared with twenty-five years ago. They no longer feel as threatened by Cuba as the once did. They have developed enormously in the interim—politically, economically, and socially—while Cuba has lagged behind. Cuba's relative weakness means it is no longer viewed as a potentially destabilizing influence, but merely as another small, underdeveloped, dependent state in the Caribbean whose revolutionary model has not worked out very well and is no longer to be viewed as a threat. The "success" of Cuban foreign policy in negotiating these new openings with Latin America and in seeking to reintegrate itself into the inter-American system may, in fact, not be so much a success as a reflection of comparative weakness. Cuba's better relations with some Latin American countries in recent years may thus be a sign of the latter's growing strength and self-confidence, and of Cuban failures.

A third related factor is whether Cuba's foreign policy successes may have already peaked and are on the decline. If a date may be assigned as the high point of Cuban foreign policy, I would say it would have to be 1979. The Grenadan and Nicaraguan revolutions had just triumphed with Cuban support and assistance; the Cuba-inspired guerrillas in Guatemala and El Salvador seemed on the verge of success; Jamaica, Suriname, and Guyana seemed ready to fall into the Cuban orbit; Cuba had launched a major military program in Angola; Cuban troops and advisers were in some twenty-five-odd other countries of the world, usually to bolster tottering Marxist-Leninist regimes or to assist in guerrilla actions; and the United States seemed sufficiently self-paralyzed as to be unable to do anything about it. But, as William LeoGrande and other close observers of Cuban foreign policy have concluded, Cuba's epoch (when a small state played an essentially global, big-power role) may have already come, and gone.[24]

Fourth, it needs to be pointed out that on some of the big issues in U.S.-Latin American relations, Cuba is essentially a marginal actor. These include such key issues as the debt, investment, trade, technology transfers, and economic interdependence. Most observers[25] are convinced that the great Cold War issues that dominated U.S.-Latin American discourse in past decades are being supplanted very rapidly (except perhaps in some Central American countries) by these political-economy issues. If that is so, then Cuba remains largely outside and marginal to this set of issues, the agenda of which is certainly fast becoming (if it is not already) the dominant one in inter-American relations. Cuba may still be fighting an ideological "war" that no one else is interested in, for in Latin America, and in the United States, the issues are trade, trade, trade; capital, capital, capital; development, development, development. As a socialist country linked closely to the (inefficient and faltering) economies of eastern Europe and the Soviet Union, Cuba is shut out from these new inter-American interconnections.

A fifth factor affecting Cuba's foreign policy in Latin America is, obviously, the Soviet Union. There are powerful indications that the Soviet Union may be turning inward to a degree, concentrating on reforming its domestic economy and dealing with its own internal pressures. The Soviets do not want to support very many more Third World economies that cannot make it on their own; they have already told the Nicaraguans they will not come to their defense if the United States invades; Latin America is far from the Soviet heartland and of marginal importance to it; and, clearly, the Soviet Union does not want to challenge the United States in the latter's own "back yard," where it has overwhelming local advantage. Such inhibitions on the part of the Soviet Union are certain eventually to put a damper on Cuban efforts to engage in new adventurism or to expand significantly its conception of "proletarian internationalism."

The Cuban domestic situation, sixth, would seem to be a further constraint. The Cuban economy is in a very difficult condition, there is considerable disillusionment with the revolution, and numerous cracks in the veneer and increased tensions have appeared. Low-level officials recognize that Cuba has overreached itself internationally, but the leadership sometimes seems eager to play a large global role regardless of the costs. Objectively, one would have to say that Cuba cannot afford much longer to play such a large international role—let alone expand that role—and this does not seem to be the most propitious time for Cuba to antagonize its Latin American neighbors by some nefarious machination in their internal affairs, or to alienate further the United States, with whom Cuba must someday reach an accommodation. Objectively and rationally, these things seem true, but it is not clear that truth is always the principle guiding Cuban foreign policy.

The historical record constitutes a seventh factor worthy of consideration. Cuba's influence on the rest of Latin America as a destabilizing force during the 1960s led to very bad relations, condemnation, isolation, and an "outlaw" status for the regime. But in the 1970s, as Cuba put aside its efforts to stimulate revolution in Latin America, or concentrated its efforts elsewhere (southern Africa, for example), its relations with Latin America greatly improved and a process of normalization began. But in 1980 and 1981, as Cuba again followed an aggressive and expansionist foreign policy in Central America, the Caribbean, and South America, its relations with Latin America again turned sour. The lessons are clear: if Cuba does not intervene in the internal affairs of its neighbors or seek to destabilize them, its relations with them improve. When it does intervene, resentments, hostility, and the desire to quarantine Cuba again increase.[26]

Eighth, and finally, we return to the crucial theme of Cuba's lack of connection with the main currents in Latin America. It is clear that the dominant thrusts in contemporary Latin America are toward democracy, development, and human rights. They are away from intense ideological disputes and toward prudence and practicality. They are toward diversifying their international relations, but also toward recognizing the need of Latin America to deal realistically with the United States. They are toward a freer trade and market system, not a closed autarchic one. The sense is widespread throughout the continent that socialism is unproductive, does not work, and leads to declining living standards, if not chaos. Democracy and freedom, not totalitarianism, seem likely to be the future of Latin America. But, on all these issues, Cuba appears out of touch, paddling against the dominant currents, still fighting the ideological wars of a quarter-century ago while everyone else has tired of them. The Cuban model seems to be the wave of the past, not of the future; the process of history has passed Cuba by. Not only is this very sad for Cuba, since its revolution no longer seems to stimulate much resonance in Latin America, but it has profound implications for Cuban foreign policy, whose capacity to influence the other countries is now very limited and whose revolutionary calls fall increasingly on deaf ears. Cuba has been marginalized by the march of events, and its international capacities to shape the future of Latin America have been greatly diminished as well.

Conclusions

The prospects for Cuban foreign policy in Latin America do not appear to be particularly bright. Cuba may increase its relations with some countries of Latin America, a policy that will be hailed as a great success by the Cubans in helping to break the U.S.-favored economic and diplomatic blockade of the island, but which we have seen as implying the strength of Latin America and the weakness of Cuba—not the reverse. On one hand, most of the Latin American countries do not think of Cuba as a particularly interesting, let alone threatening, place any more, so that if and when they reestablish normal relations with Cuba, they will do so out of boredom and self-interest and not as a symbol of approval or even of very great significance. These will be marriages of convenience and certainly not of love, or even matches carrying very much in the way of ideological, economic, or strategic meaning. Latin America is increasingly prudent, pragmatic, and realistic; their Cuba connections may enable the countries of the area to tweak the United States, thereby increasing U.S. aid to them, or to satisfy their domestic left wings by asserting their nationalism and "independence" (from the United States) at absolutely zero cost. In this way, Cuba at times also may be able to play on Latin American nationalism and anti-Americanism, and to score some points in the propaganda battle. But these eminently practical and sensible steps on the part of the Latin American states and the occasionally Cuban propaganda victories should not be thought of as implying a significant Cuban diplomatic breakthrough, or as altering fundamentally the path of Latin American development or the future of inter-American relations.

At the same time that Latin America has changed, the United States is also quite different than it was twenty-five years ago. It has finally begun to put its Latin American relations on a more mature, normal, and sophisticated basis. In its own groping way, and not without significant retrogression, the United States is developing a long-term policy toward Latin America that includes the traditional defense of its national interests, but in more enlightened ways. These include broad-ranging development policies, a more sophisticated strategic conception, and emphases on democracy and human rights. The democracy/human rights agenda implies not just a moralistic crusade, as in the past, but encompasses important strategic and political objectives as well: Latin America favors it, so do all U.S. interests and institutions, its allies are supportive, it sharply distinguishes the United States from the Soviet Union, it rallies public and elite opinion, and it causes far fewer difficulties in terms of U.S. domestic politics than does the continued propping up of aging dictators. There is widespread consensus on this more practical and sensible agenda, which means it is certain to be continued (albeit with new faces and emphases), in the Bush Administration. We do not mean here to overstate U.S. capacities or to understate the difficulties arising from the Iran-contra affair and other foreign policy debilities. But there are undoubtedly some new strengths and thrusts in U.S.-Latin America policy that offer the possibility, maybe even probability, of both better enlightenment and greater success.

The third leg of this triangular situation is Cuba. Cuba stands increasingly in Latin America as the odd country out. In recent decades, Latin America—despite some interruptions and numerous ongoing problems—has become more economically developed, more modern, more democratic, and more independent. Cuba is none of these things. Moreover, it seems to have been by-passed by the main currents of the modern western world, which are increasingly democratic. In this more democratic thrust and context, Cuba seems increasingly out of sync with its neighbors, with the Soviet Union, and, perhaps, with history. It has sacrificed its relationship with the United States at *enormous* social, economic, and political costs. One understands that it is very difficult to have a revolution in Latin America *with* the United States, but it is even more difficult to have one *without* the United States, and probably impossible to have one successfully *against* the United States.

All this leaves one very sad about the future of Cuba. My own conclusion, perhaps in the realm of justifiable speculation rather than strict social science analysis, is that Cuba made some fundamental mistakes almost three decades ago when it opted to reconstitute its society, polity, and economy along Marxist-Leninist lines and to reorient its foreign policy away from the United States and toward an alliance with the Soviet Union. It is increasingly clear to historians of that era that Cuba did so out of a combination of frustration, nationalism, bitterness, and pique, and not necessarily out of prudent and rational calculation.[27] The mistakes were fundamental; now Cuba is either too proud or its system too entrenched to contemplate some fundamental reorientations. Those earlier decision, however, saddled Cuba with a regime and system that may now be impossible to alter, but the mistakes are increasingly difficult to cover up with bluster and rhetorical flourishes. Increasingly, one is led to the conclusion that these fateful decisions have proved far too costly for the Cuban people and nation.

Notes

1. Edwin Lieuwen, *U.S. Policy in Latin America* (New York: Praeger, 1965); and Federico G. Gil, *Latin American-United States Relations* (New York: Harcourt, Brace, Jovanovich, 1971).
2. On the bases and assumptions of U.S. policy in Latin America, see Howard J. Wiarda, *In Search of Policy: The United States and Latin America* (Washington, D.C.: American Enterprise Institute, 1984).
3. See especially Ramón Ruiz, *Cuba: The Making of a Revolution* (Amherst: University of Massachusetts Press, 1965); and Hugh Thomas, *Cuba: The Pursuit of Freedom* (London: Eyre and Spottiswoode, 1971).
4. A good statement is found in Abraham F. Lowenthal, *Partners in Conflict: The United States and Latin America* (Baltimore: Johns Hopkins University Press, 1987).
5. The statistics are provided in the annual reports of the Inter-American Development Bank, *Social and Economic Progress in Latin America* (Washington, D.C., yearly); a summary and interpretation is provided in Howard J. Wiarda, "Updating U.S. Strategic Policy: Containment in the Caribbean Basin," in Terry L. Deibel and John Lewis Gaddis, eds., *Containment: Concept and Policy* (Washington, D.C.: National Defense University Press, 1986), pp. 559-579.
6. Jorge Domínguez, *U.S. Interests and Policies in the Caribbean and Central America* (Washington, D.C.: American Enterprise Institute, 1982).
7. The best book is by F. H. Cardoso and E. Faletto, *Dependency and Development in Latin America* (Berkeley: University of California Press, 1977); but see also David Ray, "The Dependency Model of Latin American Underdevelopment: Three Basic Fallacies," *Journal of Inter-American Studies*, 15 (February 1973) pp. 4-20; and Tony Smith, "The Dependency Approach" in Howard J. Wiarda,

ed., *New Directions in Comparative Politics* (Boulder: Westview Press, 1985), pp. 113-126.

8. Mark Falcoff, *Small Countries, Large Issues* (Washington, D.C.: American Enterprise Institute, 1984).

9. See the discussion in Howard J. Wiarda, *Foreign Policy Without Illusion: How Foreign Policy-Making Works and Fails to Work in The United States* (Boston: Little, Brown and Co., forthcoming).

10. Karl E. Meyer, "The Lesser Evil Doctrine," *The New Leader*, 46 (October 14, 1963), p. 14.

11. Department of State, *Democracy in Latin America: The Promise and the Challenge* (Washington, D.C.: Bureau of Public Affairs, Department of State, Special Report No. 158, (March 1987). Howard J. Wiarda, *The Democratic Revolution in Latin America: Implications for U.S. Policy* (New York: A Twentieth Century Fund Book, forthcoming).

12. See the discussion in Ronald Scheman, ed., *The Alliance for Progress: Twenty-five Years After* (New York: Praeger, 1988).

13. As in the title of the book by Seyom Brown, *On the Front Burner: Issues in U.S. Foreign Policy* (Boston: Little, Brown and Co., 1984).

14. James R. Greene and Brent Scowcroft, eds., *Western Interests and U.S. Policy Options in the Caribbean Basin* (Boston: Oelgeschlager, Gunn and Hain, 1984).

15. Howard J. Wiarda, *Finding Our Way: Toward Maturity in U.S.-Latin American Relations* (Washington, D.C.: American Enterprise Institute, 1987).

16. Howard J. Wiarda, "The Paralysis of Policy," *World Affairs*, 149 (Summer, 1986), pp. 15-20.

17. *Finding Our Way*, Introduction.

18. On these themes, see Jerome Lervison and Juan de Onís, *The Alliance that Lost Its Way* (Chicago: Quadrangle, 1970).

19. Vladimir Tismaneanu, *The Vulnerabilities of Communist Regimes* (Philadelphia: Foreign Policy Research Institute, forthcoming)—a multi-volume study that focuses on the crises of ideology, institutions, and society in socialist systems.

20. Nick Eberstadt, "Health, Nutrition, and Literacy Under Communism," *Journal of Economic Growth*, 2 (Second Quarter, 1987), pp. 11-22.

21. Robert Packenham, "Capitalist Dependency and Socialist Dependency: The Case of Cuba," paper presented at the Annual Meeting of the American Political Science Association, New Orleans, August 29-September 1, 1985.

22. Mikhail Gorbachev, *Perestroika: New Thinking for Our Country and the World* (New York: Harper and Row, 1987).

23. Howard J. Wiarda and Mark Falcoff, *The Communist Challenge in the Caribbean and Central America* (Washington, D.C.: University Press of America, 1987).

24. William LeoGrande, "Foreign Policy: The Limits of Success," in Jorge I. Domínguez, ed., *Cuba: Internal and International Affairs* (Beverly Hills: Sage Publications, 1982), pp. 167-192. See also Cole Blasier and Carmelo Mesa-Lago, eds., *Cuba in the World* (Pittsburgh: University of Pittsburgh Press 1979); Martin Weinstein, *Revolutionary Cuba in the World Arena* (Philadelphia: Institute for the Study of Human Issues, 1979); Barry B. Levine, *The New Cuban Presence in the Caribbean* (Boulder: Westview Press, 1983); Fidel Castro, *Fidel Castro Speeches, 1984-85: War and Crisis in the Americas* (New York: Pathfinder Press, 1985); Raymond Duncan, *The Soviet Union and Cuba* (New York: Praeger, 1985); Carla Anne Robbins, *The Cuban Threat* (Philadelphia: Institute for the Study of Human Issues, 1985); Pamela S. Falk, *Cuban Foreign Policy* (Lexington, Mass.: Lexington Books, 1986); H. Michael Erisman, *Cuba's International Relations* (Boulder: Westview Press, 1985).

25. Lowenthal, *Partners in Conflict*; and Wiarda, *Finding Our Way*.

26. Jorge I. Domínguez, Chapter 1.

27. Richard E. Welch, Jr., *Response to Revolution: The United States and the Cuban Revolution, 1959-1961* (Chapel Hill: University of North Carolina Press, 1985).

8

Cuba's Foreign Policy Toward Latin America and the Caribbean in the 1980s

Juan Valdés Paz

Cuba's policy toward Latin America and the Caribbean and its positions on agenda issues for the region, has, as a basic point of reference, the U.S. policy toward Cuba and toward the region. Therefore, we will examine Cuba's perception of U.S. policy and its effects on its own foreign policy. This chapter is not intended to be an exhaustive study of Cuban foreign policy; rather, it may be the beginning of a debate, from our perspective, regarding Cuban government policy. At this time, our references to other approaches will be limited pending a more detailed analysis.

Aspects of Cuba's Foreign Policy Toward Latin America and the Caribbean

Cuba's foreign policy toward the region has been called doctrinaire or ideological as well as pragmatic. Both characterizations, apart from being mutually exclusive, have been based on specific topics during a given period of Cuba's policy. In our opinion, both characterizations are incorrect; they arise from a superficial analysis of the foreign policy of the Cuban Revolution, which has now lasted for three decades. An in-depth study would show that[1]:

- Cuba's foreign policy toward Latin America and the Caribbean is part of its overall foreign policy, and an essential component of the policy of the Cuban revolution.
- Cuba's general international presence has been shaped by historical factors and circumstances, which impart a character to its policy toward the region, including, among other elements, the geopolitical situation, the multiplicity of

roles derived from its position in the international system, and the international situations generated by other nations' policies, mainly those of the United States.
- Cuba's foreign policy is based on a series of perceptions, political-ideological concepts, principles, and explicit objectives that make it highly predictable in the medium and long term.
- Cuban foreign policy is designed and implemented on the basis of norms, particularly those of international law. Interstate relations are based on mutually recognized norms and implemented by the involved parties.

Latin America and the Caribbean do not merely constitute one more region for Cuba's foreign policy. Rather, Cuba truly belongs to the region geographically, ethnically, historically, linguistically, and culturally. Cuba identifies with the region's current and future strategic interests, and considers it the natural realm for its endeavors toward economic and political integration. Latin America and the Caribbean also share the common inheritance of the liberators and of the ideals of unity and independence. Cuba's history has been marked by its Americanist vocation; this vocation is an inseparable part of its foreign policy. In addition, Cuba must play all its international roles on this continent—it is Latin American, a Third World member, socialist, and nonaligned. It must reconcile its interests with those of other American nations in a complex, strategic, and principled foreign policy.

Thus, we see that just as the general interests of the Cuban Revolution give rise to overall foreign policy objectives, Cuba's specific interests with respect to Latin America and the Caribbean give rise to specific objectives of its regional policy. These objectives are related both to the states of the region and to the region's insertion in the international system, which is marked by its dependence and its position in the system of U.S. domination. This situation determines mid- and long-term objectives:

- to ensure the survival, consolidation, and development of the Cuban revolution in its Caribbean, Latin American, nonaligned, and socialist nature;
- to achieve the full independence of Latin America and the Caribbean and abolish the system of U.S. domination over the countries of the region;
- to achieve the greatest unity and economic and political integration of the region's countries, setting Latin Americanism in opposition to Pan Americanism;

- to include the region in a new international economic order that will promote its greater economic independence and development;
- to achieve the political, economic, and social transformations that will promote these objectives; and
- to achieve unity of political and social forces that favor the struggle for independence and social change, and that oppose imperialism.

These objectives, detailed in the Cuban leadership's programmatic declarations, can also be derived from the various policies implemented by the Cuban revolution in Latin America throughout all these years. Both the objectives and the strategy have shaped a foreign policy characterized by the continuity of its objectives, the change of its strategy in keeping with its interests and principles in some cases, and its perception of continental reality and its own effectiveness in others. The artificial separation of these elements of Cuban foreign policy has allowed some to call it doctrinaire or pragmatic, as the case may be.

Two approaches help us better understand this policy: one, making a clearer distinction between Cuba's political strategy and the particular policies through which it is implemented in given situations; the other, making the distinction between a state and a nonstate foreign policy, each with its particular institutional processes and actors, which, while sharing the same strategies, do not carry out the same policies.

But the clarity and scope of Cuba's objectives do not ensure their implementation, nor even the possibility of pursuing an appropriate strategy. Hence, Cuba has had to rank one objective over another over time, adjusting its strategy in keeping with real conditions and the existing correlation of forces. The study of Cuba's foreign policy in these years serves as background for current policies and demonstrates the nature of Cuba's strategy.[2]

Some authors have observed changes in Cuba's political strategy toward Latin America and have tried to explain them as due to a variety of causes, ranging from the search for greater effectiveness to the ideological maturation of Cuba's leadership. We cannot enter this debate here, but we will state that in our opinion, a study of Cuba's foreign policy over nearly three decades shows the country's rare ability to maintain its principles in their entirety and to reconcile the multiplicity of its international roles in the pursuit of its interests in the region; moreover, the rank-order of its objectives has not meant the sacrifice of any of them.

This assessment bears up under review of current policies. However, it is important to observe how the changes in strategy reveal changes in the perceptions of realities in Latin America and the Caribbean on the part of Cuba's leadership, whose definition of the objective conditions has become more complex to the point of including the region's political and cultural dimensions. The subjective conditions of the popular struggle for change are also perceived in a more complete way, placing the role of political vanguards in specific contexts: A vanguard ought to develop a strategy of struggle that synthesizes the unity of the popular forces, their necessary link to the mass movement, and a political-military conception of the struggle.[3]

A sharper perception of the changes in the region's class structure has allowed for the incorporation into Cuba's political strategy of a more detailed view of forces and movements, of their political expressions, and of the growing importance for change of new social sectors, such as the popular Christian movement; the marginalized populations; and the feminist, ethnic, and other movements as these first become politically relevant. Furthermore, the sensitivity of the Cuban leadership has allowed it to detect the contradictory factors within the dominant classes and sectors—the entrepreneurial sectors, armed forces, and political parties—which could favor independent and nationalist positions.

This view has factored not only more effective political strategies, but also policies defined by country. Thus, the Latin American governments' policies have been differentiated according to the objectives of Cuban foreign policy and, above all, by the extent of their independence with respect to U.S. policy. This criterion stems from the perception of growing contradictions between U.S. interests and those of Latin American and Caribbean societies, even those of their ruling classes. These contradictions constitute an area of Latin American agreement and set an agenda of demands against the United States.

Coinciding with the region's growing international importance, Cuba's relations with Latin American governments have been extended and diversified, overcoming the isolation of Cuba orchestrated by the United States and supported by most of the Latin American governments in the 1960s. These relations today include fifteen of the region's governments.

With the broadening of Cuba's political and economic interstate relations with Latin America and the Caribbean, diplomacy has become increasingly important in Cuba's foreign policy. Also, as is demonstrated by the history of Cuba's relations with Mexico, Cuba subordinates its foreign policy objectives to the norms of international law that govern its bilateral relations with other states and governments.[4] In addition, Cuba's interstate relations are based on deriving mutual advantage and on reciprocity, independent from the political ideology prevailing in those other governments.

The Issues in Cuba's Policy Toward Latin America and the Caribbean

In Cuba's perception, at the end of the 1980s, the societies of Latin America and the Caribbean are immersed in one of the most serious crises of their history, expressed in the worsening economic, social, and political conditions and in the lack of alternatives within the system of dependent capitalism under U.S. imperialist domination. Cuba's foreign policy is projected from its own premises onto this setting, reorienting its political strategy or refining its implementation on each of the issues that make up its foreign relations with the region. These issues constitute its own agenda, to a large degree coinciding with the agenda of the collectivity of Latin American nations and in no sense limited to the issues that arise from its relations with the United States.

Seen as a whole, Cuba's positions on these issues express, in addition to the coherence of its roles, a certain correspondence with the issues common to the Third World. Let us examine the Cuban position on some of these issues, bearing in mind that they are closely interrelated.

Economic Dependence and Underdevelopment

Increasing economic dependence and its counterpart, underdevelopment, continue to be the region's main political problem and, consequently, one of the priority issues for Cuban foreign policy. At the end of the 1980s, the region faces a true economic and social structural crisis, where the successive partial crises—energy, trade, finance, and so on—reveal and reinforce the deformations of a structure economically dependent on the outside world and biased toward fragmentation in its domestic consequences. The economic, social, and political effects of these crises push increasingly broader sectors of the Latin American and Caribbean population into poverty and marginalization.

The foreign debt issue is part of this crisis. In early 1988, Latin American and Caribbean debt was upwards of $410,000 million, 45 percent of the world's accumulated debt, and which, during the 1980s, has averaged 325 percent of the value of the region's total exports.[5] This immense debt, the magnitude of its interest costs, and the international economic context make it not only objectively unpayable by the debtors, but uncollectible by the creditors.

Cuba's early perception of the importance and consequences of the foreign debt for the region's countries allowed it to design a strategy based on a negotiated political solution aimed at achieving the total forgiveness of the debt. The formulas proposed by Cuba included solutions for the creditors' interests and linking the settlement of the debt to a reduction of military spending. In this way, Cuba proposed an economic policy strategy that could be acceptable in the medium term by the main capitalist states in time to avert a political and social crisis of unforeseeable consequences. Cuba has strongly maintained that trying to pay the debt is a political error that will set the Latin American governments against their own peoples. Experience has shown the impossibility of addressing a problem of this magnitude and of coordinating solutions with the creditors from bilateral perspectives. It thus becomes necessary "to shift from individual to collective efforts" in the battle of the debt.[6]

Cuba's own foreign debt in freely convertible currency has not been an exception from these general trends. The only differences are the smaller amount of Cuba's debt, the political circumstances that surround it, and its limited impact on the domestic economy. Cuba and its creditors have bargained over the terms of payment for this debt. Cuba has expressed its willingness to adjust to the decisions that Latin American governments may make jointly to face up to the debt crisis.

The conditions of dependence and underdevelopment are reproduced thanks to processes within the current international economic order. Thus, the current international economic order is an objective barrier to the development of revolutionary processes and even to the mildest reform projects. Both popular as well as bourgeois governments of the region see themselves cornered by an international economic order that responds to the interests of developed capitalism.

Hence, Cuba's foreign policy expends its greatest effort on the struggle for the establishment of a new international economic order as the only alternative for the future of Third World countries. Such an order is perceived as a moment in the longer struggle of underdeveloped countries for their emancipation and against exploitation. In this sense, it is not clear whether a new international economic order will be reached by means of confrontation, or by the more logical and perhaps more utopian means of collaboration. In any event, while recognizing in Cuba's relations with the socialist community the anticipation of these new relations, Cuba also believes that it behooves the socialist states to be at the vanguard as a force for change in striving for this objective.[7]

The question of the debt signals Cuba's position with respect to the questions of peace and disarmament in general. These are necessary and extremely important goals for humanity, but they will modify human destiny only if the resources spent for military purposes are diverted to finance the development of the so-called Third World.

The arms races in Latin America and the Caribbean in the last decades have been linked mainly to interstate conflicts, to the implementation of national security policies, and to foreign attacks aimed at overthrowing popular governments. In all of these situations, U.S. policy has played a decisive role, which contributes to its standing as world leader of the arms race. In Cuba's view, the largest defense expenditures are specifically a result of U.S. attacks or threat of attack against governments or processes committed to the struggle for independence and against imperialism; as such, these expenditures are necessary for the survival of said processes.

Economic integration, one of the unavoidable alternatives for change in the external conditions of the Latin American and Caribbean economies, has been of limited scope despite broad consensus as to its necessity. Instruments such as the Latin American Economic System (SELA), the Andean Pact, and the Caribbean Common Market (CARICOM) have barely laid the institutional bases for this process. Some integration projects in international trade (the Central American Common Market, or the creation of Latin American transnational enterprises for marketing products and/or services) have not achieved a sustained development and have suffered the effects of the crisis.

Cuban policy has been and will be to support and collaborate in sustaining all institutions aiming to promote economic integration as well as fostering jointly owned state enterprises. Cuba also favors all actions that create conditions favorable for integration, as is the case of bilateral and multilateral trade, joint participation on projects, technical collaboration, and the like. But, in Cuba's opinion, it will not be possible to advance seriously toward the continent's greater economic integration—a condition for survival in the face of the world centers of economic power—without the political will of the region's governments. This will has barely shown itself beyond statements of intent and glimmerings of coordination. Thus, a greater degree of economic integration does not appear feasible absent greater political integration.

But Cuba's support for the processes and institutions of economic integration in the region does not imply its agreement with processes designed to favor or subject to the penetration of transnational capital; nor does Cuba ignore the insufficiencies and limitations of the experiences of regional and subregional integration. In the Cuban view, economic integration should serve the economic independence of all the region's countries, and should be based on certain premises, such as:[8]

- integration will be open to all countries in Latin America and the Caribbean;
- international economic relations will develop free of any political discrimination;
- the integration process will favor development more than economic growth, and it will be based on the principles of complementarity and appropriate specialization among the economies of the region;
- structural reforms will be promoted to allow for the increase of domestic aggregate demand and, with it, the formation of a common market and autonomous industrialization; and
- the objectives for integration and development must be planned and programmed for the medium and long term.

As can be observed, the economic issue has occupied and does occupy a central place in Cuba's foreign policy, not only because a greater agreement around it is possible, but also because of strategic considerations, tied to its perception of world and regional reality. However, under the current conditions and the international economic order, it will not be possible to solve the problem of development. Hence, as Fidel Castro has said, Cuba's policy is one of "unity of wills to solve this great economic crisis," giving it priority even over the achievement of the "social changes which sooner or later will have to come."

This unity of action by the Latin American and Caribbean nations will help them confront the tasks of a new international economic order, to achieve cancellation of the foreign debt, and to receive appropriate development aid. Cuba's policy in this respect has evolved on two levels: as a state policy aimed at coordinating the positions of governments, and as a nonstate policy aimed at raising consciousness and mobilizing various social and political forces in support of the historic struggle for economic independence and development.

These policies, launched with great energy by the Cuban leadership, have made a strong impact on the continent, but have not had the hoped for success. The Latin American governments have taken hesitant and defensive positions, and the level of coordination has been low and of little effect. As for the mobilization of forces, the local ruling sectors are not ready to lead a confrontation with the advanced capitalist countries, particularly the United States; notwithstanding, the Cuban government seems to understand that for the Latin American and Caribbean peoples and governments, there is, in the medium term, no alternative to a policy of open struggle against the regional economic crisis.

The Struggle for Democracy

The so-called democratic question is heavily influenced by ideological perspectives and the class position from which it is defined. We can recognize the predominance of institutionalist conceptions of democracy among the continent's political tendencies, including sectors of the Latin American left, for which democracy (and especially political democracy) amount to the lawful existence of certain political institutions—a system of parties, separation of powers, governments that result from elections, and so on—through which the majority of citizens would express their will.

Obviously, the Cuban position on the issue differs from any formal approach to this question. It is rooted in the Marxist tradition, for which democracy is a result of the greatest equality and social participation. In this way, the forms of political democracy—representative democracies, populist authoritarian governments, popular democracies, and People's Power—are seen in terms of the representation of class interests through political power. Although a political system's institutionalization and respect for law are a basis for a more effective democracy, democracy is only acheived when the majority's interests are ensured.

In this perspective, Cuba sees the struggle for democracy—political power of the majority, respect for human rights and social justice—as a process, the final objectives of which can be achieved under different forms of political and social organization. The narrowing of democracy to the bourgeois forms of representative democracy—promoted by the United States with ulterior motives—serves to cover up in our region the most blatant class exploitation and imperialist domination. While the struggle for democracy is one of the historic objectives of the nations of our continent, the political forms under which some of its goals can be achieved constitute specific problems in the democratic struggle of each country.

With regard to the first problem of the struggle for democracy—the struggle against dictatorships and other coercive regimes—Cuba's policy is firmly one of all-out struggle. This is one case in which change cannot be achieved through legal and peaceful means. The attainment of democratic rights justifies granting the most aid possible to the democratic and popular oppositions. This is also a case in which the continuation of dictatorships corresponds to the U.S. policy of support for authoritarian governments, presumed to be allies, marked by their repression of the popular movement and their self-identification as western, Christian, and anticommunist.[9]

Second, there are the processes of democratization taking place basically in South America's southern cone, which have replaced military governments that had emerged from counterinsurgency projects guided by national security doctrines, oriented to the triple goal of imposing a new model of economic accumulation, assuring the dominance of the transnationalized sectors of the economy, and crushing all popular resistance. Although these processes of redemocratization have been directed from "above" and without affecting the power bases of the new hegemonic sectors and of imperialism, under the terms of bourgeois legality, they channel the class and political struggle, opening spaces that permit the popular forces to rebuild themselves and act.

The governments emerging from these processes have managed to defend democratic rights and reorient the policies most costly for the popular masses, but they have evolved inevitably under the double fear of military threat and uncontrollable economic and social crises. Cuba's policy has been oriented toward the support of these processes, seeking their internal consolidation and greatest international support while promoting their greatest independence and integration in a Latin American community that could sustain them.

A special case in the struggle for democracy is that of governments of representative democracy, which feature serious restrictions on democratic rights of the popular masses, or which combine the persistence of democratic-bourgeois institutions with more or less sophisticated counterinsurgency projects. The so-called "façade democracies" of Central America are the extreme case in which civil power is subordinated to the counterinsurgency project. Cuba's policy in these cases is governed strictly by the norms of relations and attitudes toward Cuba that these governments observe.

The third problem refers to the popular democracies—those in which the old state has been replaced (the cases of Nicaragua and revolutionary Grenada) by a new state, resulting from a process of revolutionary struggle and the broadest popular support. The essential things in this new state are its participatory nature and the creation of a new people's army. One final problem: the democracies of people's power created in societies in transition to socialism, as in Cuba. Cuba's policy forcefully states the legitimacy of these forms of popular democracies as expressions of the interests of the majority of the people and the result of their historic struggle.

One variant of popular democracy that reveals the complex Latin American reality is the one emerging from military governments that have promoted structural transformation in their societies and reforms that benefit the great majority. This is the case of the Velasco Alvarado government in Peru, and that of Omar Torrijos in Panama. Cuba's policy has been to support these forms of democracy based on the seizure of power by patriotic military sectors when their actions have proved their will to produce radical changes in the conditions of dependency and exploitation, and when they have earned popular support.

The Cuban conception of democracy involves an uninterrupted process of democratization of the entire society, and therefore the struggle for social change. It is not necessary to study the situation of our continent's societies to understand the relevance of struggles for social change, understood as structural transformations that make possible a more egalitarian distribution of wealth, the conditions for development, and the solution to the serious social problems of health, education, housing, and so on. Without these changes, no stable democracy is possible.

The structures of domination of the local exploiting classes and of imperialism resist these changes. The economic crisis and the policies of adjustments have come to reinforce the serious situation of the masses, threatening to become a generalized social crisis. This situation has fostered a growing mass movement expressed in multiple social movements—of workers, peasants, ethnic groups, and women—in support of demands and reforms. Experience has shown that these movements' aspirations are not viable without more independence, a deepening of democracy, and structural transformations. This fact presents the need to raise the social movements to a political dimension. The political dimension of these struggles has its particular form of expression in each country of the region. The institutional space, the level of unity and political organization, the legal framework, and the formulation of correct tactics and a strategy of struggle are among the conditions of a political struggle based on a growing mass struggle.

For Cuba, these political and social processes are internal to each country; it is the masses, social movements, and political vanguards of the respective peoples that are able to promote changes favorable to their interests, which are also in the national and Latin American interest. Cuba's sympathy and solidarity is political-ideological and is framed, as in other issues, within the principles and obligations of its foreign policy. At the same time, Cuba promotes and defends, through its positions in multilateral, regional, and world organizations, the need for profound structural changes and greater social justice. Furthermore, the isolation of and discrimination against Cuba out of fear of its influence is perceived as an act of hostility, in line with U.S. counterrevolutionary policy toward the region.

We can conclude the study of this issue by noting that in general, Cuba's policy on the question of the democratic nature of the region's governments has been shaped both by the degree of their independence from the United States and by their ability to promote changes that lead to a more egalitarian, participatory society.

Security

The security issue is one of the most relevant in the foreign policy of Latin American states. Its problems are linked in some ways to the content of the other issues we examine in this chapter, insofar as they affect regional stability and the relations of the Latin American and Caribbean nations with the United States. As a result, this issue holds a central place in Cuba's foreign policy, not only as it affects its relations with the United States, but also its relations with the countries of the region.

The scope of this issue is also determined by the perception states have of their security interests, as well as by the principles and doctrines upon which they base and implement their security policies. From Cuba's extensive discussions about security problems, it is possible to derive the bases of its position on this issue, and to set them out as follows:

- All security interests should be subordinate to the norms of international law. No security interest can be exercised against the independence, sovereignty, and self-determination of peoples and states.
- Cuba does not recognize geopolitical interests, exclusive security zones, or zones of influence.
- All peoples and states have legitimate security interests; therefore, the security of each one has the security of the others as its limit.
- Shared security interests should be negotiated and be subject to the norms of international law and other sovereign agreements.
- The security of peoples and states is comprehensive. Hence, it includes not only the need for defense of their sovereignty, but of all the components of their society's security, such as economic, nutritional, and environmental security.
- Internal and external stability are part of national security.
- Security solutions must take into account the asymmetry among states, particularly between the United States and the other nations of Latin America and the Caribbean. The concept of asymmetry implies that the margins of security, the threat potential, and the measures that may be taken to attack or defend are unequal.
- Every nation and state has the right to defend its threatened security with the means available to it.

But, in addition to its principles, Cuba manifests its perception of and position on a set of security problems on our continent, concerning which it orients its foreign policy.[10] The first of these problems is the identification of the United States as the great hegemonic power whose security interests are integrated within its system of domination over the nations of the area, on which it imposes the bourgeois social order, dependence, and alignment. It is precisely one effect of this system of domination that the United States perceives every internal or external situation of the area's countries as being linked to its own national security. Thus, the United States structures and projects its policies toward the region, considering the following:

1. a set of so-called vital or national security interests—some of long standing and others of recent origin—through which it identifies a geopolitical space that must be dominated;

2. a set of means of economic, military, political, and other forms of coercion to ensure a given national and international order favorable to its security;
3. resistance to every economic, social, or political change in the countries of the region that it sees as adverse to its alliances, to the need for stability, or to the predictability of new events; and
4. identification of every regional conflict as part of or linked to the East-West conflict.

Facing these national security problems, Cuba's foreign policy demonstrates a strong commitment to principle and support for international law, not only as a condition for co-existence among nations, but as the prerequisite for solutions to security: equality among states.

For Cuba, the system of economic, political, and military domination imposed by the United States on the nations of Latin America and the Caribbean and the current security interests it harbors are the main threat and constraint on the region's security. From this perspective, Cuba postulates that there is no common identity of security interests among the United States and the Latin American nations, and that there is a basic security interest shared by Latin American nations: anti-imperialism. Cuba perceives in these shared security interests another basis for Latin American and Caribbean integration, and for coordinated action among these states.

In the Cuban view, the conciliation between the shared and the antagonistic security interests among the Latin American and Caribbean nations and the United States, a great power and hegemonic state, should be based on:

-   strict subordination to international law and to its unconditional, universal, and indivisible nature;
-   the separation of all domestic processes from external security interests;
-   co-existence among states with different political and social systems;
-   negotiated settlement of conflicts;
-   the comprehensive nature of security; and
-   nonalignment.

Cuba sees nonalignment as the situation that best reconciles the security interests of the Latin American and Caribbean nations with those of the United States in its condition as a great power.

But for Cuba, the nonaligned position does not imply a neutrality compliant with the prevalent system of domination. Rather, it means an active nonalignment committed against colonialism, neo-colonialism, and racism.

Cuba also sees efforts to harmonize U.S. security interests with those of the countries of the region on the premises of "objective inequality" or "viability," and the search for solutions based on "privileged relations," as a real subordination to the hegemonic interests of the United States. The same happens with a concept of security that accepts direct or indirect intervention of some states in the affairs of others, or any action that violates the independence, sovereignty, and self-determination of peoples.

In Cuba's view, the security of Latin American and Caribbean nations is threatened not only by U.S. interventionist actions, but also on a daily basis by the crisis that results from international economic relations and dependence. Hence, the achievement of a new national and international economic and political order would be part of regional security.

As for the subject of disarmament, Cuba's position has in general been to favor all processes that have the objective of reducing international tensions, according priority to the negotiated solution of conflicts and disarmament. In the particular case of Latin America and the Caribbean, the struggle for disarmament or the limitation of military spending cannot be considered apart from the political causes that give rise to them. Nor is the limitation of the defensive capabilities of the states separable from the policies with which the United States supports its objectives of domination. All policies of unilateral disarmament "for Latin Americans" that do not include the United States, its offensive capability, or its interventionist actions would serve to reinforce U.S. domination.[11]

Finally, we observe that Cuba's policy takes into account the increasingly relevant role that Latin America and the Caribbean play as an independent factor in international relations, and their growing importance as part of universal system of international security. This role presumes full unity of goals and the coordination of international positions on the part of the Latin American and Caribbean nations.

The Struggle for National Liberation

The existence in Latin America and the Caribbean of colonial enclaves, a system of neocolonial domination, and armed conflicts sustained by the United States makes the national liberation struggle one of the most relevant subjects of Cuba's foreign policy.

For Cuba's foreign policy toward Latin America, this issue encompasses a larger number of problems than those typically considered. This situation is explained by the nature and content of the national liberation struggle in our region, whose historical struggle for full national independence is currently centered on the struggle against imperialism and for development.[12] In this sense, the national liberation struggle in Latin America and the Caribbean today comprises the four problems discussed here.

First, there is the anticolonialist struggle. It includes the colonial cases still existing on the continent, principally in the area of the Caribbean. The colonial question has it nodal points in the U.S. colonial domination in Puerto Rico and in the United Kingdom's colonial domination of Argentina's Malvinas Islands. In the case of Puerto Rico, so long as there is one patriot who proclaims it, Cuba has made support for Puerto Rican independence a principle of its foreign policy; in the case of the Malvinas Islands, Cuba supports Argentina's claim to the islands and rejects the United Kingdom's use of force, backed by the United States, to maintain its occupation.

Second, there is the struggle for sovereignty. It includes territorial claims and claims to natural resources and maritime zones. Panama's claims to sovereignty over the canal and Cuba's own claims to the Guantánamo naval base hold a prominent place in Cuban policies. Cuba supported the signing of the Panama Canal Carter-Torrijos Treaties—the best achievement of U.S. policy in Latin America in recent decades—and fully supports Panama in its demands for treaty compliance. The actions of the Reagan administration and of sectors of the U.S. Congress to evade compliance with the treaties—above all, turning custody and administration of the canal to Panama in 1999—represent a direct act of aggression against Panama's sovereignty. The destabilizing actions aimed at undermining the Panamanian Defense Forces' support for the Torrijos system, the economic pressures, and the U.S. resistance to comply with the terms of the treaties seek to make possible the continued military-strategic presence in the Canal Zone for an indefinite time, and to change Panama's foreign policy regarding the Central American conflict. Cuba's policy supports Panamanian sovereignty and promotes the greatest Latin American support for its causes.[13]

Third, there is the anti-imperialist struggle. It encompasses all forms of struggle against neocolonial dependence, and, in particular, against U.S. domination over Latin American and Caribbean nations. This struggle includes economic, political, military, and ideological dimensions, and assumes the existence of favorable national and international conditions. Cuba's policy in the region has as its main strategic objective to break, erode, and liquidate imperialist domination of our countries. At the same time, Cuba sees two scenarios for the anti-imperialist struggle: the struggle for external independence, and the domestic struggle against denationalized ruling groups subordinate to imperialism. All the countries of the region take part in the former; in the latter are those countries dominated by power groups imposed or propped up by the United States. This case joins the democratic struggle to that against imperialism.

And fourth, there is the struggle for social transformation. It includes the struggle for the establishment of a social order that allows for the consolidation of independence and development. The unfinished nature of the liberation process, the growing dependence of the region, and its subjection to a system of political and military domination give the national liberation struggle in the current phase of Latin American capitalism, dominated by transnationalized monopoly capital, an anti-imperialist nature and an anticapitalist tendency. Thus, the path toward socialism appears as an historic option to the nations of the continent. Cuba and Nicaragua are one variant of this alternative.

Cuba's policy defends the socialist option for the peoples of Latin America with no condition other than free choice. The triumph of the Cuban Revolution began a new cycle in the struggle for national liberation in our continent. Cuba showed that it was possible to break U.S. hegemony, to begin a process of independent transformation, and to achieve a nonaligned, international role. In Cuba's perception, these processes of national liberation will have their own characteristics and their own pace in each country. The continent will become more pluralistic by reason of its social and political regimes. Respect for the self-determination and sovereignty of nations will be the condition for existence of a united and diverse Latin American community. The unity of the peoples and governments in an anti-imperialist front will be the least costly condition for all to achieve their full independence, economic development, and social justice.[14]

Cuba declares its solidarity with all the national liberation struggles of all the Latin American and Caribbean peoples. This political-ideological solidarity adheres to the norms of international law and to the norms of conduct shared among states in these countries. Even aid to the revolutionary movement would be subordinated to this principle and to U.S. commitments not to intervene by promoting counterrevolution. The premise that no one can export revolution implies recognition of its domestic nature and its subordination to the principle of nonintervention. At the same time, the premise that no one can stop a revolution implies that intervention by the United States and others in favor of counterrevolution would free other states from such restraints and would commit them to aid the revolution that confronts foreign aggression.

Thus, Cuba bases the legitimacy of its policy toward the national liberation struggle on its subordination to mutually accepted norms. The extreme situation—that of the people's movement engaged in armed struggle (the cases of El Salvador and Nicaragua)—would not be an exception; other cases, such as that of the Shining Path Movement in Peru, show that there is no participation by Cuba in a domestic matter.

Cuba focuses on the existing asymmetry between our countries and the United States as well as on the centrality of the United States in the system of foreign relations of Latin America and the Caribbean. In this perspective, the Cuban policy is oriented toward favoring all processes of coordination, association, or alliance among Latin American and Caribbean countries that raise their negotiating capacity and promote an independent, anti-imperialist position. However, Cuba does not fail to note that certain negotiation processes can head in a direction contrary to the interests of the revolutionary movement and assume, as a goal of negotiation, more centrist positions. Nonetheless, Latin American integration remains a political and material condition for Latin American independence and development.

In Cuba's perception, every process of political integration in Latin America and the Caribbean raises questions about the fate of the Organization of American States (OAS), which was once a "ministry of colonies" and is an increasingly useless tool for the goals of the United States or Latin America.[15] None of the conflicts faced by the region in the last ten years has been solvable within the OAS or within the wider, so-called inter-American system, which includes the Inter-American Treaty for Reciprocal Assistance (TIAR). The long-gestating crisis of the inter-American system, given its absolute subordination to the so-called security interests of the United States, began its definitive crisis in 1975 with the break of the blockade against Cuba; continued in 1979 with failure of the actions against the Sandinista revolution; in 1982 with the Malvinas war and the TIAR crisis; in 1983 with its inability to act in the face of the foreign debt crisis, the Central

American crisis, and so on. The key to this failure has been the loss of U.S. leverage and the growing autonomy and Latin Americanization of the processes of coordination and negotiation in the region. A revival of the OAS would require a profound modification of its procedure, at least in the sense of becoming a freestanding Latin American and Caribbean entity that would allow a coordinated dialogue with the United States and other advanced capitalist countries and international organizations. While there is no explicit Cuban position on a possible restructuring of the OAS or its own eventual incorporation into that group, it can be inferred from the Cuban position in general that it is prepared to join an exclusively Latin American-Caribbean organization.

While a new political order has not yet emerged on the continent, diverse means have appeared for coordination and negotiation to confront the region's critical problems, such as the Contadora Group and its Support Group which have focused on the Central American conflict, and, more recently, the Group of Eight.[16] This last one could be the starting point for the constitution of a Latin American political entity that would favor unity of aims and actions separate from those of the United States. Cuba recognizes the importance of this coincidence of aims and actions separate from the United States of eight Latin American governments and their commitment to peace, development, and democracy.[17]

The Central American Crisis

The Central American crisis holds an important place on the Latin American agenda of foreign relations, and is of particular importance for Cuba's foreign policy. The Central American crisis is the top foreign policy problem of the Latin American and Caribbean countries. For Cuba, at issue is a political, economic, and social crisis emerging historically and structurally in one of the zones most dominated by the United States throughout this century.

A powerful popular movement, headed by political vanguards who are the bearers of a program of change, has arisen in this context. Prolonged struggles have led to the triumph of the Sandinista revolution in Nicaragua and to powerful armed insurrections in El Salvador and Guatemala. Central America has become the center of the revolutionary, anti-imperialist struggle in Latin America and the Caribbean.

The Central American crisis is, above all, a crisis of the system of domination imposed by the United States on the region. The United States does not perceive this crisis as the result of a simple loss of hegemony, but as a real threat to its interests in the area. Thus, U.S. policy toward the Central American crisis has turned the internal struggles of the Central American countries into a "regional crisis" with geopolitical dimensions. Hence, the main component of the Central American crisis at this time is the U.S. policy towards the popular movement in the subregion.

It is in the strategic interest of Latin American and Caribbean nations that the Central American crisis be resolved by the countries of the subregion themselves, in full exercise of their sovereignty and self-determination. The survival of the Sandinista revolution and the fullest independence for Central America are also in Cuba's interest, and are an objective of its foreign policy.

Cuba's policy towards the Central American conflict has been, on one hand, to give the greatest possible support for the people's movement against U.S. counterrevolutionary policies; on the other, to support a negotiated political solution to the conflict. Thus, Cuba has expressed its support for and collaboration with the Contadora and Support Groups as well as for the peace process begun at Esquipulas II by the Central American presidents with the so-called Arias Plan, notwithstanding the differences between their two sets of proposals. Cuba has seen in the Latin Americanization of the conflict—a framework for negotiation, peace proposals, and a means for verification—one of the most important factors to achieving a negotiated solution based on the principles of independence, sovereignty, and self-determination.[18] In this respect, Cuba has said that it will support the agreements reached by the popular movement as well as the decisions made by Nicaragua—despite the dangers foreseeable in some of them—in order to support the peace process.

For Cuba, the policy of a negotiated solution in Central America has raised some basic worries: first, U.S. unwillingness to favor a solution to the conflict, without which a solution cannot be found; second, the need for any negotiated agreement to include a settlement for the Salvadoran conflict; finally, the search for solutions specific to the region, not borrowed from other regional conflicts or solutions from other parts of the world. Cuba's readiness to favor a negotiated solution does not imply its acceptance of the so-called symmetry of situations between Nicaragua and El Salvador, nor the comparison of U.S. and Cuban roles. Nor does it imply that Cuba would support a model of negotiation that was not previously accepted by the revolutionary and popular movement. Both the Sandinista government and the insurgent movements of El Salvador (FMLN-FDR) and Guatemala

(URNG) have made clear their willingness to negotiate. Given the nature of the crisis, Cuba has also pointed out the need to accompany any political solutions with international economic aid to the region.[19]

Drug Traffic

The growing magnitude of the worldwide production, commercialization, and consumption of drugs has become one of the most serious problems of contemporary society, and one of the manifestations of the economic relations between the countries of the world's center and periphery. Specifically, substantial traffic in various drugs, linked to the U.S. market, has developed in Latin America and the Caribbean. The question of drug traffic plays an increasingly important role in the international system, particularly in the interamerican system. The drug traffic issue is also increasingly noteworthy on the agenda of bilateral relations between the United States and the countries of Latin America and the Caribbean.[20]

On this issue, Cuba's foreign policy is based on the fact that it is not a country directly affected by drug traffic; however, a Latin American solution to that traffic is in its interest, provided that solution is multidimensional, coordinated, symmetrical for exporters and importers, and within the framework of international law and treaties. Cuba has accepted the need to confront this international community problem.

Precisely because of the structural and asymmetrical nature of the drug traffic issue and of the issue's significance in the growth of demand within U.S. society, the measures to be taken against it must be comprehensive, the costs of the struggle against it must be shared, and means for compensation must be devised. Each nation should adopt the economic, political, and social changes that foster such outcomes.

In Cuba's opinion, adequate developmental aid will be necessary to create options for the social groups whose survival is linked to the drug traffic. Thus, the United States should implement an economic policy toward the areas affected by drug traffic to allow them to overcome their dependence. In addition, the United States should play a decisive role in the struggle against drug traffic in its own territory because its demanding market is key for the drug trade's profitability.

Cuba has joined other Latin American countries in calling on the United States to separate the drug traffic issue from other objectives of its foreign and domestic policy, mainly from those related to its strategic military interests, to the political alignment of other states, or to its hostility toward independent governments and the revolutionary movement. Finally, with respect to the U.S. use of the drug traffic issue for aggressive purposes, as early as 1981 Cuba declared that such policies could lead its government to suspend actions favorable to the United States that Cuba had chosen to undertake of its own free will—because of its moral conviction and in compliance with international law— against boats and drug dealers. Although no cooperative agreement exists and although Cuba recognizes no obligation to the United States with respect to drug traffic, on principle Cuba's policy has been to prosecute the drug traffickers who violate its territorial space.

Aspects of the Latin American Context

Taken as a whole, the issues studied reveal a Latin American and Caribbean region devastated by a structural crisis that requires new economic and social development strategies, and that demands the broadest anti-imperialist unity in the political sphere at the national and regional levels. At one level, the issue is the crisis of dependent capitalism heading for inevitable changes, which channels Latin American and Caribbean societies toward a new capitalist development, or toward a noncapitalist development, or toward socialism. At another level, the issues are the unity of action that might emerge from the contexts in which the anti-imperialist struggle in the region is carried out today; the democratic and popular revolution in Central America; the consolidation of the processes of redemocratization and overcoming the crisis in South America; and overcoming the trauma of Grenada and the crisis in the Caribbean.

In Cuba's perception, unity of action is based on objective facts—not on the similarities of socio-economic and political structures subject to processes of differentiation among the countries and subregions of Latin America, but on their common insertion in the international economic system and their shared fate under the system of U.S. domination in the region. Both dimensions of the regional crisis and the perception that Latin America and the Caribbean are "on the eve of global changes that could lead, as in Cuba, to sudden socialist transformations"[21] require giving priority to the external over the domestic context of this anti-imperialist struggle. Thus, we try to create a front, allied ideologically though not politically, among the different social forces and countries interested in withstanding the crisis and promoting change.

In this context, Cuba's policy is to seek the broadest diplomatic, economic, cultural, and other relations with the countries of Latin America and the Caribbean. Since the mid-1970s, Cuba has been expanding its interstate relations with Latin America and the Caribbean, putting an end to the policy of isolation implemented by the United States.[22] The priority Cuba accords to its links with the region's governments does not prevent its policy from being designed and implemented on the basis of its multiplicity of roles—Latin American, nonaligned and socialist—and compatible with each one of them.

Seen as a whole, it could be said that in the 1980s, the position of the Latin American and Caribbean countries has shifted more toward Cuba than toward the United States. Some analysts have said that the three main limits and obstacles to Cuba's relations with these countries are bilateral issues between Cuba and countries in the region; differences of approach to multilateral questions; and Cuba's ties to radical domestic opposition forces in countries of the region.[23]

In fact, rather than limits and obstacles, these situations could be accidents in the relations between any states. In practice, Cuba has not conditioned its interstate relations beyond international law, and has never promoted the break of established relations. The obstacles mentioned become insurmountable only within the framework of the great obstacle that is not mentioned: U.S. policy toward the region and toward Cuba in particular. Only alignment with U.S. imperialist policy makes insurmountable the obstacles that may exist between Cuba and the countries of Latin America and the Caribbean.

U.S. Policy Toward Latin America and the Caribbean

Its characteristics as the most developed capitalist country and the world's leading military power, rather than its condition as hegemonic leader of the world imperialist system and as the dominant power on the continent, make the United States and its policy the key reference point for the foreign policy of the region's countries. In the design of its own political strategy, Cuba has had to take into account U.S. policy toward Latin America and the Caribbean. This triangular perspective is sustained in the midst of a crisis of U.S. domination in the region, and of a growing contradiction between its interests and those of the region's countries; paradoxically, the greater the region's dependence, the lesser is U.S. hegemony over the region.

In Cuba's view, moreover, U.S. interests in the region increasingly have a geopolitical and military dimension without the "economic advantages" the United States had offered before. These U.S. interests are expressed through asymmetrical relations that require political stability and total alignment, the two pillars of U.S. foreign policy toward the region. The net transfer of capital, the denationalization of the productive apparatus, and the loss of markets are the features of the region's current links with the U.S. economy which form part of the region's crisis. The perception of this crisis has led U.S. administrations since Carter to try out strategies to re-establish hegemony. The essential feature of these strategies has been recourse to force and to direct or indirect intervention. In light of these intensifying contradictions, the Reagan administration made explicit the nature of this policy.

Thus, U.S. policy has been a sustained effort to contain the popular movement and to subvert the anti-imperialist governments in the region. U.S. roles of the past three decades—organizer of the counterrevolution and aggressor against Cuba, invader of the Dominican Republic and Grenada, organizer of the overthrow of the government of Salvador Allende, political and military leader of the Nicaraguan counterrevolution and of the Salvadoran counterinsurgency, leader of destabilizing actions in Panama, and so on—say more about the nature of its policy than its declarations of principle. In the face of U.S. policy of support for the counterrevolution and against the popular movement, Cuba has defined a policy of support for revolution and the people's movement, which is, in the final analysis, a policy of defense against U.S. intervention.

U.S. efforts to recover its hegemony from positions of force or through policies aimed to modernize its domination—more economic dependence, more rationalization, political systems of representative democracy, more cultural-ideological influence, and the like—have failed to the extent that the United States sought to subject the domestic politics of the region's countries to its foreign policy and security interests, and to the extent that its local allies have resisted such modernization and have rejected negotiations as a way to solve regional conflicts.

But the Cuban leadership believes that concealed behind this basic nature of U.S. policy, there is a growing inability to deal with the problems troubling the region's countries and its imperial order. Unlike the 1960s and 1970s when it functioned with some strategic sense and tried solutions based on consensus, U.S. policy currently lacks any strategy or capacity for solving or settling issues on the Latin American agenda. Thus, the U.S. recourse to force tends to become more frequent, as we see in the Central American conflict and in Panama, for example.[24]

The absence of strategy condemns U.S. policy to short-term "solutions" and to ad hoc responses hidden behind the alibi of an East-West conflict. U.S. actions express veiled threats against all proposals for change in the region, and they reinforce the loyalties of the local ruling sectors. In the same sense, the proposals for a "modernization of domination" by the United States find themselves up against the insurmountable obstacle of the U.S. material incapacity to fund controlled change in the region. This is evident in the fate of proposed policies of strategic support, such as the Caribbean Basin Initiative or the Kissinger Report on Central America. Thus, Cuba understands that the United States will not be able to modify the Latin American situation in its favor in the medium term, and will face a crisis of independence in the long term.

For some authors, the traditional U.S. domination of Latin America and the Caribbean is in a crisis of transition toward more "complex interdependence" between a different United States and a more differentiated region. This situation will not modify the natural asymmetry, but it will favor dialogue. Cuba's policy must inevitably adapt itself to this new situation or be left behind, given that "ideological arguments" will no longer carry weight in Latin America or the United States. In Cuba's perception, this scenario is nothing more than wishful thinking on the path to hell.

Cuba's policy toward Latin America and the Caribbean with respect to U.S. policy has one fundamental objective: to achieve the necessary unity to oblige the United States to negotiate over a Latin American agenda. This agenda of Latin American consensus could be addressed by the United States with realism and at lower cost in the new conditions of détente in the arms race, provided that the political will is there. However, for Cuba, the necessary process of global détente between the great powers—a condition of peace and disarmament—is not yet an irreversible process, nor will it automatically guarantee a solution for the so-called regional conflicts, or for peace and development in the nations of the Third World. Rather, Cuba perceives that for some imperialist strategies, détente will be the opportunity to make war on the world's periphery.[25]

With respect to the United States, Cuban policy makers do not ignore the degree of unpredictability in U.S. politics nor the risky influence on it of domestic public opinion, which is more sensitive to failures than to injustice. For this reason, Cuba considers an effective anti-imperialist policy to be one based on the unity of action and integration of Latin America and the Caribbean.

Conclusions

The issues examined here, taken as a whole and in the Latin American context, indicate that the achievement of the political and economic integration of Latin America is the only alternative to U.S. domination over the region, and to the international economic order imposed by the developed capitalist centers. At the same time, this policy seeks negotiated political solutions on multilateral, fair bases, in keeping with international law. In this sense, Cuba supports the negotiation of a Latin American agenda on these issues and promotes actions leading to such negotiation. This Cuban policy notes the lack of a U.S. strategy aimed to solve the region's problems.

Cuba's policy is based on the conviction that its destiny is tied to that of Latin America and the Caribbean. Union with Latin America will reduce the costs of the defense and development of the revolution, and raise its capacity of negotiation over its own agenda. But Cuba interprets its own success in the consolidation and construction of socialism as a contribution to the region's capacity to overcome dependency and underdevelopment.

Notes

1. Here we summarize a more extensive treatment of the characteristics of Cuban foreign policy contained in the brief essay "La formación de la política exterior de Cuba," a paper presented by the author at the Group on Comparative Policies of Latin America and the Caribbean at the Sixth Annual Meeting of RIAL (Brasilia, November 1987).
2. Luis Suárez Salazar, "La política exterior de la revolución cubana hacia América Latina," *Cuadernos de Nuestra América*, No. 6 (Havana: 1986); Juan Valdés Paz, "La formación de la política exterior de Cuba"; William LeoGrande, "The Limits of Success" in Jorge I. Domínguez, ed., *Cuba: Internal and International Affairs* (Beverly Hills: Sage Publications, 1982); Heraldo Muñoz and Boris Yopo, "Cuba y las democracias latinoamericanas en los 80,"

Working Papers, PROSPEL No. 9 (Santiago de Chile: CERC, March 1987), Jorge I. Domínguez, Chapter 9, unpublished; Fidel Castro Ruz, *Main Reports to the 1st, 2nd and 3rd Congresses of the Cuban Communist Party* (Havana: Editora Política, 1976, 1981, 1986 respectively).

3. A more detailed explanation of this approach is found in Manuel Piñeiro Losada, "La crisis actual del imperialismo y los procesos revolucionarios en América Latina y el Caribe," *Cuba Socialista*, No. 4 (1982).

4. Fidel Castro expressed the historic and normative aspects of this policy when he said:

> Nor do I hide that revolutionary Cuba has offered its active solidarity to other Latin American revolutionaries in countries where—such as Somoza's Nicaragua—any democratic action and any possibility of protest that was not armed struggle was obliterated by a brutal terror. Nor do I hide that when an important group of Latin American countries, acting under the inspiration and guidance of Washington, not only tried to politically isolate Cuba, but also blockaded it economically and contributed to the counterrevolutionary actions that sought to overthrow the Revolution, we responded in legitimate defense by aiding all those who in those years wished to struggle against such governments. . . . But in the same way, I can categorically state—and I challenge anyone to try to show the opposite—that no government that has maintained correct and respectful relations toward Cuba in Latin America has failed to have in turn the respect of Cuba.

From interview granted to Patricia Sethi in *Bohemia* (February 6, 1984).

5. U.N. Economic Commission for Latin America, *Report* (1987).

6. Carlos Rafael Rodríguez, speech at the Conference on the Foreign Debt sponsored by the Third World Foundation (Brasilia: May 1980).

7. *Informe central al III Congreso del Partido Comunista de Cuba* (Havana: Editora Política, 1980), Chapter 11.

8. Carlos Rafael Rodríguez, speech at the meeting for the XL Anniversary of the U.N. Economic Commission for the Latin America, Rio de Janeiro, April 25, 1988.

9. See note 6.

10. We follow the themes of the Latin American-U.S. Agenda Project of RIAL's United States-Latin America Working Group.

11. Obviously, the struggle for peace and general disarmament must have a universal nature and serve not only the great powers. The processes of peace and disarmament must guarantee the security of everyone. *Informe central al I Congreso del Partido Comunista de Cuba* (Havana: Editora Política, 1976).

12. The Movement of Nonaligned Countries defines the national liberation struggle as a struggle against colonialism and for national political independence.

13. Fidel Castro, Interview with Maria Shriver, NBC News, *Granma*, Supplement, February 29, 1988.

14. Fidel Castro, Interview with Patricia Sethi, *Bohemia* (February 6, 1984); also interview with the EFE News Agency, February 13, 1985; see also, Manuel Piñeiro, "La crisis actual."

15. See RIAL, note 10.

16. Founding document of the Group of Eight: Acapulco Commitment to Peace, Development and Democracy (November 1987).

17. Fidel Castro, Letter to the Latin American Presidents participating in the Acapulco Agreement (November 1987).

18. Juan Valdés Paz, "Cuba y Centroamérica," *Cuadernos de Nuestra América*, No. 2 (1984).

19. Foreign Minister Isidoro Malmierca's Speech before the 42nd General Assembly of the United Nations, *Granma*, September 24, 1987.

20. Given their participation in drug traffic, this is the case of Bolivia, Colombia, Mexico, Belize, and Honduras; and because of U.S. foreign policy, these plus Nicaragua, Peru, Cuba, and others. *Idem.*

21. *Informe central al I Congreso del Partido Comunista de Cuba*, Chapter 11.

22. Some authors have seen in this opening a change in Latin America's perception of Cuba (Muñoz and Yopo) or a lessened concern about its influence (see Wiarda in Chapter 7 of this book), whereas Cuba has perceived a greater

independence of the region with respect to the United States and the recognition of Cuba's importance in the international and Latin American context.

23. Muñoz and Yopo, "Cuba y las democracias."
24. Fidel Castro, Interview with Maria Shriver, NBC News.
25. "However, international détente does not in any way mean that imperialism has lost its aggressive essence," *Informe central al I Congreso del Partido Comunista de Cuba*, Chapter 11.

9

U.S.-Cuban Economic Relations in the 1990s

Kenneth P. Jameson

Clearly, few instances can be found where economic relations are so "uneconomic" as those between the United States and Cuba. The countries are separated by the oft-noted ninety miles, yet for the most part, direct commercial contacts are banned, no commercial airline flights are scheduled, and direct financial relations are strictly limited. Interestingly, the one major exception has been in the "labor market," where the United States has been ready to allow Cuban migration at rates far higher than those of other Latin American countries because of the political implications. While devices have been found to evade the U.S. embargo of Cuba, direct relations are indeed minimal.

The absence of economic interchange has been reflected in the academic sphere as well. In the period during the 1970s when there was a move toward normalization of relations, efforts were made to sort out the economic implications of renewed relations in terms of the settlements of outstanding claims, the effect of Cuban access to the U.S. sugar quotas, and the effect of the embargo on the Cuban economy.[1] The cooling of relations froze treatment of these issues.[2]

Many of these same issues remain today, and will be an element in Cuban-U.S. relations in the 1990s. However, consideration of economic relations during the 1990s needs to put these matters aside and to accept two premises as points of departure.

The first is that the Cuban economy is clearly viable, even though currently it may be having difficulties and though it remains heavily dependent upon its negotiated arrangements with the eastern bloc's CMEA (Council for Mutual Economic Assistance).[3] It has shown growth, most notably in the period in the first half of the 1980s, when the other Latin countries were facing severe recessions; it has successfully mechanized most of the harvesting of its key export crop, sugar; and it has clearly provided for the basic needs of its population.[4] (Data supporting these assertions appear in Table 9.2.)

The second point of departure is that Cuba will continue to be a socialist economy, with substantial state control over the economy, predominantly social ownership of the means of production, and careful attention paid to equity. Nonetheless, as in most of the eastern-bloc economies today, continual experimentation occurs with the economic mechanisms. The change in Cuban economic policy that led to Cuba's "rectification" program predated the Soviet perestroika, and on the surface seems to have moved in the opposite direction. The free farm markets have been severely restricted, a strong push has been made toward agricultural cooperatives and away from private farms, and the initial program of incentive payments in enterprises has been greatly limited. Efforts to provide agricultural and industrial enterprises with greater latitude of decision while becoming more individually accountable are examples of countervailing tendencies. The constant is that the economy is and will remain socialist.

Therefore, any effort to understand the likely economic relations between Cuba and the United States in the 1990s must take as given a viable socialist economy in Cuba confronting a very different, viable, and capitalist U.S. economy. It also must start from the reality of current economic relations. Why are direct economic relations in 1988 virtually at a zero point? The reason is politics. For the United States there is probably no case in which politics so dominates economics, and is likely to continue to do so. Israel would be the closest parallel. My claim is that political factors dominate because economic factors are objectively secondary in U.S. Cuban relations and that, at least in the case of the United States, little is to be gained economically from better commercial relations with Cuba.[5] Much the same case could be made about Cuba, though the argument is more complex.

Primacy of Politics Over Economics in U.S.-Cuban Relations

In the United States, economics generally enjoys considerable autonomy from politics, and in many cases dominates politics. Even in the case of those implacable U.S. foes, China and the U.S.S.R., commercial gain has subtly subverted political stance. The close relations of Armand Hammer, and now of Donald

Kendall and other U.S. capitalists, with the Soviet Union show that possibilities for economic gain will lead to modifications, or at least nonenforcement, of political regulations on economic relations. The counter-examples, such as President Carter's restrictions on the sale of Caterpillar pipe-laying equipment to the Soviet Union and the political firestorm those restrictions unleashed, are further proof of the dynamism of economic relations when faced with political constraints.

So why are politics dominant in the case of Cuba? There are two appealing explanations. The first is that the political differences and enmity are so great as to submerge any mutual economic interest that might exist. The history of the relations is well known, and the basis for mutual suspicion and distrust cannot be denied. While not discounting this explanation, I would like to explore the other alternative: that there really is very little to be gained by the United States from better economic relations with Cuba, nor are Cuba's potential gains as significant as one might presume. This seems to me the better explanation and it has definite ramifications for future relations.

The case that no compelling basis exists for better economic relations has three elements. First, the economic disparity between Cuba and the United States implies that Cuba has at most a peripheral importance for the larger country in economic terms. Second, the proper economic context for viewing Cuba is as the most important Caribbean island country. This perspective reiterates the marginal importance of the Cuban economy to the United States; however, it also suggests that U.S.-Cuban economic relations in the 1990s may take on added importance, given the potential role that Cuba may play in the Caribbean. Finally, a realistic appraisal of the potential gains from better relations shows that there is little benefit for the United States as a whole, though individuals and specific businesses might reap gains; the direct gains for Cuba are similarly small.

Economic Disparities: The United States and Cuba

The U.S. economy is the largest in the world on most indicators of economic activity. Although its conventionally measured per capita GNP has fallen relatively with the dollar depreciation, it remains nearly the highest in the world. Cuba's status within the Caribbean is similar: Its economy is the largest and its per capita GNP is at or near the top. However, the Caribbean and the world scales are quite different, as shown in Table 9.1.

Table 9.1

Indicators of Relative Size of Cuba and the United States

	U.S.	Cuba
GNP (1980)	$2,732.00 billion	$11.95 billion*
Exports (1982)	$373.00 billion	$1.16 billion
Imports (1982)	$478.70 billion	$ .62 billion
GNP per capita (1980)	$12,035	$1,222
Population (1985)	239,000,000	10,100,000
Area (000 km sq.)	9,363	115

*See footnote 6 for a description of the exchange rate regime; the official exchange rate of $1.19 per peso was used in the conversions.

Sources: U.S.: *Economic Report of the President, 1988* (Washington: U.S. Government Printing Office, 1988). Cuba: Banco Nacional de Cuba, *Economic Report*, August 1982, as reprinted in Jack Hopkins, ed., *Latin America and Caribbean Contemporary Record, 1983-84* (New York: Holmes and Meier, 1985), pp. 1153-1204.

The disparities can be measured on the order of hundreds:[6] The United States has 770 times the imports, 320 times the exports, 230 times the GNP, and is 800 times the size of Cuba. Only in GNP per capita is the U.S. magnitude smaller—in this case, about 10:1. The magnitude of these differences gives some indication of why economic factors do not dominate the political. From the U.S. standpoint, Cuba's economic importance is small—at best, quite marginal. Thus, U.S. losses from interrupted economic relations with Cuba are small, as are the potential gains from their restoration.

The size of the U.S. economy would suggest large potential Cuban gains, for even though transportation costs have shrunk in importance in international economic relations, a newly opened market of the size and proximity of the United States should provide important opportunities. However, the minimal economic gains argument can also be made for Cuba. The size of the Cuban economy should allow it to obtain needed inputs and imports from a variety of sources without affecting their prices; and the evidence suggests that Cuba's exports are not demand constrained—supply factors limit them far more than demand. Cuba's exports should be able to enter the international marketplace and find buyers at the existing international prices.[7]

One exception is the sugar market, where Cuba does produce approximately 7 percent of world sugar. Even sugar may not be an exception, since Cuba has recently had difficulty fulfilling its sugar export agreements and has been forced to buy sugar in the international market. As recently as June 1988, Cuba upset international sugar markets by announcing it was canceling its shipments for two months because of flood damage to its port facilities. So, even in this case, the addition of a large U.S. market would have few direct economic benefits.[8]

The other possible exception is the labor market. Cuba's small size and U.S. political enmity has allowed Cuba to use the United States as an outlet for its disaffected population, with the most celebrated example the Mariel episode.[9] No other country has the possibility of such a massive emigration, except perhaps South Vietnam after 1975; it results from the abnormal relations between the two countries concerned. In Cuba's case, the migrations are aptly characterized as "politicized expressions of regional underdevelopment."[10] As the migration agreement, renewed in December 1987, comes into effect, the regularity and size of the migration flow should increase. A normal emigration quota, plus a family reunification procedure, should bring emigration to well above 20,000 persons per year. Such flows will have little effect on the U.S. labor market, though they may alleviate Cuba's tendency toward the underemployment found in many socialist countries.

A whole range of other disparities arises between the United States and Cuba. The structure of the U.S. economy is quite different in its capacity to generate its own technology and to produce its own capital goods. The service sector has attained a much higher level of development and of technical sophistication. At the same time, the United States produces many of the same goods as Cuba. For example, in 1985-86, Cuba produced 7.1 million tons of sugar, while the United States produced 5.6 million tons. In 1984, Cuba produced 302 million cigars, compared with the United States' 3.7 billion. Cuba's 1984 production of nickel was, however, substantially higher—reaching 35,100 tons, compared with the U.S. production of 14,500 tons.[11]

The development of the financial and service sectors is another area of substantial difference. The United States has been and continues to be the financial center of the capitalist West, and its banking and finance system is highly developed, highly integrated, and very active, for good or ill. Similarly, the shift to information-based services and consumer services has been notable in recent years, and has accounted for much of the job creation since 1980. Cuban advances in these areas are much fewer, with tourism exhibiting the most activity. This in part is because of the ambiguous role of such services in socialist economic thinking, where they are generally seen as nonproductive and, in many cases, do not even enter the accounting of Global Social Product. Thus, the possible relations in this area (e.g., Cuban provision of data input services to financial corporations) are unlikely to be accepted by the Cuban government.

The list could continue, but the basic claim would hold in each case. There has been no major pressure to remove the embargo and no significant evasion because Cuba is economically marginal to the United States in terms of both size and structure. The United States is economically peripheral in importance to Cuba because of the nature of its needs, and because Cuba can develop the same type of economic relations with many other countries (e.g., Canada, Mexico, Europe, or Japan).[12] Thus political factors naturally are primary in the relation of Cuba and the United States, dominating economic factors.

The case would be overstated, however, if one other dimension were not specifically noted. For, although the bilateral relation of the U.S. and Cuban economies may be marginal, Cuba's actual and potential role in the Caribbean may serve to enhance that country's economic significance, especially if one looks ahead to the 1990s. At this point it is important to situate Cuba within the Caribbean, noting its relative economic predominance.

Cuba in the Caribbean

Table 9.2 underlines Cuba's predominance among the Caribbean nations. On all measures, size, growth, or per capita income, Cuba stands out as the most important of the Caribbean economies.[13]

Table 9.2

Cuba in the Caribbean

	Haiti	Dominican Republic	Jamaica	Trinidad & Tobago	Cuba
Population (million)	5.9	6.4	2.2	1.2	10.1
Area (1,000 km^2)	28	49	11	5	115
GNP/ capita	$310	$790	$940	$6,020	$1,222
GNP Growth (1965-1985)	.7%	2.9%	-.7%	2.3%	5.7%*
Life Expectancy	54	64	73	69	73
Primary Enrollment**	76	112	106	96	106
Population/ Doctor	820	1,400	2,700	1,500	720
Daily Calories	1,855	2,461	2,585	3,006	3,122
Infant Mortality	123	70	20	22	16

* (1970-1980)
** (Ratio of pupils to the population of school-age children)

Sources: Cuba: See Table 9.1 and social indicators as below. Other countries: IBRD, *World Development Report, 1987* (New York: Oxford University Press, 1987)

The magnitudes of difference are not as great as in the Cuba-U.S. comparison, but Cuba's dominance is quite apparent. If other indicators, such as literacy or health care, were used, the same pattern would appear.

It is important to note that every piece of data on Cuba is hotly disputed, though the conclusions of this section should be quite robust. The debate on GNP growth rates has been the most active, but the differences have narrowed substantially: There is a consensus that the Cuban economy did not grow in the 1960s, grew rapidly in the early 1970s, and more slowly in the late 1970s. The economy was in recession in 1979-80 and recovered in the early 1980s, only to slow in later years. The debate is about the growth rates in each subperiod, but its resolution does not affect the claims in this paper.

One way of viewing the Cuban economy, then, is as an important success story in the development of a small, island economy. Despite major dislocations at the time of the revolution and then the subsequent political and economic conflict with the United States, Cuba has been able to maintain its position and performance at the top of the Caribbean group, despite the disadvantages of the small island economy (e.g., absence of scale economies and the minimal development of economic linkages that characterize larger economies, even those with the same level of per capita GNP as Cuba). One contributor to Cuban performance has been Soviet support, accepted by all sides of the Cubanist debate as significant. But Cuban performance cannot be dismissed as simply a result of this aid.

In examining Cuba's relative position in the Caribbean, Kalecki's construct of the "intermediate regime" is useful to characterize the other Caribbean economies and their comparison with Cuba.[14] Kalecki suggests that any viable economic policy in intermediate regimes (intermediate between capitalism and socialism), such as those of the Caribbean, is predicated upon the need to build and maintain a base of support among the lower-middle class, while attacking the upper-middle class and avoiding alienation of the lower class. The key mechanisms in this effort are three: change in the pattern of ownership; structural transformation of the economy; and provision of basic human needs.

On the first of these, Jamaica made tentative efforts in areas such as bauxite, which are now being reversed, and Guyana made a number of statist changes as a means of ethnic control. However, Cuba has moved farthest in changing the pattern of ownership, initially with its expropriation of foreign assets and then through its extensive agrarian reform. Since 1980, Cuba has continued its movement away from private ownership to state or social ownership and control, though the rectification campaign shows that the efficiency costs of breaking the mold of the intermediate regime cannot be overlooked. Nonetheless, Cuba's policy toward ownership differentiates its pattern from that of the other countries.

In the case of the structural transformation of the economy, primarily through industrialization,[15] the results in Cuba have been mixed, reflecting the limitations of an island economy in moving beyond an intermediate regime. On the positive side, Zimbalist's[16] examination of the various estimates for Cuban industrial growth rates concludes that the best estimate is a 1965-1980 annual growth rate of 6.3 percent--"very healthy, if not impressive." Brundenius[17] estimated even higher growth rates in engineering goods industries (roughly the capital goods industry): an average annual growth rate of 10.3 percent from 1976 to 1980 and 15.6 percent from 1981 to 1985. While these may be optimistic estimates, the significant accomplishments of the Cuban economy in developing capital goods for agriculture are carefully documented by Edquist.[18] The contrast between Cuba's ability to develop designs and some production of harvesting equipment and Jamaica's almost complete reliance on international sources is striking, and it favors Cuba as the most successful Caribbean economy in this area.

However, the limitations of Cuban industrialization should also be noted, reflecting the constraints of a small island economy. Measures of the sectoral share of industry do not indicate a notable transformation in the structure of the economy since the revolution. Other indicators, such as the shares of the labor force in various sectors, Cuba's trade dependence, trade concentration, and export composition, similarly show a modest transformation. Much of the initial impetus for industrial growth was the imperative of a war economy and the need to substitute for imports that were no longer available. The limitations of such steps are clearest in the minor role that manufactured exports play in Cuban trade. So, results must be deemed mixed.

The other mechanism for dealing with the intermediate regime problem is through the provision of basic human needs to a much broader segment of the population, thus building support as well as fulfilling aspirations more widely. In this case (Table 9.2) Cuba has generally attained a higher degree of success on the measured indicators, such as life expectancy, infant mortality, available calories, and school enrollment rates. Indeed, the Cuban advantage has grown during the 1980s as the others have suffered much more severe downturns, reflecting the general international disorder of the capitalist system.[19]

So a comparison of Cuba with other Caribbean countries shows its accomplishments as well as its limitations. It is the largest, most successful of all of those economies, and it has moved farthest from the intermediate regime status that afflicts all such economies, most directly through changing the ownership structure in the economy, and most successfully in providing for the widespread basic needs of its population. However, the reality of the small island economy continues to place real limitations on its development.

Considering Cuba as a Caribbean economy adds two dimensions to the argument for the primacy of politics over economics in U.S.-Cuban relations. On one hand, it emphasizes the real and binding economic constraints on the directions and accomplishments available to the Cuban economy. So politics should dominate, for it could provide the resources that would allow some relaxation of the economic constraints.

On the other hand, viewing Cuba as a Caribbean nation emphasizes its real accomplishments and its potential predominance in the area. Its size and dynamism, as well as its relative success in transforming the economy, set it apart. So, the economic importance of Cuba for the United States rests much more on its importance within the Caribbean than on any bilateral relation. This is particularly true if we look ahead to the 1990s.

Let us assess the gains that might come from a renewal of normal relations between the United States and Cuba. Again, the case will be made that these gains are not strong enough to force a change in political relations; they are subsidiary.

Economic Gains from Normalization of Relations

Were relations to be normalized, there would clearly be some gains, but they would most likely be quite small and might come from somewhat surprising directions. This case must be made taking as a given the current political economy of the western hemisphere and examining the pure "economic" gains that could be had through normalization. More pertinent, finally, to Cuban-U.S. economic relations in the 1990s is what the gains would be in a world economy that evolved beyond its present form in the next decade, and how Cuba and the United States might fit into that evolution.

Under such circumstances, economic relations between the two nations might take on greater importance. Before dealing with these issues, let us examine the likely gains under present economic circumstances.

The global gains for the United States would be small, especially in the trade area. Cuba is and will be a high-cost supplier of products simply because it is a relatively high-income area, and so its wage costs will remain high relative to those of Haiti, Central America, or Mexico. The exception might be Cuba's main export crops. However, the international sugar market is in surplus, and access to Cuba's production would have no effect on the United States, whose policy is to maintain a high support price for its own domestic producers, and to support its friends among the sugar producers. Even this latter effort diminished under the Reagan administration, which reduced the sugar quotas to the lowest level since 1975. This reduction has lowered the Latin American and Caribbean revenues from sugar sales to the United States by almost 90 percent over the last six years.[20] Nickel is also in oversupply, and the citrus crops that Cuba produces are deemed of inferior quality. In any case, the tremendous growth of the Brazilian citrus industry indicates that willing suppliers to the United States, at prices more favorable than those of domestic producers, are not scarce. Cuban tobacco may be an exception, but competition from new suppliers is significant, and Cuban tobacco sales—even to traditional demanders—are no longer assured.

There would be few global gains for U.S. exports, because Cuba's trade is highly constricted and controlled, and because convertible exchange constraints prevent its already small market from playing a role of any significance in U.S. exports. In addition, Cuba is probably able to purchase the goods it wants from other suppliers, from U.S. subsidiaries, or through dummy corporations.

What might the United States gain from normalization of relations? Paradoxically, the effect of normalization on the resources provided to subsidize stability in the Caribbean might be the most significant. The Caribbean Basin Initiative, the allocation of sugar quotas, and the foreign assistance program are designed to maintain stability and friendship in the area and to counter Cuban and other insurgent influences. Normalization could remove some of the pressures that generate these revenues, minuscule though they be, and could free them for other uses. More importantly, it might allow their reorientation toward development efforts that would be more successful than has been the case. Another indirect and minor gain would come by freeing the resources dedicated to monitoring the Cuban-American community and to encouraging their continued opposition to the Cuban regime. Were a true normalization to take place, these resource expenditures could diminish, and a more natural involvement of the Cuban-American community with Cuba might occur.

The payment of indemnifications for expropriated U.S. property has received much interest and treatment. Claims allowed by the Foreign Claims Settlement Commission totaled $1.8 billion, with $267 million to the Cuban Electric Company and $130 million to International Telephone and Telegraph the largest amounts involved.[21] But such private gains would have little effect on the overall U.S. economy, and the actual amount of payment would certainly be far less than the amounts claimed.[22]

This situation raises the important question of whether individuals or specific corporations might reap benefits from the normalization of relations. The answer is surely yes, for any increase in economic relations would provide opportunities for some producers or some economic agents.[23] When the U.S. Treasury issued licenses for subsidiary exports to Cuba between August 1975 and the end of 1976, their value totaled $345 million, around $200 million of which was for grains. Some 94 products were involved.[24] While one need not share the 1977 optimism of Business International that "Cuba is emerging as a land of new trade and investment opportunities for international companies,"[25] activity in many areas would surely increase, as they correctly noted. However, it would not be very important for any major sector of U.S. business; thus, the political situation is unlikely to be moved by these economic issues. So, the search for possible economic gains from the normalization of relations finds little advantage for the United States.

On the Cuban side, the potential for gain may be larger, but is likely to be offset by losses. One benefit to Cuba would be the cessation of the trade embargo. The Banco Nacional de Cuba estimated the capital costs of the embargo at $9.1 billion, with the main costs in trade disruption ($5.2 billion) and national defense ($2.9 billion).[26] But these costs, which have been paid, are not relevant because they are not recoverable, unless taken as an offset to the U.S. claims for expropriated property, as Cuba would certainly demand. Costs of inefficiency continue because Cuba cannot select U.S. suppliers or purchasers. However, the diminished U.S. role in international trade indicates that Cuba could find other suppliers and other markets for most goods, and so Cuba's benefits might be small.

Perhaps the largest potential gain would be access to U.S. tourist dollars. In 1982, 100,340 tourists visited Cuba, 28 percent from Canada, 18 percent from Europe, and 24 percent from the socialist countries.[27] Rapid growth has continued in more recent years, with an estimated 250,000 tourist entries in 1987. Although there may be short-run supply constraints, the added convertible foreign exchange earnings would increase Cuba's economic possibilities.

Inclusion in the Caribbean Basin Initiative (CBI), which has provided a series of facilities to Caribbean nations, such as better access to the U.S. market and aid flows, would also be of benefit to Cuba were that part of normalization. However, most analyses of the CBI have found the benefits to participation to be minor.[28]

In addition, Cuban gains might well be offset by losses. Any normalization of relations with the United States is likely to be predicated upon, or to encourage, a reduction in Soviet assistance to Cuba, which has been variously estimated at $3 million to $5 million per day. Because some of the gains to Cuba might be offset, it is not clear that Cuba would come out a winner from the normalization.

Thus, once again the available information suggests that, in general, the gains to Cuba from a normalization of relations would not be large enough to override more purely political factors. As we have seen, this statement is even more true for the United States.

Conclusions

We can conclude that politics has dominated, and indeed should be expected to continue to dominate, U.S.-Cuban economic relations. The economies are vastly different, and even though Cuba is an important Caribbean economy, it has little to offer the United States. Similarly, from a purely economic perspective, the gains to Cuba from normalized economic relations do not seem great.

This conclusion allows us to turn to a political-economic understanding of potential developments in the 1990s which could influence U.S.-Cuban relations.

Cuba and the United States in the World Economy of the 1990s

Little in the economies of the two countries drives them to greater relations today, but what are the likely outlines of Cuban-U.S.

economic relations in the 1990s? The starting point: The evolution of their economic relations will be largely determined by the nature of the world economy in the 1990s. Therefore, it is necessary to understand how the world economy will evolve in the next decade. This treatment must be somewhat speculative, but from previous work I think that some tendencies are clear and suggest a probable evolution of the world economy of the 1990s.[29]

In outline, the argument is that the United States is in the process of reestablishing its economic dominance or hegemony in the Western hemisphere, relying on financial mechanisms to create a type of "dollar bloc," which has its domestic counterpart in the Latin American countries' dollarization.[30] This dollarization is an adjustment to the reality of Japanese and European challenges to the United States elsewhere in the world. It corresponds to an implicit agreement on how the world economy will be controlled after the Pax Americana, and after the disruptions of the 1980s have made it clear that the free-market and free-trade approach is incapable of providing a stable and prosperous world economy in all regions. In the 1990s, U.S. adjustment to challenges to its worldwide economic control will be an attempt to exert ever-greater economic sway over the Latin American countries, recreating a dependency that seemed to disappear during the 1970s. The basis for this reassertion of U.S. power is the growing autonomy of the Pacific under the leadership of Japan and of China, and the virtual disappearance of Africa from the world economic scene, as the African economies decline and turn inward.[31] Europe will exert increasing influence in Africa, while Japan and China will exercise dominance in Asia. The mechanisms have been put in place by the internationalization of capital markets and by the extent of dollarization throughout Latin America, with Cuba the major exception.[32]

Two points emerge with particular importance for economic relations between Cuba and the United States. First, the stability and prosperity of the western hemisphere will become much more important to the U.S. economy. After World War II, when the world was the U.S. oyster, one particular region had little more importance than another. But in the 1990s, the performance of the western hemisphere will grow in importance for the United States, whose own prosperity will depend more on the other countries of the area. Secondly, the mechanism or regime that will organize this system will be financial, in this case an informal dollar bloc, which will stand against the yen bloc and the EMS (European Monetary System) bloc. In this western-hemisphere bloc, Cuba will play a special role for several reasons: its predominance in the Caribbean, its development within a socialist context, and its relationship with the CMEA.

Thus, a western hemisphere might evolve that has two foci: one would be the traditional U.S. dominance which will play a central role in the financial sphere and in much of the area's trade. The second focal point would be a Cuban-led Caribbean, able to participate partially in the dollar bloc but with a wider range of options reflecting Cuba's uniqueness. So, the 1990s might well see a very dynamic and positive period of Cuban-U.S. economic relations, even in the absence of major and extensive economic relations between the United States and Cuba. Let us turn now to specific consideration of these developments.

The Outlines of U.S. Hegemony in the 1990s

The basis for restoring U.S. hegemony is the widespread dollarization in Latin America. Broadly defined, dollarization is the decision by citizens of other countries to hold or to use U.S. dollars, or assets denominated in U.S. dollars, such as bank accounts, Treasury bills, bonds, or securities. The practice of holding dollars inside and outside of the home country has grown rapidly, beginning with the recycling of petrodollars through the international financial system. The World Bank estimated that for the 1974-1982 period the citizens of Argentina, Mexico, and Venezuela chose to increase their overseas assets by between $59 and $76 billion.[33] Also, dollars have taken on a series of new and unaccustomed roles in many countries that allow private dollar-denominated deposits in their banking system. Such deposits have grown rapidly in some cases. For example, in Peru, these dollar accounts reached 73.7 percent of the total time deposits in the banking system in 1984.

Especially since early 1988, Panama shows that the dollarized economy is dependent on the United States and can have its development greatly affected by that relation. Even in countries that have undergone a much less extensive dollarization, the effects are quite substantial, generally leading to a loss of policy control by authorities of the country. There are four main effects: loss of control of the domestic money supply; loss of control of exchange rate policy; loss of seigniorage, the increase in government resources from minting or printing the domestic currency; and limits on the effectiveness of capital controls. These four effects of dollarization make domestic economic policy much more difficult and much less effective. The reality of dollarization will be a central element in restructuring the economic relations of the western hemisphere during the 1990s.

With dollarization, the United States has laid the base for development of a new currency bloc, much along the lines of the British and French currency blocs of previous years. Control of dollar emission gives the United States basic control over the financial situation of the hemisphere and, therefore, substantial influence over the economic policies of dollarized economies. The system operates much less formally than other currency blocs such as the franc bloc, and it does not entail their reciprocal obligations. The United States has taken very little responsibility for ensuring the stability and prosperity of the Latin countries under its sway. To this point the system has encouraged instability and has not forced upon the United States the role of disciplinarian, either of its own behavior or that of other countries. Similarly, there were no obligations placed directly on the United States to develop a coherent policy that would take the Latin countries into account, nor to make domestic adjustments to facilitate this. So, the bloc has not performed in a positive manner for the Latin countries, especially in the difficult times of the 1980s.

Nonetheless, many efforts are underway to redefine the rules of participation in the dollar area, from the unilateral and ineffective decision of the Alan García government of Peru to limit interest payments to 10 percent of export proceeds, to Brazil's February 1987 moratorium on interest payments on its bank debt. The latter step forced the U.S. banks to begin to shoulder some of the costs of keeping the bloc in operation, in this case by setting aside massive loan loss reserves of over $17 billion, which generated accounting losses of over $7 billion during the second quarter of 1987.

Therefore, we are currently in a period that is redefining the dollar bloc. On one side is an increased assertiveness of the Latin American countries who are seeking--and increasingly finding-- new mechanisms that can force on the United States and its banks greater portions of the costs of keeping the dollar bloc functioning, and that can restore their control over domestic economic policy.[34]

Changes are also being encouraged from the U.S. side, reflecting a greater willingness to deal with the imbalances with Asia and Latin America. These changes will come about partially because U.S. prosperity is more closely linked to the prosperity of Latin America, and adjustments must be made toward greater economic coordination so that stable growth returns to Latin America. The key will be a gradual working down of the debt overhang and a gradual stabilization of the financial system within a context of greater capital controls. The Brady Plan for dealing with the debt is a first step in the evolution of new relations in this arena. The United States will be forced to take the role of the positive hegemon, a role that even the Cubans feel could be acceptable.

Cuba and the Caribbean in the 1990s

The next important issue is the role of Cuba during the 1990s. In the first place, Cuba will have to deal with its debt drain in order to avoid being drawn into the dollar bloc. Presumably, this action would be through political resolution of the debt problem with the hard-currency bloc, or perhaps through long-term agreements for commodity exchanges, such as Cuba has with the Soviet Union. My presumption continues that there is no strong basis for better U.S.-Cuban economic relations and it is doubtful that Cuba could enlist the United States in any effort to solve its debt problem.[35]

Cuba's presence as an alternative to the dollar bloc may be the most important element, for three main reasons. First, it is the least dollarized of the western-hemisphere countries.[36] As a result, Cuba will be in a unique position to provide an alternative to the dollar bloc, to develop economic relations with other Caribbean countries that take place outside of the dollar channels. The Cubans already have a wealth of experience with compensation balance trading, most with the CMEA, but also with countries as diverse as Brazil and Trinidad-Tobago.[37]

Secondly, as noted above, Cuba has developed into the predominant Caribbean economy in terms of its industry, its human resources, and its satisfaction of basic human needs, even abstracting from the economic accomplishments of Cuban-Americans. To the extent that Cuban industry continues to grow and the capital goods industry is successful in developing machinery appropriate for these intermediate regimes, it could become a very dynamic relationship with wide implications. It has the potential to contribute to the development of countries that are dollar-constrained through its industrial base, its capital-goods industry, and its educational and health acumen.

Finally, Cuba has a unique and integral relation with the Eastern bloc, and will be integrated more closely into its economic program in coming years. If the CMEA can overcome its stagnation problems to become a dynamic force, the Cuban economy will receive a growth impulse that can again enhance its situation in the Caribbean.

If regularization of relations between Cuba and other Caribbean countries continued, and if the United States reduced its interference in Cuba's international economic relations, Cuba might indeed be able to develop a number of reciprocal economic relations with other Caribbean countries that would take place outside the dollar bloc, perhaps on a barter basis; and these might in turn be beneficial to both sides, helping them escape the strictures of the dollar bloc. These relations would be stronger and more beneficial to all concerned the more advanced Cuban industrial and capital goods production becomes; therefore the benefits of commercial interchange would increase. In a very real sense, this situation could provide the true measure of Cuba's industrial transformation, and reveal whether it has moved beyond the stage of an "intermediate regime." The actual possibilities must be left speculative at this point, though a more detailed analysis of Cuba's production as compared with Caribbean production would provide insight into these possibilities.

Under this optimistic scenario, Cuba would play a very important role during the 1990s in the Caribbean, not through its direct U.S. relations, but as an example of an alternative mode of organizing economic interchange. Such a development is likely to be beneficial in several dimensions, not the least of which is the pressure it would put on the United States to shoulder its responsibilities for the operation of the dollar area and for ensuring the prosperity of the whole area. In this way, Cuba's dominance in the Caribbean would multiply its economic importance to the United States and could force a reorientation of bilateral economic relations as a result.

Cuban-Americans: What Role?

Just as Cuban-Americans have played a central role in maintaining the political enmity between the United States and Cuba, they will have a major influence on any developments during the 1990s. In my mind, the most likely scenario sees that enmity continuing, with the two different foci in the Caribbean more important than the link between the United States and Cuba. However, notable changes are certainly conceivable.

For example, Cuban-Americans are clearly well placed to benefit and participate in any increase in economic relations between the two countries. The language, the knowledge of the country, and the set of contacts all provide them with an advantage that could be exploited to their benefit. Even with the low level of contact that currently exists, there are ample examples of the gains to some Cuban-Americans from greater contacts.[38]

A more optimistic scenario takes into account the unique position of the Cubans vis a vis the U.S. economy. They are vibrant and important participants in the U.S. economy, with growing links throughout that economy. They could be seen as a sort of Latin American beachhead on the North American continent, in much the same way that Hong Kong was mainland China's beachhead in the Western capitalist economies. It is conceivable that the Cuban-Americans could play the same role of facilitators of trade and financial relations, and eventually of brokers for ever-larger and more important economic contacts as a process of mutual adjustment takes place. This scenario would certainly result in the highest level of economic relations between the two countries, though its occurrence will remain dependent on political factors.

Summary

Cuban-U.S. economic relations in the 1990s are likely to remain subsidiary to political relations. No overwhelming economic logic from either side demands improved economic relations. Yet, the reality of Cuba's prominence in the Caribbean opens an avenue for developments during the 1990s. I see that decade dominated in the western hemisphere by a dollar bloc under U.S. guidance and control, not clearly to the benefit of the Latin American countries. Adjustments may occur in a positive direction, which may be accelerated by a growing Cuban role as the center of a Caribbean non-dollar-bloc where commercial relations take place outside the constraints of the dollar bloc, to the mutual benefit of the countries involved.

I suspect that U.S.-Cuban economic relations will gradually increase, but always in the context of their competition for place in the Caribbean. In a very real sense, Cuba has the luxury of gradually defining a relationship with the United States that takes Cuban interests as its starting point, a unique possibility in Latin America. Joan Robinson once said that the only thing worse than being colonized was not to have been colonized. We might paraphrase her: The only thing better than being independent of the United States, as Cuba has been, is to be able to compromise that independence on your own terms.

Notes

1. See the materials included in *U.S. Trade Embargo of Cuba*, Hearings of Committee on International Relations, House of Representatives (Washington, D.C.: GPO, 1975).
2. In recent years the economic issue that has occupied the U.S. Cubanists has been the performance of the Cuban economy at the macro level in agriculture, industry, and planning. Skeptics such as Jorge Domínguez and Carmelo Mesa-Lago have published widely and a collection of critical articles appeared in the *Caribbean Review* in 1986 (Vol. 15, No. 2). The proponents have been led by Andrew Zimbalist and Claes Brundenius, who had their most extensive forum in *World Development*, 15, 1 (January 1987).
3. See Richard Turits, "Trade, Debt, and the Cuban Economy," *World Development*, 15, 1 (January 1987), pp. 163-180, for a treatment of these relations, and their effect on the Cuban economy and its ability to mitigate the austerity pressures on Latin America. According to our interview with Vice President of the Council of Ministers, Carlos Rafael Rodríguez, Cuba has recently signed the agreements that will govern these relations over the next fifteen years and will ensure Cuba's coordination with the CMEA.
4. At the meetings of the Latin American Studies Association (March 1988), Claes Brundenius presented initial results of a comparison with Taiwan in which Cuba compared quite favorably in all areas except export growth. This is certainly a far more positive view than that implied by the data of Table 9.2, though they cast Cuban performance in a relatively positive light.
5. Some individual businesses and even some industries in the United States would benefit from better relations with Cuba, as will be noted below. However, their influence in setting overall U.S. policy toward Cuba is far less at this point than the interests that oppose improvements.
6. Of course, the magnitudes are very rough because of the difference in exchange rates. The peso was fixed at 1.19 per dollar during the period of the Table; however, other evidence indicates that a free rate would be higher. The street rate in Cuba is perhaps five to ten pesos per dollar. It is a very thin and imperfect market, however; a better

market would probably generate a rate between one and five pesos per dollar and most likely closer to one than five.

7. There are, however, some *political* constraints on Cuban exports and imports derived from U.S. embargo policies that affect Cuban trade with other countries. For example, shippers charge higher insurance rates. And Western European steel producers cannot export to the United States steel that uses Cuban nickel, with the result that they obtain their nickel from other sources.

8. If Cuban sugar sold in the United States at the artificially high price that results from the quota system, there would be added economic benefit. However, this is a highly unlikely occurrence.

9. This has been a two-edged sword because the initial Cuban emigrations took large segments of the professionally trained population, and the Mariel episode may have taken segments of skilled labor that Cuba could ill afford.

10. Robert L. Bach, "Socialist Construction and Cuban Emigration: Explorations into Mariel," *Cuban Studies*, 15, 2 (Summer 1985), pp. 18-36, makes a convincing case for internally generated pressures for emigration. Other articles on the same issue deal with the experience of the migrants in the United States.

11. The sole remaining U.S. nickel mine was closed for an indefinite period in August 1986. See *Commodity Yearbook, 1987* (New York: Commodity Research Bureau, 1987), p. 163 and p. 251.

12. It should be noted that this was much less the case in the early years of the embargo, when U.S. sanctions made Cuban access to spare parts very difficult, and countries were much less ready to resist U.S. pressure to support the embargo.

13. The exception, the per capita GNP of Trinidad-Tobago, is a result of its oil production, which is currently declining, and therefore proves the rule. The proper comparison would be in terms of "purchasing power parity," the average income expressed in terms of its command over actual goods and services. No such estimates are available for Cuba, however. In general, socialist countries' purchasing power parity is higher relatively than their per capita income.

14. Much of this section draws on Kenneth P. Jameson, "Socialist Cuba and the Intermediate Regimes of Jamaica

and Guyana," *World Development*, 9, 9/10 (September/October 1981), pp. 871-888.

15.   The centrality of industrialization was emphasized by T. Skouras, "The 'Intermediate Regime' and Industrialization Projects," *Development and Change* 9 (1978), pp. 631-648, and more recently has been central to the "Cambridge model of development." See, for example, Ajit Singh, "The Interrupted Industrial Revolution of the Third World: Prospects and Policies for Resumption," *Industry and Development*, 12 (1984), pp. 43-68, or Francis Cripps and Wynne Godley, "A Formal Analysis of the Cambridge Economic Policy Group's Model," *Economica* (November 1976), pp. 335-348.

16.   Andrew Zimbalist, "Cuban Industrial Growth, 1965-84," *World Development*, 15, 1 (January 1987), pp 83-93.

17.   Claes Brundenius, "Development and Prospects of Capital Goods Production in Revolutionary Cuba," *World Development*, 15, 1 (January 1987), pp. 95-112.

18.   Charles Edquist, *Capitalism, Socialism and Technology: A Comparative Study of Cuba and Jamaica* (London: Zed, 1985).

19.   It would be useful to update this information and the comparisons. However, comparable information has been much more difficult to obtain in recent years because the international agencies have little access to Cuban statistics for a reliable comparison. A variety of critiques of the Cuban statistics have been made, though Cuba's performance would have to be measured as quite good, even if the critiques were accepted.

20.   "New Blow from U.S. Sugar Quota Cuts," *Latin American Weekly Report* (March 3, 1988).

21.   Estimates are from Table 1 of Arthur Downey, "United States Commercial Relations with Cuba: A Survey," Appendix VI in *U.S. Trade Embargo on Cuba*, Hearings in the House of Representatives (Washington, D.C.: GPO, 1975).

22.   Susan Fernández, "The Sanctity of Property: American Responses to Cuban Expropriations, 1959-1984," *Cuban Studies* 14 No. 2 (Summer 1984), pp. 21-34, provides extensive background on the issue and reaches the conclusion that compensation for expropriation has not been an important issue, especially since tax credits already transferred much of the cost to the U.S. taxpayer.

23. Even the small openings that have occurred to date have benefited some, such as those involved in making the travel arrangements. In addition, the Cubans mention that they frequently receive letters from firms asking to be remembered if relations are ever renewed.

24. See Business International, *Cuba at the Turning Point* (New York: Business International Corporation, 1977).

25. *Ibid.*, p. i.

26. Cuba, Banco Nacional de Cuba, *Economic Report*, August 1982, as reprinted in Jack Hopkins, ed., *Latin America and Caribbean Contemporary Record, 1983-84* (New York: Holmes and Meier, 1985), pp. 1153-1204. Casanova and Monreal (Chapter 10) extrapolate the amount to $11.5 billion by 1987.

27. *Caribbean Tourism Statistical Report, 1986* (Caribbean Tourism Research and Development Centre, 1986), p. 79.

28. Clayton Yeutter reported that after two years of operations, Caribbean exports to the United States had fallen by 23 percent, though, if petroleum exports were removed from the data, there would have been an increase of 11.3 percent. See "Review of the Impact and Effectiveness of the Caribbean Basin Initiative," Hearings in the House of Representatives (Washington, D.C.: GPO, 1986). Joseph Pelzman and Gregory Schoepfle, "The Impact of the Caribbean Basin Economic Recovery Act on Caribbean Nations' Exports and Development," *Economic Development and Cultural Change*, 36, 4 (July 1988), pp. 759-796, find very small effects from the trade preferences and suggest that a program to encourage U.S. manufacturing investment and human resource development in the area would have more positive effects on development. In actual fact, much of the funding has gone for security assistance to the Central American countries supported by the United States, which should explain the summary U.S. rejection of the Mexican suggestion that Cuba be included in the Caribbean Basin program. A similar conclusion is reached by Gerardo González, "La Inciativa para la Cuenca del Caribe en República Dominicana," *Cuadernos de Nuestra América*, 3, 6 (July-December 1986), pp. 99-136.

29. The whole framework is developed most extensively in my "Latin America in the 1980s: A New Dollar Bloc?" Working Paper #102, The Helen Kellogg Institute of International Studies (January 1988). Specific treatment of the

dollarization of Latin America is contained in a manuscript, "The Dollarization of Latin America" (December 1987), and a specific case study of the effect of dollarization is presented in "Macro Policy in a Dollarized Economy: The Experience of Bolivia," Working Paper #89, The Helen Kellogg Institute of International Studies (December 1986).

30. This analysis differs somewhat from the treatment of María C. Tavares, "The Revival of American Hegemony," *CEPAL Review*, 26 (August 1985), pp. 139-146. She argues that the United States, through financial mechanisms, has succeeded in restoring international hegemony over Japan and Europe. My view is that a far higher degree of international parity exists, and that hegemony will be partial for any one of the three.

31. The increasing efforts to control international trade, misleadingly lumped under the term "protectionism," will lead to a reorientation of trade toward "intra-bloc" exchange.

32. The U.S. pressure on the Noriega regime in Panama was possible because of the particularly extreme form of dollarization that Panama exhibits. The degree to which the United States could affect other Latin American countries is much less, though the same mechanisms are available. Ironically, the actions taken in Panama may be damaging to the reassertion of U.S. authority because they are so obvious—and they have been ineffective.

33. Mohin Khan and Nadeem ul Haq, "Capital Flight from Developing Countries," *Finance and Development*, 24, 1 (March 1987), pp. 2-5.

34. This has led to increasing tension between the U.S. banks and their government, since the banks want these costs borne by the government. Their current goal is for the government to guarantee a portion of any new loans to Latin nations. Thus they are balking at participating in the concessions envisioned in the Brady Plan. The Cubans see these problems increasing as movement toward greater Latin American unity continues, as the *concertación* becomes a reality through the Cartagena group, the Group of Eight, and the Contadora group.

35. One mechanism that would help in this regard would be an increase in remittances from Cuban-Americans; but this again is a very political question not dealt with here.

36. The major exception to this is the Cuban hard currency debt, which transmits a dollar scarcity to the economy and

which forces it to seek dollars. On the other hand, the extensive use of dollars in other Latin American countries has not occurred in Cuba. Nonetheless, how Cuba deals with its hard currency debt will affect how it relates to the dollar bloc.

37. Silvia Rodríguez, "Utilización en Cuba de las nuevas formas de comercio y colaboración con América Latina: Dificultades existentes y líneas a seguir," *Temas de economía mundial: Revista del CIEM* 20 (1987), pp. 59-98.

38. The Cuban-Americans are very different from other U.S. Hispanic groups in terms of their education, their demographics, and their income, and a number of these elements would also position them well for an active participation in any increase in economic relations. See the articles on Cubans in the United States in *Cuban Studies*, 15, 2 (Summer 1985).

10

Cuba and the United States: The Potential of Their Economic Relations

Alfonso Casanova Montero
and Pedro Monreal González

> Commerce is like a tree which grows
> wherever there is peace, as soon as there
> is peace, and so long as there is peace.
>
> —Ralph Waldo Emerson

Since the end of the past century up to 1960, Cuba's relations with the United States were characterized by an extreme economic and political dependence. For more than half a century, the activity of U.S. business and its local allies decided the evolution of Cuban society. The former Spanish colony became a U.S. neocolony.

U.S. business controlled strategic sectors of Cuba's economy, the structure and growth rate of which were subordinate to U.S. interests. As a result, trade relations between Cuba and the United States conformed to the typical model of neocolonial exchange. Cuba offered easy access—thanks to a favorable tariffs code—to U.S. agricultural and industrial products, and, in turn, obtained a guarantee—subject to change at U.S. discretion—to export limited quantities of sugar to the U.S. market. This dependent relationship prevented, rather effectively, any attempt to diversify the Cuban economy, and perpetuated the role of Cuba as producer and exporter of only one product.

The United States was a trade "partner" that decided, unilaterally, the volume and the price of Cuban exports, and controlled Cuba's internal market; hence, the chronic deficit in Cuba's balance of trade with the United States and its financing by European countries and other nations of the world. Obviously, this situation could not have been maintained indefinitely, for Cuba's income was based solely on the export of sugar, a product for which the world market has shrunk during the past decades.

Maybe even worse than this economic dependence was the absence of a comprehensive and balanced investment program aimed at channeling internal resources and external financing toward the transformation of the economic-productive structure of the country. The goals of such a program would be to permit future export expansion, to substitute imports with national products, and to improve the living standards of the people.

With this background, and bearing in mind the significant changes that the revolutionary process has promoted in Cuban society, it is obvious that—given its nature, structure, and limited reach— this pre-1959 pattern of economic relations between Cuba and the United States, which was abruptly severed with the implementation of the economic blockade against Cuba, cannot serve as a model if economic relations are renewed between both countries. The main objective of this paper is to explore the potential of these economic ties and to project a plausible scenario for their implementation.

The Evolution of the Cuban Economy During the Revolutionary Period

In every assessment of the possible scenarios in the event of renewal of relations between Cuba and the United States, one element cannot be overlooked: Cuba's economic progress in these last thirty years.

It is true that from the economic point of view, Cuba cannot be considered a developed country. Economic progress has not been as noteworthy as in other spheres of Cuban social development, such as public health or education.

In spite of the objective restrictions—internal and external—of the costs imposed since 1959 by the aggressive attitude of the U.S. government, and the mistakes made by the Revolution itself, Cuba's economy has not only grown, it has been comprehensively diversified during these years, with a favorable reorientation toward the socialist community. Cuba has transformed its economic structure, diversified its industrial and agricultural production, created an economic and social infrastructure, and improved the educational, scientific, and technical standards of its people, among other social benefits.

The main results in industrial development have been:

- reconstruction, modernization, and expansion of the factories already existing at the triumph of the Revolution, and technological adaptation of industrial facilities.
- creation and promotion of new and important industries that were nonexistent or barely developed in 1958—for example, the construction of machinery, development of electronics, and the production of nitrogen-based fertilizers and sugar-cane derivatives. Industries such as that of manufacturing construction materials, which existed before 1959, were also expanded.
- concentration and centralization of productive entities.
- development of a nationwide industrialization policy, which attempts to transform the rural areas of the country. This development has led to the creation of network of industries distributed throughout the nation. Cities like Holguín, Nuevitas, Cienfuegos, and Santa Clara have become centers of industrial development.
- mass introduction of science and technology in all spheres of production through the educational, scientific, and technical development of human resources, the incorporation of foreign technologies, and national technological development.

The economic transformations in Cuba have not limited themselves to the industrial sphere. During the last thirty years, there has also been an impetuous advance in the agro-livestock sector, based on a radical transformation of land ownership. The productive characteristics of the agricultural sector have been substantially modified, humanizing agricultural labor with the introduction of large-scale mechanization, the use of chemicals, and irrigation techniques. A profound scientific and technological revolution has taken place in Cuban farming that, together with better attention to the soil, has brought about a significant increase of productivity. In most of the activities of the agricultural sector, higher production levels have been progressively reached and sustained.

Also outstanding has been the genetic improvement of cattle through a cross-breeding policy directed toward obtaining high milk yields, under the country's existing weather conditions. We have seen great progress in the creation of the necessary economic infrastructure for development. Much has been done to promote the development of electric energy, to build up the merchant marine, and to improve the communications network, the construction materials industry, and the highway system.

Of particular importance in these three decades is the nation's development of the tourist infrastructure, making tourism fourth in order of economic importance, given the income it generates in hard currency, superseded only by sugar exports, re-export of oil, and the fishing industry.

The most strategic investment of the Revolution has been in the creation of conditions for the development of human resources who enjoy an increasing educational level, good health, and who are well-nourished. The result is an ever-increasing number of young professionals with a high educational, scientific, and technical level that represents an invaluable resource in today's world. It has enabled Cuba to score victories in the field of advanced technology such as the electronics industry, including software production, the medical-pharmaceutical industry, and genetic engineering and biotechnology.

All these transformations have had an impact on the so-called external sector of the Cuban economy. As a result, Cuban exports have been diversified, in spite of the fact that sugar still carries considerable weight.[1] Cuba has developed the following exports:

- food products and live animals, mainly fresh, frozen, or canned seafood; citrus fruits; canned fruits; vegetables; honey; coffee and cacao;
- rum and cigars;
- nickel, copper, and chrome;
- naphtha;
- animal and vegetable oil;
- manufactured products;
- nonmetal mineral products (cement and marble blocks);
- machinery and transportation material; and
- other manufacturing products: sanitary commodities; heating, lighting, and water systems accessories; textiles; footwear; professional instruments.

The difficulties confronted by Cuba in these years have not truncated the progress achieved in its economy, nor have they brought about the "failure" of the Cuban economy. Undoubtedly, the national economy's development has been affected to a certain extent; the pace has been slower, and a series of the Cuban people's aspirations have not been met to the extent they require. Therefore, a "rectification process" has been initiated to make

Cuban society advance in the present conditions of external restrictions and guarantee the social and economic development levels already attained.

The achievements of the past thirty years prove the failure of the economic blockade imposed by the United States, though at a very high cost for the Cuban people, of up to 11.5 billion dollars (until 1987).[2] But the cost has also been high for U.S. business firms. According to some specialists, the isolation policy maintained by U.S. administrations has cost U.S. business 30 billion dollars between 1960 and 1985. [3]

To conclude, it could be stated that the absurd and mutually harmful nature of the economic blockade, the progress achieved by Cuba, and the political consolidation of the Revolution favor the renewal of diplomatic and economic relations between Cuba and the United States, but on a basis qualitatively different from that of 1959.

Perspectives of the Economic Relations Between Cuba and the United States

In the same way that severing economic ties between Cuba and the United States was part and parcel of a more general deterioration of the relations between the two nations, the eventual renewal of economic links would have to take place, necessarily, within the framework of the renewal of political relations between Cuba and the United States. Of course, this renewal of political relations could have, among its most immediate results, the establishment of mutually advantageous economic links. For Cuba, these relations would supplement policies fostering its economic and social development. This process of renewing economic relations would include the solution and definition of various matters, such as compensations for expropriated U. S. property; the mutual granting of the status of most favored nation; the concession of all benefits required for a preferential treatment of Cuba as an underdeveloped nation, in the case of exports to the United States; Cuba's access to the U.S. market and to U.S. development aid credit; the possibility of having official U.S. guarantees to U.S. business firms exporting to Cuba; customs and immigration agreements; and so on.

In the case of one of the most controversial aspects—that of compensation for U.S. property expropriated by Cuba—a solution could be reached, bearing in mind that Cuba has reached agreements on this problem with other countries. However, the United States must expect that Cuba will present as an agenda item for negotiation the compensations it is to receive for the damages caused by the actions taken by U.S. administrations and by certain U.S. enterprises.[4]

Opportunities for economic relations exist between Cuba and the United States in the fields of trade and investments, even though the Cuban market may not appear as generally attractive for trade and investments as markets in other countries do. The opportunities in certain sectors of the Cuban economy would undoubtedly represent advantages for a series of enterprises and for consumers within the United States.

Because of the existence of wide and stable economic ties among Cuba and the socialist countries that constitute the Council for Mutual Economic Assistance (CMEA), only 25 percent (at most) of Cuba's foreign trade has been estimated by the Cuban government to be appropriate for Cuba's relations with market-economy countries. Trade between Cuba and the United States would have to be carried out within the limits of this 25 percent. Given the scope of Cuba's trade with the socialist countries, this 25 percent should represent around 3.8 billion dollars annually.[5]

With fewer external restrictions than those that now exist, the proportion of Cuba's foreign trade with market-economy countries would approximate this 25 percent. However, during the present decade, due to the economic difficulties that Cuba has faced—particularly the loss of purchasing power and hard currency credit restrictions—Cuba has been unable to reach this figure. Between 1981 and 1986, Cuba's trade with market-economy nations reached an annual average of 1.7 billion dollars—approximately 12 percent of its total foreign trade, which means only half of its potential. [6]

This situation will continue in the immediate future, even though a slight improvement has been foreseen. Therefore, we consider it possible to expect Cuban trade with market-economy countries to reach a total of approximately 2 billion pesos in 1992. Supposing that the structure observed between 1981 to 1985 is maintained (imports represent 63.5 percent and exports 36.5 percent of Cuba's total trade with market-economy countries) in 1992, imports would reach 1.27 billion pesos, while exports would reach 730 million.[7]

We must take into account the notable reduction of Cuban hard currency imports during 1987 and 1988 that resulted from the circumstances that the Cuban government addressed by means of the policy of rectification. This policy had to be adopted to solve certain short-run problems. Any improvement of the external restrictions that Cuba now confronts would tend to re-establish a structure of trade similar to that prevailing with the market-economy countries in the 1981-1985 period. The 1981-1985 period also faced restrictions, but less than those of the last three years (1986-1988).[8] In any event, it must be taken into account that in the case of a country such as Cuba, import reductions beyond certain limits could be counterproductive for the reduction of the imbalance of external accounts and for economic growth itself, given the weight imports have within the Cuban economy.

It is rather difficult to forecast the trade level that Cuba and the United States could reach if relations are eventually renewed. But, if the previously described scenario is accepted, some estimates could be made, assuming that this bilateral exchange might represent approximately one-third of Cuba's foreign trade with market-economy countries. In such a case, it would be possible to forecast, for 1992, a trade potential between Cuba and the United States of around 670 million pesos (245 million in Cuban exports to the United States and 425 million in imports from the United States).[9]

These figures only represent an estimate of such relations because, possibly, the structure of trade between Cuba and the United States would not be similar to that which already exists between Cuba and the other market-economy nations. The geographic proximity and the extent of the U.S. market are factors that could generate a somewhat different Cuban trade structure, unlike that which exists between Cuba and its market-economy trade partners.

These levels seem to indicate that not only in the case of exports, but also in that of imports, the United States could become—soon after the renewal of relations between both countries—Cuba's main trade partner among the market-economy countries. We must not lose sight of the fact that Spain, Cuba's main trade partner in this area, imported, in 1987, 84.8 million pesos from Cuba and exported 163 million pesos to the island. These figures, even though they will surely increase by 1992, would still lag far behind the potential forecasted for the United States.[10]

Perspectives on Cuban Imports from the United States

U.S. exporters to Cuba would have to compete mainly with twelve nations: Spain, Argentina, Japan, Mexico, the United Kingdom, the Federal Republic of Germany, France, Italy, Switzerland, Canada, Holland, and Sweden, which account for 85 percent of Cuba's market-economy imports (783.3 million pesos in 1987).

This figure includes subsidiaries of U.S. corporations in these countries due to the U.S. administration's 1975 partial modification of the economic blockade regulations that had existed against Cuba.[11] Even though these new regulations that permitted trade between Cuba and U.S. subsidiaries continued being quite restrictive, exchange between these entities and Cuba reached 1.554 billion dollars between 1982 and 1987 (685 million in exports toward Cuba and 869 million in imports from Cuba).[12]

As a result, the renewal of relations between Cuba and the United States would mean, partially at least, the possibility of substituting Cuba's present trade with the subsidiaries of U.S. firms in third countries with direct trade with U.S. enterprises established in the continental United States. This situation would represent a total trade potential of approximately 300 million dollars a year.[13]

According to some U.S. experts, in a series of sectors, U.S. enterprises seem to have competitive advantages over certain current suppliers to Cuba, so that one could expect their rapid displacement by U.S. exporters in areas such as cereals, food products, chemical products, and medical instruments. According to estimates, these spheres alone represent a potential of between 300 and 400 million dollars in U.S. exports to Cuba.[14]

There are also possibilities that in some of these sectors—for example, in the chemical and pharmaceutical industries and in the manufacturing of medical equipment—relations between Cuba and the United States could go beyond the field of trade to include investments and joint ventures. In this way, U.S. suppliers of capital goods would also benefit.

Given the present external financial limitations of Cuba, progress of an eventual trade relation would depend on Cuba's export earnings in the U.S. markets and its access to U.S. credit markets and to the mechanisms of economic cooperation in the United States. Without this cooperation, it would be impossible to think of a sustained level of U.S. exports to Cuba, nor other advantages in the economic field that the development of these links would bring about to enterprises and consumers in the United States.

Perspectives on Cuban Exports to the United States and on U.S. Investments in Cuba

Within the framework of the eventual renewal of economic relations between Cuba and the United States, the latter would receive around 250 million pesos' worth of Cuban export products by 1992. Even though the United States will surely substitute already existing markets for Cuban products, it has to be taken into account that Cuba aspires to optimize these economic relations through the creation of new markets, and not just the displacement of those that already exist.

Some specialists have stated that present trends in the reduction of transportation costs have decreased the advantages that U.S. consumers would have from Cuban imports. Nonetheless, one must not forget that in the cases of sugar, nickel, agricultural produce, and seafood, the geographical proximity between Cuba and the United States would represent important transportation cost reductions, as well as reductions in fresh produce preservation costs; the availability of high-quality fresh products combines these advantages.

Among other products, Cuba could export the following:

Sugar. If the higher level of sugar production is stabilized (around 9 million metric tons a year), there would exist a new export supply potential to the United States. Some specialists consider that in spite of the progressive reduction of the quantities of sugar that the United States buys, there is an export potential in crude sugar, which could be shipped to U.S. sugar refineries, of about 500,000 tons yearly.[15] In this case, the United States would become the second or third largest importer of Cuban sugar (measured according to the shipping volume), ahead of current important buyers such as Bulgaria, the German Democratic Republic, Romania, and Czechoslovakia. This forecast is based on three main factors:

- U.S. national sugar production cannot cover the refinery potential of the United States;
- transportation costs reduction—especially in relation to current Asian suppliers—would be around 13 dollars per ton, representing savings of about 6.5 million dollars if, for example, half a million tons of sugar were imported from Cuba;[16] and
- the elimination of political obstacles, present only a few years ago, in relation to U.S. import quotas and what this would have meant if a new exporter were introduced. The substantial reduction of these quotas in itself has contributed to minimize these difficulties, inasmuch as it might have reduced the diplomatic and political significance that for many years characterized the U.S. sugar market.

Nonetheless, it must be very clear that Cuba's potential to export sugar to the United States should not be estimated based only on economic factors. Cuban foreign trade has also been conceived of as an instrument for international cooperation. Therefore, access to a new market such as that of the United States cannot be achieved with detriment to other underdeveloped countries, especially in the case of Latin American and Caribbean nations.

Nickel. In 1987, Cuba produced 35.8 thousand tons of nickel and exported 25.9 million pesos to market-economy countries, which totaled only 8 percent of the total export value of this product.[17]

The refurbishing of the two plants that already existed in 1959 and the opening of two new facilities will triple the present volume of production for 1992, representing somewhat more than 100,000 tons a year.[18] This increase in production levels will permit the creation of an export supply potential for the United States, which purchases, in foreign markets, all the nickel it processes and consumes. This would save U.S. importers between 500 and 800 dollars per ton.[19]

At present, Cuba exports between 30 and 40 percent of its nickel physical volume to market-economy countries (11,000 to 14,000 tons). If these percentages are maintained, by 1992 the total volume of Cuban exports to market-economy countries would be between 30,000 and 40,000 tons. At today's prices, that amount would represent three times as much income for Cuba than it now obtains in hard currency for exporting this product. It is possible that the United States would purchase between 30 and 50 percent of this total, representing around 30 million dollars' worth of Cuban nickel.[20]

Seafood. In 1987, all Cuban seafood exports (144.3 million pesos) were purchased by market-economy countries, of which 138.5 million pesos were of fresh frozen seafood.[21]

Cuba is one of the main world suppliers of quality lobsters and shrimps. Its main markets are Canada, France, and Italy. However, at present, Cuba is producing these products nearly at full capacity. Future increases of production volume will be possible only with the improvement and increase of the artificial culture of shrimp, recently begun in Cuba, which in 1988 reached a production of only 500 tons.[22]

For all these reasons it is possible to expect that exports of products—where there is an increasing demand for these products—would mean a reduction of Cuban exports to its present clients—bearing in mind that, even if there is no significant price increase, the total value of Cuban seafood export products should maintain the present level during the next few years.

The development of tourism in Cuba will be another factor that will limit the future availability of seafood for exports. The sale of seafood in Cuba's national network of restaurants and cafeterias renders four times as much hard currency as that which would be obtained by exporting it to market-economy countries.[23]

Fruits and Vegetables. In 1987, Cuba produced 885.5 million metric tons of citrus fruits. Half a million tons of this total (fresh fruits, frozen concentrates, and canned fruits and vegetables) were exported.[24] Nonetheless, citrus exports to market-economy countries have been very limited (6.1 million pesos in 1987), representing only 14 percent of the agricultural exports to that group of countries.[25]

The United States could become an important market in the future for the simple reason that U.S. importers would benefit from savings in transportation costs.[26] What is more, Cuban citrus production should significantly grow during the following years, mainly as a result of the increase of the number of plantations that are reaching their productive peak. For example, at the citrus enterprise Victoria de Girón (in Jagüey Grande, Matanzas), the largest of this type in the world, the current average plantation age is nine years, so in six more years the plantation will begin its period of ten years of maximum capacity. Its average yield is 11.5 tons per hectare, relatively low compared to the 32 tons per hectare achieved by the first plantations to reach their productive peak. Currently, this enterprise is producing 414 million tons of citrus fruit; it is expected that in 1990 it will reach half a million tons.[27]

On the other hand, if a flow of exports to a market such as that of the United States, characterized by its largescale and geographic proximity, is stabilized, Cuba would increase the citrus cultivation area. Besides citrus fruits, Cuba could supply fresh vegetables to the United States, especially if we take into consideration the different growing seasons that exist in the two countries.

Other Export Products: Possible U.S. Investments in this Field. Geographical proximity and the very existence of a large Cuban community in the United States—mainly in Florida—could favorably impact the export of certain products to the United States (alcoholic beverages, fresh or canned fruits and vegetables, footwear, clothing, handicrafts, and the like), even though the amounts would not be as significant as those of the other export products.

There is yet another export potential based on the already existing industrial capacity and that being built in various sectors of the economy. Let us analyze this potential. It is true that at present, Cuba faces difficulties that limit the exporting of industrial products, especially to market-economy countries. In 1987 "nontraditional exports" to these countries were mainly manufactured products; they represented only 1.13 percent of Cuba's industrial production.[28]

The persistence of some organizational deficiencies and misconceptions has been aggravated by other material difficulties, hardly to be solved on a short-term basis (such as the inability to obtain certain raw materials and spare parts, and especially the obsolescence of a large and important segment of the productive apparatus, which detracts from the competitiveness of Cuba's industrial products). So, part of the installed capacity—in use or idle—does not represent an export potential because these products cannot compete in international markets.

But recently created industries do exist in an entirely different situation, even though they still face some problems. Among them we find paper and sugar-cane derivatives, which can compete at an international level, but one of the most promising areas of Cuban industry is the field of avant-garde technologies, particularly microelectronics, computer science, biotechnology, and the production of certain medical equipment—industries that were practically nonexistent in Cuba ten years ago.[29]

The electronics industry is one of the clearest examples in this respect. Since 1984, considerable investments have been made, especially in the field of computers and microelectronics, that have rendered possible the take-off of production and the exporting of microcircuits, displays, and, recently, microcomputer network switches. At the CMEA level, Cuba obtained the mission of specializing in displays and keyboards; this focus has enabled Cuba to make considerable progress in this industry. Agreements to produce and commercialize these articles have also been reached with enterprises of Brazil, Argentina, Venezuela, Spain and Italy.[30] Lately, progress has also been achieved in the production of computer software, especially for specific applications. Cuba is also improving its capacity to design and produce basic inputs in this industry.

In tourism, joint ventures with foreign enterprises have brought about favorable results. The Cuban government is willing to do the same in the field of industrial production to promote export industries. The very existence in Cuba of young industries in the field of advanced technology constitutes an important starting point to develop these joint ventures.[31]

In addition, the existence of a large, young, qualified, and not very expensive labor force would represent an advantage for U.S. enterprises interested in producing competitive articles of a certain technological complexity. Given the excellent educational level and the relative abundance of highly qualified technicians and professionals, certain enterprises could carry out research and development programs at lower costs in Cuba than in the United States or other countries. These advantages were clearly outlined by Otto Wolf von Amerongen, an entrepreneur from the German Federal Republic and Honorary Chairman of the German Chambers of Industry and Commerce (DIHT) during his October 1988 visit to Cuba.[32]

Tourism. The tourism sector is probably one that would benefit most from the renewal of relations between Cuba and the United States, particularly bearing in mind that 70 percent of tourists now visiting the Caribbean come from the United States. U.S. citizens would have access to the natural beauties and a sandy coastal strip far longer and better than that found elsewhere in the Caribbean, while enjoying the hospitality and security Cuba offers its visitors. Geographical proximity and the development Cuba is working to achieve in this sphere constitute undeniable factors that could result in relatively cheap and varied opportunities for U.S. tourists. Thus, Cuba would multiply its tourism earnings to invest them in the economic and social development of the country, and also increase and stabilize its economic links with the United States.

In 1987, Cuba received 237,300 tourists from market-economy countries, which meant an income of 111.7 million pesos. This figure represented 94 percent of the total value of international tourism that year.[33] Nonetheless, the current level is only a small fraction of Cuba's tourism potential. Cuba's tourist sector suffers from management deficiencies and lack of initiative, problems in the quality of tourist services, and an inadequate infrastructure, among other difficulties. These problems have limited the possibilities of development in this field. But, since 1986, the Cuban government has given tourism top priority, and, currently, a comprehensive development program is under way to overcome, as soon as possible, the existing problems, in particular those related to deficiencies in management, organization, quality of services, and the attention offered to tourists.[34]

Important investments have been made to expand and modernize the tourist infrastructure; even at a time of serious economic restriction, Cuba has given top priority to such investments.[35] At the beginning of 1988, Cuba had around 8,000 rooms to offer international tourists; with the new investments, by 1992 it will have 20,000 rooms, and 30,000 by the year 2000. This expansion will allow Cuba to receive more than a million tourists annually by 1992. The investment plan also includes the construction of facilities of a quality previously nonexistent in the country, to attract high-income tourists. The construction of the first five-star hotel has already begun in the city of Havana.[36]

Joint ventures with western firms cover approximately 70 percent of the foreseen constructions. As can be seen, this cooperation would also benefit U.S. enterprises if relations between the United States and Cuba are renewed. Furthermore, Cuba's tourism development would represent potential advantages for U.S. enterprises specializing in tourism and/or construction, and for equipment and facilities suppliers that, given the geographical proximity and the technological uniformity of its products, would compete in advantageous conditions with European and Asian enterprises. Other U.S. tourist-oriented service enterprises (telecommunications, information services, catering services, aviation, financial services, and repairs) could also benefit with the development of Cuba's international tourist trade.

Other Services and Possible Forms of Economic Relations Between Cuba and the United States. To the large Latin community within the United States, Cuba could offer a series of services in the United States, among which we could find medical services, Spanish language lessons or lessons on other subjects in Spanish (including computer science, for example), vocational training, sports and cultural training (dance, theater, and the like), and specialized professors in education of Spanish-speaking children with visual, walking, hearing or mental impairments. Cuba could also service the commercial airplanes traveling from the United States to Latin America and the Caribbean.[37]

The larger experience and greater flexibility of the Cuban institutions in charge of foreign economic activities (the Ministry of Foreign Trade, the State Committee for Economic Cooperation, the Chamber of Commerce of Cuba, and the National Bank) as well as the recent development of various nongovernmental enterprises and institutions have made possible different modalities of economic exchange, such as:

- joint productions in Cuba with foreign imports of technologies and/or raw materials,

- trade in specialized professional services,
- joint ventures in tourism,
- different forms of compensated trade (barter, countertrade, buyback agreements, etc.),
- seasonal compensated trade in agricultural produce,
- joint ventures in third countries, and
- joint development of research projects, including feasibility and investment studies.

Final Considerations

Many of the forms of economic interaction currently foreseen between Cuba and the United States surely represent only part of the relations that will one day exist between the two countries. Eventually and in a short time, the United States could become an important trade partner among the market-economy countries, even superseding, in volume, Cuba's trade in some product lines with several socialist countries.

The renewal of trade relations would permit the flow of Cuban exports to the U.S. market—not only traditional products, but also new industrial products. An important participation of the United States could also be expected in the field of tourism, as a market as well as a joint investment. Also, joint ventures could cover industrial production, among other areas.

This improved situation would offer Cuba new financing opportunities that would expand the possibilities of increasing trade with the United States, and would favor Cuba's socio-economic development. Cuba, on the other hand, would not only be a competitive supplier of commodities and tourist services for the United States, but also could offer a wide range of services that would benefit certain sectors of U.S. society, especially the Latin community. The establishment and consolidation of commercial ties would foster additional forms of economic cooperation and cooperation of other types, and would represent an important contribution to the aspirations for peace of the people of both countries.

Notes

1. Sugar continues as the main export product (74.3 percent in 1987) because of the CMEA's specialization policy and the

substantially higher prices—compared to those of the world market—that Cuba obtains for its sugar exports to the socialist countries, among other reasons. If Cuban sugar were sold to the socialist countries at world market prices, sugar would only account for around 40 percent of Cuba's total exports.

2. The cost of the blockade and aggressive measures and sabotage against Cuba was estimated at around $9.081 billion up to December 31, 1981 (Banco Nacional Cuba, *Informe económico*, August 1982). A linear updating for the 1982 to 1987 period would increase this figure to more than $11.5 billion, undoubtedly an underestimate if we take into account the toughening of the blockade, the increase of the Reagan administration's threats, and what those threats meant in terms of the measures that had to be taken for the defense of the Cuban Revolution.

3. Johns Hopkins School of Advanced International Studies (SAIS), Cuban Studies Program, *Opportunities for U.S.-Cuban Trade*, June 1988. This study was carried out by Kirby Jones and Donna Rich.

4. One must bear in mind that Cuba's claims would not only include the United States government, but also a number of U.S. enterprises that caused damages to the Cuban economy during the first years of the Revolution with the intentional breaking of equipment, unjustified interruption of productive processes, the refusal to process raw materials from the socialist countries, the "brain drain" of qualified technical cadres, manipulation of accounting data to hide their true earnings, and so on.

5. The estimate was constructed as follows: Take the total amount of Cuban trade in 1987 with socialist countries (roughly 11.5 billion pesos). This is the part of Cuba's foreign trade that was less affected by the restrictions of the past few years. Were this figure to represent 75 percent of Cuba's potential total foreign trade, then Cuba's potential trade would have been 15.333 billion pesos; 25 percent of this potential trade would be with market economies (about 3.833 billion pesos). In 1987 the exchange rate was 1.00 peso to $1.00 U.S. Source: Banco Nacional de Cuba, *Informe Económico*, June 1988.

6. During this period, the peso-dollar exchange rate was different than that of 1987.

7. The assumptions for this forecast are: a foreign trade total value of 13.012 billion pesos in 1987; an annual average growth rate of 1 percent on the total foreign trade during the 1988-1992 period; that trade with market-economy countries would account for 15 percent of the total foreign trade of Cuba in 1992. (If we consider a yearly growth rate of 2 percent of the total foreign trade, the total value of Cuban trade with market-economy countries in 1992 would be 2.115 billion pesos.)

8. Even though the essence of the economic constraints, as it seems, will be maintained, in 1989 certain improvements will come about in relation to the three previous years. An efficient and large sugar harvest in 1989 will permit Cuba to cover its sugar export agreements without having to import this product in order to fulfill its own export obligations. This will reduce imports and increase the availability of sugar to export at a moment when there has been a certain recovery in prices. While this chapter was being drafted, the Cuban government announced the overfulfillment of the sugar plan up to December 31, which represents good prospects for the first months of 1989.

9. The value of Cuba's total trade with market-economy countries was assumed to be 2 billion pesos in 1992; the trade structure was assumed to be similar to that of 1981-1985 (in exports and imports).

10. Banco Nacional de Cuba, *Información estadística seleccionada de la economía cubana*, June 1988.

11. *Ibid.*

12. U.S. Treasury Department, Office of Foreign Assets Control, May 1988. Quoted by Johns Hopkins, SAIS, *Opportunities for U.S.-Cuban Trade*. The figures correspond to fiscal years.

13. During the fiscal year 1987, Cuba's total trade with U.S. subsidiaries came to 243 million dollars, but the previous year it had been 354 million. U.S. Treasury Department, Office of Foreign Assets Control, May 1988.

14. Johns Hopkins, SAIS, *Opportunities for U.S.-Cuban Trade*, p. 2.

15. *Ibid.*, p. 18.

16. *Ibid.*, p. 18.

17. Banco Nacional de Cuba, *Información estadística seleccionada de la economía cubana*, June 1988.

18. *Bohemia*, 38, September 16, 1988, p. 48; *ibid.*, 30, July 22, 1988, p. 50.
19. Johns Hopkins, SAIS, *Opportunities for U.S.-Cuban Trade*, p. 16.
20. This statement assumes that the present average price for nickel products that Cuba exports to market-economy countries be maintained.
21. Banco Nacional de Cuba, *Información estadística seleccionada de la economía cubana*, June 1988.
22. *Trabajadores*, December 26, 1988. (Interview with Jorge Fernández Cuervo, Cuba's Minister of the Fishing Industry.)
23. *Bohemia*, February 6, 1987, p. 47.
24. Banco Nacional de Cuba, *Información estadística seleccionada de la economía cubana*, June 1988.
25. In 1987, coffee accounted for 80 percent of a total of 43.6 million pesos exported in agricultural products to market-economy countries. Banco Nacional de Cuba, *Información estadística seleccionada de la economía cubana*, June 1988.
26. These savings have been estimated as $150 per ton of frozen concentrates—namely $34 million if the 200,000 to 250,000 tons that the United States currently purchases from Brazil were substituted by Cuban products. (Johns Hopkins, SAIS, *Opportunities for U.S.-Cuban Trade*).
27. *Bohemia*, November 25, 1988, p. 51; *Granma*, December 24, 1988, p. 2.
28. Banco Nacional de Cuba, *Información estadística seleccionada de la economía cubana*, June 1988.
29. The interest of Western European firms in Cuba's potential in these industries has led to different studies, among which the most outstanding are those made by Cuba Business Research Consulting Firm (London), which publishes *Cuba Business* magazine and a series of specialized studies on sectors of the Cuban economy.
30. Alfonso Casanova, "La industria electrónica cubana," *Serie de estudios de la estructura económica cubana*, published by the Centro de Investigaciones de la Economía Internacional, University of Havana (CIEI), 1988; José Luis Rodríguez, "El desarrollo de las técnicas de computación en Cuba: Evaluación preliminar," *Temas de economía mundial*, no. 22, Centro de Investigaciones de la Economía Mundial (CIEM), 1987.

31. See Fidel Castro's speech at the regular session of the National Assembly of the People's Power, *Granma*, December 26, 1988, p. 3.

32. *Granma*, October 22, 1988, and *Cuba Business*, vol. 2, no. 5, December 1988.

33. Banco Nacional de Cuba, *Informe económico*, June 1988.

34. *Bohemia*, February 6, 1987, p. 47; *Cuba Business*, vol. 2, no. 5, December, 1988, p. 15.

35. See Fidel Castro's speech at the regular session of the National Assembly of the People's Power, *Granma*, December 26, 1988, p. 3.

36. *Bohemia*, 34, August 19, 1988, p. 10; *ibid.*, 47, November 18, 1988, p. 19.

37. Professor Jorge I. Domínguez, Center for International Affairs, Harvard University, suggested several of these service modalities to the authors of this chapter.

11

International Law
and U.S.-Cuban Relations

Miguel A. D'Estéfano Pisani

This work is based on various considerations: (1) it is conceived
sine ira et studio—that is to say, alien to all emotional bias; (2) it
fits a legal framework, although we do not believe in the existence
of *pure* law, just as there are no pure politics and no pure
economics; (3) we address ourselves to facts, so that analysis and
legal meaning coincide with reality; (4) our main belief is that all
disputes can be settled by solutions befitting the observance of the
UN Charter, which calls for peaceful solutions in its third
paragraph and rejects threats or the use of force in its fourth
paragraph; and (5) concerning its legal scope, the issue at hand in
this exchange goes beyond the bilateral framework, to acquire an
undeniable regional or international relevance.

If political negotiations can be—and in fact are—shaded by
more or less subjective perceptions, law is based in more or less
objective elements. Therefore, to state and elucidate legal aspects
is a useful contribution to every dialogue. International law is an
instrument based on principles and norms that must be strictly
observed. Its purpose is not to promote discrepancies, but to
clarify and resolve them. It imposes a language and avails of a
given hermeneutic. We agree with Professor James P. Rowles in
considering it "a neutral ground" on which to find solutions.[1]

All serious negotiations must be directed toward the
identification of the various aspects of the dispute under
examination; *identification* leads to *clarification*, to the search of a
logical and, when possible, common language. According to law,
one must look for an agreement on issues over which both parties
could or should coincide, and, for possible identification or
clarification, consider the adoption of further agreements or
measures.

Those in the United States who expect from Cuba "an acceptable conduct" are not few, and that is fair, providing that the United States also upholds an acceptable conduct; above all, that our country is not treated differently so as to bring about a different international legal situation. We must assume that both countries—irrespective of all asymmetry between them—honor their obligations and commitments, prompted by the principle of sovereign equality, which must rule over all relations between states.

Many U.S. interlocutors are intent on constantly demanding from Cuba much more than they are willing to concede. In regard to the legal side of the issues at stake, this demand is even more erroneous. The bulk of information about and against Cuba has tended to minimize the violations of international of law targeted against our country, and, at the same time, exaggerated alleged violations on our part. It is therefore appropriate to ask how, by whom and for what purposes this "information" is produced. The arguments that follow are indispensable reflections stating the legal problems that Cuba and the United States must identify, analyze, and resolve.

A "Dossier" of Aggressions

It would be impossible to list, however briefly, the aggressions of all types perpetrated against Cuba by the United States. They would compose a voluminous dossier that cannot be adequately summarized here. We mention them not because we intend to delve into the dispute; on the contrary, we seek an approach through legal means, which will lead to clarification of the issues.[2]

It can be said that political aggressions have become a means to precipitate other aggressions. When the United States severed diplomatic and consular relations with Cuba on January 3, 1961, it meant a turning point as well as another method of aggression, for which instructive antecedents can be found in prerevolutionary Cuba.

Besides that severance of relations, the serious violations and aggressions perpetrated against Cuban diplomats and its diplomatic headquarters in several countries are listed in various documents. In addition, many documents issued by the Committee on Relations with the Host Country at the UN headquarters refer to denunciations formulated by Cuba with regard to very serious acts of aggression.[3]

Military Aggressions

Military aggressions against Cuba go even beyond those included in resolution 3314, dated the December 14, 1974, about the definition of aggression.[4] However, we would like to cite three clear cases: (1) the April 1961 invasion of Playa Girón (known as the Bay of Pigs in the United States); (2) the "quarantine" of October 1962; (3) the maritime aggressions.

Playa Girón. After the invasion plan of Brigade 2506 failed, the White House issued a statement on April 24, 1961, expressing that "The President has stated from the very beginning that, as president, he assumes full responsibility for the events of these past days." Many statements and confessions have been issued about U.S. responsibility in those developments. Professor Fenwick asked himself: "Was the invasion of Cuba . . . a violation of International Law? Technically considered, it is a violation, but not in regard to the principles of equality and justice." It is difficult to understand this reasoning.

The "quarantine." According to an announcement by President Kennedy on October 22, 1962, "a quarantine" was imposed upon Cuba; the United States claimed the right to stop and turn back on the high seas ships that would carry "offensive armament" to Cuba, making those rights extensive, "if necessary," to other types of cargo and means of transportation. What Kennedy forced upon Cuba was not a quarantine, nor, had it been one, can any state unilaterally establish such a blockade against another state in times of peace. Several U.S. international law experts took upon themselves the impossible task of justifying it. Thus, for Christol and Davis, the principle of freedom of the seas "is not useful as a prescription . . . against a reasonable restriction of the free use of the seas by every state," and for MacDougal it was "the lesser possible interference in the territory of another state. . . ." There was talk about "a limited coercion . . . to limited areas on the seas." But, in that regard, jurisprudence and international law are very clear.[5]

Maritime aggressions. Many aggressions were carried out against Cuban fishing boats, as well as against Cuban and foreign merchant ships.[6] Several perpetrators of such attacks—which caused death and injury to the crews—returned immediately to the United States and made statements to that country's media, giving detailed accounts of the events and their participation in them. U.S. complicity in those aggressions would reach such a point that, when answering one of our government's notes of protest, it was said those individuals had been "warned" that they "could be prosecuted" for violating U.S. laws "if they committed those acts again"; that is to say, they were not to be prosecuted, as if sanctions to crime required recidivism as an essential element—notwithstanding the fact that none of those aggressions was punished later on.

Aggressions Against Civil Aviation

Besides the attack against a civilian aircraft over Barbados—to which we will refer later—and other attempts and assaults against Cuban civil aviation and Cuban airline agencies in several countries, other types of violations were and still are committed by the United States concerning international civil aviation, about which very little is said. Let us cite just three: (1) the violation evident in Ordinance 81.541, May 8, 1981, adopted by the U.S. Civil Aeronautics Board because it is discriminatory and it contradicts the principles set forth in the International Civil Aviation Charter, signed at Chicago in 1944, insofar as it changes the framework that governs charter flights and services; (2) the violation evident in Regulation 91.105 of U.S. Federal Aviation Agency because it breaches the agreements with regard to international aviation services insofar as it limits Cuban civil aviation to the use of scheduled flight services in the United States, thereby weakening the availability of needed security protection; and (3) the denial to use the Kindley Field (Bermuda) facilities, which prevents Cubana de Aviación from making technical stops, thus flagrantly violating the 1944 Chicago Convention and the Air Traffic Agreement.[7]

Aggressions Against Broadcasting Systems

The United States takes it upon itself to violate radio frequencies allotted to radio amateurs and to maritime and fishing security communications. Many U.S. broadcasters transmit to Cuba in frequencies other than those allotted to regular broadcasting services, violating the International Telecommunications Union's stipulations to that effect. The Guantánamo base still uses electric radio frequencies to hinder Cuban communications and our sovereignty over the spectrum of electric radio frequencies.

It is in this context that the so-called Radio Martí appears, adding to the aforementioned violations the insult of appropriating the name of Cuba's national hero as its own. To this insult must also be added the issue of illegal U.S. television broadcasts to Cuba as still another gross violation of regulations.

Cuba's protests have only been answered by the U.S. Federal Communications Commission, asking for "complementary data," which, in all cases, has been supplied, without further response. However, it must be pointed out that in those cases in which the United States has asked for Cuban technical aid to solve any type of radio interference, Cuba has given a satisfactory solution to those requests.[8]

Economic Aggressions

It is evident that international economic relations are not simply a *mode* for developing relations between peoples, but that they are the *means par excellence* to develop them. Before going into that issue, we must clarify the concepts of *force* and *aggression*. According to Kelsen, article 2, paragraph four of the UN Charter must be interpreted in the sense that states are forbidden to use not only armed force, but even non-armed force, exemplified by any illegal action against a state without its consent.

Thus, aggression includes not only action of a military nature, but also of other types—which is confirmed in the Cuban case. Armed force—the threat to use it and its use—has become only one kind of force. During recent decades—as in Cuba's case—the use of non-armed force has become especially common. All through the first half of this century, resorting to the "marines" was the norm. However, this tactic has now become an exception because the forms of non-armed aggression have taken on astonishing and institutionalized proportions.

Among other documents, the UN General Assembly's Declaration of October 24, 1970, established the duty of states to abstain from exerting military, political, economic, or any other manner of coercion. Among the various types of aggression and force, we can highlight the following: (1) economic coercion; (2) commercial coercion; (3) coercion through monetary-financial means; and (4) coercion by external debt, unpayable and uncollectible for historical, political, economic, moral, and legal reasons. Thus, for purposes of our discussion, it is necessary to delve further into the legal side of economic relations.

Since 1973, the legal aspect has gained even more weight in international economic relations, thanks to three UN General Assembly resolutions: 3201 (S-VI), which includes the Declaration of the New International Economic Order; 3202 (S-VI), which contains the Action Program (both of these adopted on May 1, 1973); and 3281 (December 1973), which comprises the Charter of Economic Rights and Duties of the States. Article 32 of this last document decrees that "No state shall use economic, political or other means or promote their use with the purpose of compelling another state to make it subordinate in the exercise of its sovereign obligations."

However, the United States insists that said Charter was adopted by the General Assembly as a resolution, and that there is no consensus on the scope of its legal standing. It dismisses the fact that the Charter resulted from prolonged negotiations that sought to impart it with legal value, and that it was attained by voting, marked by agreement on a document more limited than the previous May's Declaration.

Besides that fact, there are GATT's regulations; UNCTAD's decisions; successive Decades for Development statements, adopted since the 1960s by the UN General Assembly; an International Strategy for Development, also adopted by that same body; as well as decisions taken in other international organizations, the aims of international cooperation and development that have been given priority by the UN Charter, and the constant activity of the UN system. All that leads to the existence of a body of law, from which no member of the international community is estranged and which none can violate.

Cuba well exemplifies the various forms of U.S. economic aggression.[9] In June 1960, for example, a U.S. refinery refused to refine crude oil from the Soviet Union, disregarding our government decrees consistent with the Law on Minerals and Fuels of May 9, 1938, which compelled refineries to process crude oil supplied by Cuba. For that reason, it was necessary to seize these refineries. On July 6, 1960, President Eisenhower cut the Cuban sugar quota. It was the first in a series of measures arbitrarily amending regulations contained in Section 408 of the 1948 U.S. Sugar Act. That was followed by U.S. obstructions to negotiations about loading and shipping, embargoes, sabotage, and even piracy against our merchant fleet.

Let us examine some of the mechanisms contained in the U.S. national law—to which we will refer again later—regarding economic aggression, considering that all economic aggressions and coercion against Cuba have been based on internal U.S. regulations adopted at different levels (the Congress, the President, or various Departments), a step that is frequently contrary to international law and obligations. Picturesque situations have taken place, such as the one referred to by Olga Miranda: ". . . on the one hand, the Cuban Government is in the hands of the Congress which amends Section 620a of the Foreign Assistance Act; on the other hand,

Cuban trade is in the hands of the President, according to Decree 3447 of February 3, 1962."[10]   According to her, U.S. imports of Cuban products are regulated by the secretary of the treasury, and U.S. exports to Cuba fall under the secretary of commerce. Decree 3447 establishes an embargo on Cuba, arguing that the Eighth Meeting of Consultation of Foreign Affairs Ministers of the American Republics resolved that "the present Government of Cuba is incompatible with the principles and objectives of the inter-American system. . . ."   We will return to this "incompatibility," but not before pointing out that when, in July 1964, at the Ninth Meeting of Consultation to sever economic relations with Cuba, the United States had already unilaterally done so. It had been previously announced, in March 1961, that the Trading with the Enemy Act, which established a total embargo of imports and exports, would soon be implented against Cuba.

Violations of Cuban Air Space

For decades, hundreds of violations of Cuban air space by U.S. airplanes or by airplanes coming from that country have occurred, thus violating the sovereignty of the state's air space according to the principle of *aer causum* contained in international law. It is worth mentioning the year 1964 in that respect, for, on the face of such violations, our country reiterated its rejection of such practices. What did the United States answer? President Johnson warned that if Cuba tried to "obstruct" these "reconnaissance flights," "a very serious action" would follow. McGeorge Bundy, his national security advisor, would then say that the United States would continue its "surveyance flights" and that any "interference" would create "a serious danger," while Secretary of State Dean Rusk warned that "if our surveyance were hindered . . . a highly dangerous situation . . . would ensue." The situation was such that, since November 1963, the Defense Department publicly decorated sixteen pilots for flying over Cuba.[11]

State Terrorism Against Cuba

Cuba has been the target of numerous acts of well-planned state terrorism, directly enacted by the CIA or by counterrevolutionary groups and mercenaries originally founded under the umbrella of the CIA. However, we refer only to two well-known and abominable cases: the blasting of a Cuban civilian airplane near Barbados and the assassination plans against President Fidel Castro Ruz.

The blasting of a Cuban civilian airplane near Barbados. On October 6, 1976, the Cubana de Avación airplane CUT-1201 fell into the sea minutes after it had left Seawell airport on the island of Barbados. It had suffered violent explosions that killed seventy-three persons. The following day, two Venezuelans arrested in Trinidad-Tobago acknowledged having blasted the airplane using a delayed-action bomb. One of them acknowledged being a CIA agent, and the other one admitted having been employed by a counterrevolutionary gang leader of Cuban origin, Luis Posada Carriles, in his Caracas office, which was a cover for CIA activities.

On October 15, 1976, at the victims' funeral, Commander-in-Chief Fidel Castro said, "Three years ago, the Cuban government signed an agreement on air and maritime piracy and other crimes with the U.S., which was an important contribution from us to the solution of the serious world problem of airplane hijacking. . . . The agreement signed by the governments of the U.S. and Cuba on February 15, 1973, cannot survive this brutal crime. The Government of Cuba is forced to cancel it."

Assassination plots against President Fidel Castro Ruz. We quote a report on the CIA's activities, published by a U.S. Senate committee, which states, "we have uncovered concrete proofs about at least eight plots to assassinate Fidel Castro between 1960 and 1965, in which the CIA has been involved." Numerous reports, documents, books, and statements confirm these and other plots against Fidel Castro.[12]

Mechanisms for Violations and Aggressions Against International Law

Besides establishing responsibility for violations and aggressions contrary to international law committed by United States against Cuba, legal analysis calls for examination of the equal responsibility of the United States for resorting to pretexts and artifices in its laborious attempts to find a "legal basis" for evidently illegal activities. "Legitimate defense" and "security" are found among the pretexts while the so-called "hemispheric system" is included among its means.

The concept of legitimate defense is clearly described in article 51 of the UN Charter, but certain U.S. theoreticians resort to all sorts of bizarre interpretations and some, like Jessup, state that article 51 limits states' "freedom of action" according to international law. For example, the United States stated before the International Court of Justice that Nicaragua asked for measures to be imposed that "could hinder the right to self-defense inherent to states according to article 51 of the Charter." Cuba could not help but feel concern about those and other interpretations, such as the ones from some U.S. international law experts, considering the enforcement of a "quarantine" against our country as a legitimate defense.

In regard to security, to speak about it in its different manifestations demands that it be placed within the framework of a purpose contained in the UN Charter. The United States seeks to reserve for itself the definition of what it considers "its" security. But no state may freely interpret the meaning of its own security without frequently clashing with that of other states. That U.S. concept of "security" has nothing to do with international security as demanded by international law.

During the 1940s, the United States accepted the principle of nonintervention, as approved by the Eighth Inter-American Conference (Montevideo, 1933), in exchange for the later introduction of the concept of "hemispheric security"; in other words, intervention under the guise of security and with the consent and complicity of the victims themselves.

This type of security has been used time and again against Cuba; thus, according to the aforementioned decree 3447 (1962), the Cuban economy was attacked because "the U.S., according to its international obligations, is prepared to take all necessary measures to promote national and hemispheric security isolating the present Cuban Government . . ."

Therefore, the act of referring to revolutions and to socioeconomic changes on one hand and to security on the other hand as antithetical terms, could not in theory or practice be interpreted as anything but the exultation of the "doctrine of national security." Cuba has made repeated efforts toward a system of world security.[13]

Within the context of this spectrum of illegal activities, the United States has repeatedly resorted to a docile hemispheric mechanism in regard to the Cuban case: the Organization of American States (OAS) and the Inter-American Treaty for Reciprocal Assistance. It is virtually impossible to follow anti-Cuban activities displayed by these means during the years 1959 to 1964, which consist of numerous meetings, conspiracies, vote-tradings, illegal decisions, violations of its own statutes, and so on. It is a strategy of formal concepts aimed at finding pseudo-legal arguments against Cuba and, at the same time, trying to prevent the application of the framework of the UN and international law.

The role the United States had envisaged for the inter-American system was confirmed: that it be kept separate from and not subjected to the then-emerging United Nations.

We can dispense with the OAS anti-Cuban comings and goings from 1959 to 1962. In February 1962, the Eighth Meeting of Consultation decreed Cuban "incompatibility" with the so-called inter-American system, and Cuba's separation from the OAS; it was agreed there to "immediately exclude the present Cuban Government from the Inter-American Defense Board" (from which it had already been excluded). It was a legal absurdity to expel Cuba and legalize that penalty afterwards. Expulsion,[14] by the way, was not foreseen in the OAS statutes, but it was accomplished via the reasoning that "the adherence of any member of the OAS to Marxism-Leninism is incompatible with the inter-American system." Secretary of State Dean Rusk then made a truly unique speech in the eyes of any law expert, demanding that Cuba be separated from the system. He stated: "It is true that there have been different viewpoints in regards to what has been termed as a legal problem, but none of those who supported this resolution (expulsion) thought or believed we were acting illegally . . . the Constituent Charter does not foresee this situation, but the Charter can be amended according to the general principles of natural law. . . ." One cannot help but wonder at the use of the phrase "natural law."[15]

In July 1964 the Ninth Meeting of Consultation, held in Washington, adopted agreements against Cuba that were completely devoid of legal meaning. In short, the elements that generally shape the hemispheric system's acts can be summarized as follows: (1) the assertion of the principle of anti-communism; (2) the thesis of the "incompatibility" between Marxism-Leninism and the OAS; (3) Cuba's alleged "acts that display the characteristics of aggression"; (4) Cuba's separation from the OAS; (5) the severance of diplomatic, consular, and economic relations with Cuba; (6) the "exhortation" to counterrevolutionary intervention; and (7) the insolent "warning" to Cuba. These decisions lacked an ethical or legal basis.[16]

The inventory of the inter-American system's actions against Cuba was shaded by irregularities and illegalities. Several law experts have analyzed at least some aspects of this problem and, more than once, U.S. officials commented that the experts were hiding behind "exaggerated legalisms and formalisms." One of Cuba's most valuable contributions to international and regional law is having unmasked the inter-American system. Due to that unmasking, in 1967, the so-called OAS "modernization" process began. In April 1973, the organization agreed upon "ideological pluralism" as a basis for hemispheric solidarity; in 1975, it established the right of its members to every type of relation with Cuba. Perhaps these changes have to do with the fact that the United States is no longer paying in full its financial obligations to the OAS. In 1988, President Fidel Castro said in regard to the OAS that Cuba's stance is not dogmatic, and that the OAS can be a useful tool; therefore, we would be willing to examine Latin American proposals inviting Cuba to reenter.[17]

But if the hemispheric mechanism proved to be inadequate, or if it were necessary to disregard it, the United States has resorted to other means. Let us not forget its national law. Legal or executive measures cannot assume the right to interpret, make reservations, and add amendments that are detrimental to international law and to the fulfillment of U.S. obligations to other states or to other international actors.

Resorting to such measures against Cuba has been frequent and evidently illegal. In the case of U.S. Congressional amendments, we present two of utmost relevance: according to the 1901 Platt Amendment, a status of quasi-protectorate was imposed upon Cuba, in virtue of the U.S. claim to a right to intervene, and a U.S. base was established on our territory. The 1964 Hickenlooper Amendment tried to deny our right to nationalize, even though the U.S. Supreme Court had acknowledged our right that same year (we will return to this later) and overthrew the theory of the Act of State, in spite of its brilliant historic tradition in the United States. (According to this Amendment, the right to nationalization was conditioned upon immediate compensation—that is "just, prompt, and in cash.")

A dictum issued on December 6, 1923, by the Permanent International Court of Justice established that an obligation imposed by an international treaty cannot be interpreted according to just one of the signatories' laws. The United States frequently resorts to a peculiar interpretation of the principle *ut res nacis valeat quam pareat*, called the principle of useful effect, interpreting the treaties in a manner contrary to the meaning of their terms. As a way to minimize this generalized and arbitrary trend, the United States holds the position that its domestic law is of "secondary importance" and must not be an obstacle to the settlement of disputes with other states.[18]

It must not be forgotten that on grounds of domestic law, the United States can avail of two elements that it frequently and traditionally wields, often unfairly: the law on neutrality, turned into an instrument applicable in circumstances that often are not related to international law's concept of neutrality; and the law of enemies, which the United States applies to Cuba with no regard whatsoever to the international concept of the term "enemy." (The concept of "enemy," in law, cannot be applied to a country with which one is not at war.) Lastly, the United States decides to act according to its own judgment.

The Guantánamo Naval Base

It would be indeed interesting to follow developments from April 18, 1898—when the Joint Resolution stated that "the people of Cuba are and by right must be free and independent"—and March 2, 1901, when the Platt Amendment was enacted, by which the United States claimed the right to intervene in the future of the Republic of Cuba, and which states in its article VII: "To enable the United States to maintain the independence of Cuba, and to protect the people thereof, as well as for its own defense, the Cuban Government will sell or lease to the United States the lands necessary for coaling or naval stations, at certain specified points, to be agreed upon with the President of the United States." The Platt Amendment was imposed upon the Cuban Constituent Assembly by an ultimatum: either it was included as an appendix to Cuba's new constitution, or there would be no independence. Thus, the principle of consent was violated; morally and legally, there was no consent. Together with this lack of consent went the fact that the Cuban convention members were not endowed with the legal capacity to agree on something that went beyond their power.[19]

According to article I of the February 1903 agreements, complementary to that of July 2, 1903, it was decreed that: "The Republic of Cuba hereby *leases* to the United States, for the time required for the purposes of coaling and naval stations, the following described areas of land and water situated in the Island of Cuba." In the May 1934 Reciprocity Treaty, which abrogates the Platt Amendment, the Guantánamo Naval Base is, nevertheless, preserved.

According to the Platt Amendment, the reason for leasing was "to enable the United States to maintain the independence of Cuba and to protect the people thereof," as well as for its own defense; however, the 1934 treaty states that such lease was inspired "by the desire to fortify the relations of friendship between the two countries and to modify, with purpose, the relations established between them by the treaty on relations signed at Havana, May 22, 1903. . . ."

The U.S. presence in the Guantánamo base is illegal. If the treaty was valid at any time, it is no longer, for it is not now a gift in response to "the relations of friendship between the two countries"; what is more, referring to the 1903 treaty as conceived to "maintain the independence of Cuba" deprived it of value, for what was and what has become the real purpose and cause of the aforementioned documents?

The lease is mentioned in such documents, but a lease is a consensual, onerous, and commutative contract through which one party *temporarily* obligates itself to enjoy or use something or to render certain services to another person. It is a legal absurdity to think that someone who owns something that is leased cannot recover the property and the ability to use it. Article I of the May 29, 1934, treaty on relations states that the 1903 treaty "shall cease to be in force and is abrogated," but, in its article III it states that "until the two contracting parties agree to the modification or abrogation of the [1903] agreement signed in regard to the lease to the United States of America of lands in Cuba for coaling and naval stations . . . the stipulations of that agreement with regard to the naval station of Guantánamo shall continue in effect." The supplementary arrangement referring to another coal or naval station in Bahía Honda (the rights to which the United States could exchange for more land in Guantánamo) would still be valid in its original form and conditions. It is reiterated in the treaty of 1934 that "so long as the United States of America shall not abandon the said naval station of Guantánamo or the two governments shall not agree to a modification of its present limits, the station shall continue to have the territorial area that it now has. . . ."

It is evident that the 1934 treaty on relations is as flawed as the 1903 treaty. It is null from the very beginning; nothing and no one can validate it after the fact. But even if, for the sake of argument, the whole process leading to the establishment of the base, and the 1903 and 1934 treaties mentioned above were valid, there would at least be two elements that cause its absolute legal nullity: (1) the *ius cogens* principle; and (2) the *rebus sic stantibus* clause; that is, a fundamental change in circumstances.

The Law of Treaties (Vienna Convention, 1969) includes *ius cogens* in two circumstances: 1) declaring null all treaties opposed "to an imperative regulation of international law" (article 53.2); and (2) if a new imperative principle of international law were to appear, according to article 64, "every existing treaty which opposes that regulation will be declared null and will be extinguished." It is not necessary to delve into a theoretical and practical analysis of *ius cogens* and of its scientific and doctrinal meaning; it is a norm that warns states that they should agree with other states to certain obligations according to fundamental principles of international law; a treaty that violates such principles is declared fully null thereby. The military bases established in circumstances similar to those found in Guantánamo have been denounced by the international community.

Article 62 of the Law of Treaties summarizes the *rebus sic stantibus*, or "fundamental change in circumstances," clause, which considers a treaty ineffective, inapplicable, or null when the circumstances in which it was signed have changed so much that it can be said that, had they existed when the treaty was signed, it would not have been signed. International law includes many cases in which this clause has been applied; in the case of *Rothschild and son vs. Egyptian Government*, it states that the clause applies to contracts and obligations of indefinite duration (Egyptian Joint Committee of Appeals, 1925).[20]

It is not necessary to spell out how much the circumstances have changed in the case of the Guantánamo naval base, which is indeed a case of *de facto* occupation. The last paragraph of article 10 of Cuba's 1976 Constitution states that "The Republic of Cuba repudiates and deems illegal and null the treaties, pacts and concessions agreed upon on conditions of inequality or that disown or diminish its sovereignty over any portion of the national territory."

It is a legitimate and unrenounceable demand of the Cuban people that there be awareness regarding the significance of this issue for Cuba's national sovereignty and for the respect that should be accorded to international law, so that it can adequately be solved in due time.[21]

Nationalization of Property

The issue of the nationalization of U.S. properties in Cuba is as well known as it is badly analyzed. The United States holds the general belief that (1) those nationalizations have a "retaliatory" nature; (2) compensation is a necessary condition in all negotiations about these issues; and (3) all problems to be discussed and settled revolve around only these two points. It is argued that Cuba acted in "retaliation" toward the United States by nationalizing its citizens' properties; the State Department and other agencies state that our nationalization was "retaliatory." It was not.

As is well known, the properties of citizens of other western countries were also nationalized; subsequent settlement agreements have been reached with them.[22]

It has been said that a total of 5,911 U.S. citizens have valid claims against Cuba—as quoted in a report by a committee authorized by the U.S. Congress in 1964—totalling 1,799,548,690 U.S. dollars, to which a 6 percent annual interest rate is added. This would raise the total to approximately 3.5 billion.

It has been clearly established by international law that every state has the right to political and economic self-determination. We are not dealing here with abstract law, but with a tool of international law: the right to nationalize, which is also inherent to every process of structural changes in society.

The U.S. Supreme Court itself, while dealing with a historic international law case (the case of *Banco Nacional de Cuba vs. Sabbatino*) wisely ruled, on March 23, 1964, that it acknowledged the international legal validity of our nationalizations, establishing that: "In spite of how costly an expropriation of this type may be for the public norm of this country and for the states that constitute it, we have concluded that the national interest and advancement towards the goal that international law should prevail among nations are best served by keeping the doctrine of the act of sovereignty intact so that this case is governed by its application." Cuba had sustained two essential and irrefutable points: (1) the decisions made by a foreign government cannot be legally judged if they violate international law; and (2) the acts of the Cuban government did not violate international law.

It is evident that, being subject to international law, no state is subordinate to another's legal framework, but only to international law, according to the *par in parem non habet imperium* principle. But the United States violated international law through an immediate response to the verdict of its Supreme Court, when Congress adopted, in October 1964, the Hickenlooper Amendment, which—according to its own author's definition—"seeks to dissuade the act of expropriation from taking place in the absence of compensation for foreign investment, by means of preserving the original owners' rights to attack any seizure that violates international law." International law and the doctrine of the act of state—valuable precedents in U.S. courts and legal doctrine since the beginning of the past century—were violated.[23]

U.S concern is less with nationalization and the undeniable right to nationalize and more with regard to the compensation that should follow. We shall examine this topic with the most amicable intentions. However, it is essential, first, to delve into the domain of international responsibility. When a state violates an obligation or an international regulation, it incurs such a responsibility. In the case of the violations and aggression referred to earlier, the required elements coincide to shape international responsibility: (1) damages caused; (2) infraction of international law; and (3) the existence of means to establish such a responsibility accurately. The notion of responsibility is not only limited to the duty of redressing or restoring the damages, but also extends to other legal consequences that may stem from the violation or nonfulfillment of certain obligations. In the case of U.S. responsibility to Cuba, the principle of *ubi emolumentum ibi onus* must rule; that is, when a state is benefitted by a given act or by a given omission, it is fair that it takes responsibility for the consequences of that act or omission. The U.S attained—or has tried to attain—benefits or gains of a diverse nature in its continued activities against Cuba, which are far more numerous than those listed in this work, but this is not the place to refer concretely to the types of U.S. responsibilities (political, moral, and material) in regard to the Cuban case.

That is why, for decades, the international community, and especially the International Law Committee, has been paying attention to different aspects of international responsibility. There is also the continuous development of other norms regarding the legal consequences of the nonfulfillment of established obligations and internationally illegal acts that, according to international law, can have consequences for the state that committed them. International jurisprudence is abundant in this regard.[24]

Having said all this, let us refer to compensation. Cuban nationalization laws foresee ways of compensation; thus, the Agrarian Reform Law of May 17, 1959, established payment through bonds payable in thirty years, at a 4 percent interest rate; the July 1960 Law 851 established payment in bonds of the Republic and created a fund to be nourished yearly with 25 percent of the hard currency obtained from U.S. yearly sugar purchases in excess of 3 million long Spanish tons for its own internal consumption, at a price not less than 5.75 U.S. cents per English pound (FAS). Those bonds would earn at least 2 percent interest yearly, while amortization would take place in not less than thirty years. According to Law 891 (October, 1960), partners or shareholders of legal persons or of dissolved or extinguished enterprises have the right to compensation.

It is clear that the United States has not received such compensation. It would be asking too much from the victim. The fact that all our nationalizations seek to change Cuba's socioeconomic structures is something nobody can seriously deny, for they are fully valid under international norms. It is also no secret that the formula of "fair, prompt and in cash" compensation has not been upheld in decades. Although it is clearly established that compensation due to nationalization is regulated by the national law of the nationalizing states, we believe it is an effective contribution to any U.S.-Cuban negotiation to pursue the practice of the lump-sum agreement. International experience of the past decades—and this has been confirmed by many studies, even those from respected U.S. research centers—points to the fact that payments are done within a period of twenty to twenty-five years, without charging additional rates of interest, without reducing the amount to be nationalized, and with compensation in kind; thus, Cuba might compensate by delivering sugar and its by-products, nickel, tobacco, citrus fruits, electronic components, and other articles.

However, it must be clear that the United States has a premise: that it has not attacked or violated international law in regard to Cuba, nor, therefore, has it incurred any international responsibility whatsoever for damages inflicted. But, in every negotiation—whether the lump-sum agreement formula or any other formula is accepted—the sum total of Cuba's claim on account of aggressions and violations, of which it has been and continues to be a victim, must be clearly borne in mind. Cuba's competent agencies have carefully evaluated those claims, which already total more than $10 billion.

Cuba's Internationalist Presence

The presence of Cuban internationalist troops in Angola has been a permanent topic in the context of the U.S.-Cuban dispute. The best answer can be found in the historic agreements signed on December 22, 1988, at the UN headquarters in New York: the trilateral agreement among the People's Republic of Angola, the Republic of Cuba, and the Republic of South Africa, which offers guarantees for Angola's sovereignty and territorial integrity and for the implementation of Security Council resolution 435 (1978) regarding Namibia's independence and the maintenance of peace in South West Africa; and in the bilateral agreement between the governments of Angola and Cuba, which terminates the internationalist mission and establishes a calendar for the withdrawal of about 50,000 Cuban soldiers, in a process that will culminate on July 1, 1991.[25] These agreements fully answer those who have questioned Cuba's acts, and could eventually lead, together with our presence in Angola, to an interesting international law analysis.

The international community has reiterated the legitimacy of national liberation movements and the legitimacy of support to those struggles and movements. The illegitimacy of all situations of dependency and of all aid to those who purport to maintain it, including apartheid, is equally reiterated.

The United States has denounced Cuba for its solidarity with the cause of independence for Puerto Rico, a country under intervention. The U.S. government demands that Cuba stop such solidarity. Since 1972, the UN Decolonization Committee has reiterated that people's inalienable right to self-determination.[26]

The thesis of supporting "legal nonviolent opposition" is quite commonplace in the United States. Reasoning thus, never-ending nonresistance would be the only way to get rid of colonialism and racism. The struggles for independence undertaken by George Washington, Simón Bolívar and José Martí—just to mention some names—would therefore not be justified. For example, when one follows the forty-year UN debate over apartheid, it can be seen that for the ideologues of nonviolent solutions, there is no other alternative than "nonviolent legal opposition." But the right to rebel is centuries old, and the 1948 Universal Declaration on Human Rights states in its preamble that it is the "supreme resource against tyranny and oppression."

Drug Traffic

Cuba and the United States have cooperated in fighting this serious crime and it is well known that Cuban and U.S. coast guards have taken anti-drug actions during the 1970s and 1980s. Cuba does not produce, consume, or export drugs. However, we are very close to the United States, a great consumer and producer of drugs, and the first nation to commercialize such substances.

Between 1974 and 1985, Cuba alone caught 306 drug traffickers, seized 599,162 pounds of marijuana and 1,024 pounds of cocaine and captured 25 airplanes and 56 ships, of which 61 were U.S. vessels. Detailed information can be found about all cases and punishments imposed. It would be pertinent for the United States to consider the active Cuban presence in the international effort to control illegal drugs.

An agreement on the suppression of drug traffic befitting international law, which leads to its control through cooperation between both countries, is feasible. It would have a favorable impact on both our peoples' public opinion: on U.S. public opinion for what everything related to drugs means to that people; and on Cuban public opinion because it is taxing to mobilize resources to prevent and repress this problem, which affects us only because of our nearness to the United States.

Human Rights

It is usually said in the United States that the issue of human rights in Cuba is an essential element of any change in relations between the countries. In truth, it should be an issue of interest to both parties. The 1948 Universal Declaration on Human Rights is a historic document: For the first time, an international document included human rights, and—also for the first time—economic, social, and cultural rights were coupled with civil and political rights.

But that declaration was only a starting point. The international community has reiterated that the image of the free man cannot be alienated from its economic, social, and cultural rights. In the process of progressive development of human rights, those pertaining to human collectivities as such have been added (political and economic self-determination, equality, no discrimination against women or on the grounds of race, apartheid and some remaining forms of slavery) as well as those rights pertaining to mankind as a whole (the right to live, to have peace, to develop). The current valid approach to human rights thus includes the promotion and protection by every state—internally as well as internationally—of the three aforementioned categories. Cuba can clearly reason how it fulfills these three categories of human rights.

Cuba, of course, rejects that this issue be turned into a foreign policy battle horse—to turn it into still another form of aggression to be added to the spectrum of ill-fated aggressions, of which we have been a target.

Agreements Based on a Quid Pro Quo

It has been argued that some issues pertaining to certain relations between Cuba and the United States can lead to a rapprochement on the basis of a *quid pro quo*, in which context international law would only have a more concrete or technical presence, although, even regarding these issues, its norms are always to be considered. Let us examine some of these issues.

Agreements on Maritime Borders

In April 1977, Cuba and the United States signed a treaty, which went into effect on January 1, 1978, on the delimitation of their respective maritime borders according to what would be the new Law of the Sea. The treaty's temporary implementation was extended in December 1985, and it is obviously very important that it be ratified by both countries.

Fishing Agreement

This agreement was signed on April 27, 1977 and was valid until, in 1982, it was interrupted. It is of common interest that it be renewed.

Migratory Agreements

On December 14, 1984, Cuba and the United States signed an agreement that Cuba had to suspend on May 20, 1985, due to the beginning of broadcasts by the so-called Radio Martí. In November 1987, the agreement was reactivated, and it was decided to continue negotiations on radio and middle-wave broadcasts in order to reach another mutually acceptable agreement.

Much has been said in the United States about migratory problems related to Cuba; these are not necessary to analyze. The truth is that the U.S. migration mechanisms and regulations have turned into another form of aggression. The United States forbids its citizens to visit Cuba, the Socialist Republic of Viet Nam, and the People's Democratic Republic of Korea. Regulation 515-560 deprives U.S. citizens of their right to travel—part of their freedom, of which they cannot be deprived without due process under the Fifth Constitutional Amendment. On the other hand, the issue of U.S. citizens visiting Cuba on a scale still to be established would be an advance in regard to the Cuban-American community.[27]

Tourism

The United States forbids tourism with Cuba. However, travel was allowed between 1977 and 1982. It was then interrupted by the policy of new restrictions and aggression against Cuba. Some steps can be taken in that direction.

Environment and Pollution

These are among the "global issues" faced by the international community that Cuba is interested in actively considering. Measures can and must be taken if geographical proximity is added to the seriousness of these issues at the international level. In this context, the issues of nuclear safety, on a basis of reciprocity, should also be taken into consideration. Cuba abides by the norms and regulations established by competent international bodies.

The United States' stand on the treaty for the prohibition of nuclear weapons in Latin America requires a separate comment. Cuba has always acknowledged Mexico's sound purposes in encouraging the so-called Treaty of Tlatelolco. But we object that the United States arrogates to itself the right to station nuclear weapons in large quantities in the Latin American area, and that, more recently, the United States supplied to England nuclear means used in its war of colonial reconquest of the Malvinas Islands, which were under Argentine sovereignty. Furthermore, we are not the only reluctant Latin American country in regard to that treaty.

Diplomatic Relations

This is an issue that requires further analysis, for it has to do with the theory of recognition in international law. If one were to follow the trajectory of U.S. practice in the recognition of states and governments, we would have to refer to J. Basset Moore's well-documented work entitled *A Digest of International Law*, which deals with two centuries of his country's history on the issue of recognition.

It is well known that in January 1961, the United States severed diplomatic relations with Cuba. It was not until 1977 that the respective "interests sections" were established. One more step can be taken—and this would involve a purely political decision—to raise their status to the highest diplomatic level. That would expand possibilities for contacts and negotiations.

Cuba has always upheld the principle that it is the duty of all states to maintain normal relations with other nations on the basis of mutual respect. The fact that we have diplomatic relations with more than 120 states—which is more than twice the 1958 figure—in spite of well-known pressures exerted by the United States to prevent those relations to be established or re-established, speaks for itself. On principle, we are not interested in relations with some regimes in Latin America and in other parts of the world.

It must be clearly understood that normalizing relations with the United States would not add one iota to our government's legitimacy; it already has full legitimacy. For many years during the past century, our people waged wars for independence. Nevertheless, our governments-in-arms were never recognized by the United States.[28]

In conclusion, a legal approach allows the exploration of valid means for conciliation. Much can and must be done *sine ira et studio*.

Notes

1. See James P. Rowles in Chapter 12 of this book.
2. Miguel A. D'Estéfano Pisani, *Cuba, Estados Unidos y el derecho internacional contemporáneo* (Havana: Editorial Ciencias Sociales, 1983).
3. Among these documents see A/AC. 154/97 (December 5, 1975); A/AC. 154/144 (June 7, 1976); A/AC. 154/173 (September 14, 1978), and A/AC. 154/178 (January 4, 1979).
4. J. M. Díaz Escrich, "Las agresiones militares del imperialismo yanqui contra Cuba y el principio de la renuncia a la amenaza o el uso de la fuerza," in *Agresiones de Estados Unidos a Cuba Revolucionaria* (Havana: forthcoming).
5. "According to the principle of the freedom of the seas, that is, absent of all territorial sovereignty on high seas, no state can perform acts of jurisdiction over foreign ships." (The *Lotus* case, Permanent International Court of Justice, 1927). In *The American Journal of International Law*, special issue (57, 1963) about the quarantine over Cuba, there appear works of international law experts Olner, Marker, Christol and Davis, Wright, Fenwick, MacChesney, and McDougal.
6. Alonso Expósito Alvarez, "La agresiva política marítima de Estados Unidos en la guerra del Caribe y en particular hacia Cuba," in *Agresiones de Estados Unidos a Cuba Revolucionaria*.
7. Angel Arango, "Los actos discriminatorios de los Estados Unidos de América contra la aviación civil cubana," in *ibid*.
8. Manuel Yañes Quiveiro, "Las agresiones norteamericanas contra Cuba por las frecuencias radiales," in *ibid*.

9. Alfonso Martínez Parada, "Agresiones económicas del imperialismo contra Cuba," and Aída de Puzo, "Agresiones de Estados Unidos contra la economía de Cuba," both in *ibid*.

10. Olga Miranda Bravo, "La legislación norteamericana como instrumento de agresión imperialista contra Cuba," in *ibid*.

11. In the case of *Nicaragua vs. the United States*, the International Court of Justice ruled that U.S. flights over Nicaraguan territory violated Nicaragua's right to national sovereignty.

12. Tomás Almodóvar, "El terrorismo de Estado como política de agresión del imperialismo yanqui contra Cuba," and Ivonne R. Diago and Manuel A. Longo, "El mercenarismo como instrumento de agresión contra Cuba," both in *Agresiones de Estados Unidos a Cuba Revolucionaria*. UN General Assembly's resolution 39/159 (December 17, 1984) on the "Inadmissability of the policy of state terrorism and of all actions to undermine the sociopolitical system of other sovereign states" was adopted by an overwhelming majority, with the abstention of the United States.

13. Cuba has said that it "favors all efforts toward the creation of a world security system, but believes that the validity of this system is subject to the fact that no exceptions are made and no privileges offered to anyone." (Note to the UN General Assembly, October 7, 1963).

14. Whatever the formal label, in fact this amounted to an "expulsion."

15. Dean Rusk's speech at the VIII OAS Meeting of Consultation, held in Punta del Este (Uruguay) in February 1962.

16. Miguel A. D'Estéfano Pisani, "OEA: 'subversión' cubana y legalización de la subversión yanqui," *Política internacional*, no. 18 (April-June 1967).

17. Miguel A. D'Estéfano Pisani, "Los mecanismos hemisféricos de Estados Unidos como instrumento de agresión a Cuba revolucionaria," in *Agresiones de Estados Unidos a Cuba Revolucionaria*.

18. "It is not a generally accepted principle of international law that, in relations between states that are parties to a treaty, the domestic laws would prevail over the obligations of the treaty." Consultative opinion, *Greco-Bulgarian* case, Permanent International Court of Justice, July 31, 1930.

Cited in Miranda Bravo, "La legislación norteamericana como instrumento de agresión imperialista contra Cuba."

19. Among documents cited: A/AC. 154/97 (December 5, 1975); A/AC. 154/144 (June 4, 1976); A/AC. 154/173 (September 14, 1978), and A/AC. 154/178 (January 4, 1979).

20. "In reference to international law, the extinction of a treaty, as a result of a profound alteration of the factual circumstances which served as its basis, is possible." (*Lawsuit between Bremen and Prussia*, verdict issued by German Supreme Court on June 29, 1925).

21. Miguel A. D'Estéfano Pisani, *Derecho de Tratados* (Havana: Editorial Pueblo y Educación, 1977), Chapter 13; Fernando Alvarez Tabío, "La base naval de Guantánamo y el derecho internacional," *Cuba Socialista*, no. 11 (February 1962); Gilberto Toste Ballart, *Guantánamo: USA al desnudo* (Havana: Editorial de Ciencias Sociales, 1983).

22. A note from the revolutionary government, issued on August 10, 1960, states that nationalization cannot be characterized as retaliation, adding that "if it had been adopted as such, even then the Revolutionary Government would not have violated international law principles or decrees."

23. Miguel A. D'Estéfano Pisani, *Casos de derecho internacional público* (Havana: Editorial de Ciencias Sociales, 1974; the case: *Banco Nacional de Cuba vs. Sabbatino*; Olga Miranda Bravo, "Las nacionalizaciones cubanas ante los tribunales norteamericanos y la Enmienda Hickenlooper," *Revista cubana de derecho* (October 1972).

24. Miguel A. D'Estéfano Pisani, *Casos de derecho internacional público*, Chapter 6. "Even if the nature of contractual rights is denied by national law, a government's responsibility is determined exclusively according to international law" (*The Issue of German Interests in Polish Upper Silesia*, Permanent International Court of Justice, 1926). "A State cannot invoke, opposing another state, its own constitution to evade obligations imposed by international law or by treaties in effect." (Dictum by Permanent International Court of Justice, February 4, 1932). "It is a principle of international law that the violation of a commitment leads to the obligation of adequately redressing the offense thus committed." (The case of the *Charzow Factory*, verdict

issued by Permanent International Court of Justice on July 26, 1927).

25. James P. Rowles in Chapter 12 of this book.

26. Miguel A. D'Estéfano Pisani, "Puerto Rico: análisis de un plebiscito," in *Tricontinental* (1967).

27. Olga Miranda Bravo, "Las relaciones migratorias entre Cuba y Estados Unidos," in *Agresiones de Estados Unidos a Cuba Revolucionaria*.

28. Miguel A. D'Estéfano Pisani, *Historia del derecho internacional* (Havana: Editorial Ciencias Sociales, first volume, 1985; second volume, 1988); Miguel A. D'Estéfano Pisani, *Cuba en lo internacional*, Volume I (1510-1898) (Havana: Editorial Ciencias Sociales, 1988).

12

Dialogue or Denial:
The Uses of International Law
in U.S.-Cuban Relations

James P. Rowles

Introduction

The current state of U.S.-Cuban relations is the product of fundamental differences between the ways state and society are organized in the two nations, the pursuit of foreign policy objectives that are often fundamentally opposed, constraints imposed by domestic interests and politics that sharply restrict the kinds of agreements and understandings that might be reached through negotiation, and a history of antagonistic relations that deeply affects perceptions by each of the other's motives and behavior.[1]

The most important issues that divide the two countries are essentially political in nature. Nonetheless, legal issues and considerations have played an important role in shaping perceptions in each country of the legitimacy of behavior by the other. The expropriation of North American properties by Cuba, Cuban support of revolutionary movements in Latin America and elsewhere, and the introduction of Cuban troops into Angola and Ethiopia, for example, illustrate the fact that perceptions of the legitimacy of a state's behavior may be influenced by views of international law—or failures to take international law into account.

International law is also important in terms of the more or less technical substantive issues involved in reaching agreement on matters such as delimitation of the maritime boundary, fisheries management, the prevention and punishment of air hijacking, or the allocation of radio frequencies and the prevention or limitation of interference on medium-wave frequencies.

More important, international law represents a common framework of accepted principles that may be drawn upon in order to reach agreement on important substantive issues dividing two countries, even on issues with a predominant political or military content. For example, the most important elements of the 1962 U.S.-Soviet understandings following the Cuban missile crisis could be confirmed in agreements between the United States and Cuba, and through other bilateral and multilateral agreements.

At the same time, the fact that the terms of an agreement simply restate accepted principles of international law should make them more acceptable in domestic political terms. For example, it might be difficult, politically, for the United States to agree publicly not to engage in overflights of Cuban territory (assuming they occur) as a simple concession to Cuban demands, whereas it might be much easier for the United States to reaffirm in an international agreement its acceptance of the international law principles governing sovereign control over a nation's airspace.

For its part, domestic law may both reflect policy and serve as an essential instrument for its implementation. The policy of the United States to exert economic pressure on Cuba by denying it important benefits, such as trade in commodities, imports of capital and technology, income from tourism, and other means of earning hard currency, has been made effective through regulations with the force of law.[2] Obviously, U.S. legal prohibitions of trade and other economic transactions represent a serious "legal problem" for Cuba.

However, from the point of view of the United States, the "legal" problem may simply be that there is a need for adopting new legislation. In the case of economic sanctions against Cuba, not even this appears to be required, since the regulations establishing the embargo and other restrictions may be lifted by executive decree. The obstacles to their removal are not legal, but rather political in nature. Thus, U.S. domestic law appears in the context of U.S.-Cuban relations to be of secondary importance.

With respect to Cuba, its domestic law may pose no problems in terms of normalization of relations, except as it may relate to questions of compliance with its international human rights obligations, the issue of the Guantánamo naval base, and possibly as it may affect the settlement of expropriation and foreign claims issues. As in the United States, whether such obstacles can be overcome will ultimately depend on political decisions and legislative action.

In sum, at least from the point of view of the United States, the legal considerations of greatest importance for improved relations involve questions of international law.

U.S. Negotiating Strategy: Two Approaches

The United States may employ one of at least two different approaches in future negotiations with Cuba aimed at solving current problems, and possibly normalizing relations. The first addresses present issues that represent problems for the United States, without abandoning the current strategy of economic isolation and denial. The second relies more heavily on international law in addressing both technical and broader issues, as part of a strategy aimed at improving and, perhaps, ultimately transforming the nature of the relationship between the two countries.

Technical Negotiations Within a Strategy of Economic Pressure

One approach would be to engage in negotiations to resolve issues that represent current irritants or problems for the United States, without abandoning the general strategy of economic pressure and denial directed against Cuba. Using this approach, issues would be dealt with on a quid pro quo basis, with international law being used only in a technical sense and as necessary in order to resolve problems such as the return of excludable aliens who entered the United States during the 1980 Mariel boatlift, or the interference on medium-wave frequencies resulting from the failure of the two countries to reach agreement on technical issues—a failure that includes but also predates plans for and the initiation of broadcasting by Radio Martí, and Cuban reactions to these developments.

Under this approach, the United States might also seek to negotiate other agreements of direct benefit. Reestablishment of the anti-hijacking agreement, or an agreement for cooperation in combatting drug trafficking, would fall within this category. However, the overall strategy of economic denial would not be changed, at least initially. Some relaxation of the economic sanctions in place against Cuba could conceivably evolve under this approach, but only in exchange for foreign policy behavior the United States deems desirable.

The anticipated advantages of such an approach are to deny the Cuban government resources needed for development, thus increasing internal pressure; to deny Cuba resources that might be used for foreign policy actions detrimental to U.S. interests; and to avoid actions that might serve to legitimate the Cuban regime in the eyes of other countries. One possible disadvantage, on the other hand, is that such an approach might offer few positive inducements for Cuba to modify its behavior. Another is that it might hold little promise for redefining the relationship between the two countries in ways that could afford the United States opportunities for exercising greater influence over Cuban policies and actions through a broader and more richly textured set of economic and other relationships. Finally, the perception of what foreign policy behavior by Cuba might justify a further relaxation in sanctions would remain subjective to a large degree, not being related to standards and perceptions of legitimate behavior held by other states.

Negotiations on Both Technical and Broader Issues Relying Generally on Norms of International Law

A second approach would address a broader range of issues while relying more heavily on international law, both to identify elements of potential agreement and to define expectations regarding each nation's foreign policy behavior. The general framework of international law would be considered relevant both in terms of selecting problems or issues on which to seek agreement, and in terms of the solutions deemed to be acceptable. Not all issues would be settled by recourse to international law, but some would be. Others might simply require straight political bargaining.

Such an approach would attempt to bring the behavior of each government into compliance with clear norms of international law by reaffirming existing norms. It would have different advantages and disadvantages for each. U.S. overflights of Cuban territory would be a ripe subject for discussion and possible agreement, particularly in view of the World Court's holding in *Nicaragua v. U.S.* that such overflights violate a nation's right to sovereignty.[3] But Cuban compliance with international human rights norms, including those articles of the Universal Declaration on Human Rights that now represent customary international law, would also be a subject for discussion, probable contention, and, perhaps, agreement.

Of particular importance is the fact that customary international law prohibits the provision of arms or logistical support to revolutionary forces, a point now clarified by the World Court in its judgment on the merits in *Nicaragua v. U.S.* Reaffirmation of such a norm in a bilateral agreement, and perhaps a multilateral agreement to which both states are parties, could contribute to the easing of both U.S. and Cuban fears regarding the behavior of the other in Central America and the Caribbean, and even elsewhere.

In the Central American context, such an accord might form an important element in an agreement by outside countries pledging to support and uphold a Central American peace agreement. "Acceptable Cuban behavior," in U.S. eyes, would be more sharply and objectively defined. At the same time, a clearer definition of "acceptable U.S. behavior"—embodied in an international agreement recognized as legally binding by other states—might help assuage Cuban fears, while adding incentives for greater restraint in Cuban foreign policy actions. Other matters not regulated by general international law, such as the size of the military forces placed on the territory of another state with its consent, would consequently be viewed not as illegitimate behavior, but rather as political issues to be negotiated.

In general, by drawing on principles already accepted by the overwhelming majority of states, such a negotiating strategy would facilitate agreement on more than technical issues. Consequently, it might be considerably more promising in terms of achieving a normalization of relations between the two countries. Because the United States lost the merits judgment in the *Nicaragua* case, current U.S. attitudes are not particularly supportive of such an approach, though this might change if and when the peace process in Central America achieves further results, or with the new Bush administration.

Disadvantages of this second approach include the fact that there is always a danger of getting bogged down in legal arguments, particularly when negotiators concentrate on who was right or wrong in the past instead of focusing on potential agreements that might help shape the future. This danger may be reduced, perhaps, by a conscious effort to avoid the rhetorical use of international law to condemn and ridicule, and to state arguments in a neutral tone more likely to elicit serious response and continuing dialogue. Second, there may be a risk that such an approach would contribute to a legitimation of Cuban behavior that does not clearly violate international law in an area where the lines are not always clear. Such disadvantages would have to be weighed against the possible benefits to be gained in constraining Cuban actions, including acts that the norms governing material support of guerrillas now clearly prohibit.

A Sequential Strategy for Negotiating Improved U.S.-Cuban Relations

The two approaches to negotiation sketched above are not mutually exclusive in the early stages of negotiating improved relations. In theory, the first would simply stop with limited agreements, but Cuba could enter such agreements at least partly in the hope of broadening the subjects under negotiation, with a view toward eventually securing a relaxation or lifting of the embargo and increased access to capital and technology.

Similarly, the second approach would logically lead toward the normalization of relations between Cuba and the United States, but it could easily be derailed by abrogation or failure to comply with the terms of one of the early agreements, such as the 1984 agreement on immigration procedures that was reinstated in November 1987. Should that occur, U.S. proponents of the second approach might be persuaded to retreat to the first, or lose the battle for policy control.

Improved relations, and a broadening of the subjects that are successfully negotiated, will require the slow accretion of confidence through firm observance of even technical agreements, particularly when sharp disagreements or differences erupt between the two countries. Given their differing social systems, interests, and objectives, such disagreements are sure to occur from time to time.

Following a negotiating strategy that includes at least a major part of the second approach sketched above, issues should be negotiated in accordance with certain sequences to increase the chances of success. It could be a serious mistake, for example, to take up the issue of Guantánamo or that of the settlement of claims for expropriated properties in an early phase of the negotiations. The former would be likely to engender strong political opposition within the United States, while the latter involves issues of considerable difficulty that will require a good deal of political will and ingenuity to resolve. With these considerations in mind, the following sequence is illustrative of the kind of approach to negotiations that may hold the greatest promise.

Immediate Technical Issues

Immigration Procedures Agreement (1984 and 1987). On December 14, 1984, Cuba and the United States reached an agreement providing for (1) the U.S. issuance of preference immigrant visas to up to 20,000 Cuban nationals residing in Cuba per year, and in particular to relatives of U.S. citizens and Cuban permanent residents in the United States; (2) continued issuance of immigrant visas to residents of Cuba who are parents, spouses, or unmarried children under twenty-one years of age of U.S. citizens, whose numbers will not be counted against the annual 20,000 limit; (3) Cuban acceptance of the return to Cuba of 2,746 named individuals who entered the United States during the Mariel boatlift, but who are excludable aliens not eligible for legal entry into the United States; and (4) establishment of a program for the emigration to the United States of former Cuban prisoners having completed sentences for "offenses against the state," up to a limit of 3,000 persons during 1985, with the size of the program in subsequent years to be agreed to in the future.[4]

Cuba suspended the agreement when Radio Martí began broadcasting on May 20, 1985. In November 1987, the accord was reactivated as a result of an agreement reached by U.S. and Cuban officials in Mexico City. It was also agreed at that time that the two countries would continue negotiations over radio transmissions on the medium-wave band directed from one country to audiences in the other, in order to reach a mutually acceptable agreement. They also agreed that a systematic effort should be made to reduce technical interference resulting from congestion of the medium-wave band and the proximity of the two countries. Finally, the two parties agreed that discussions aimed at the solution of these problems should continue, in strict conformity with international law, including the applicable international radio law and regulations.[5]

The reactivation of the immigration procedures agreement has contributed significantly to a mild thaw in U.S.-Cuban relations, opening the way for discussions on other issues. Particularly significant was the agreement's success in decoupling the migration and radio broadcasting issues, suggesting an approach that should be useful on a wide range of questions.

Medium-wave Radio Transmissions and Interference. The subject of medium-wave transmissions and interference appears to be one on which agreement might be reached, provided Cuba does not insist on a cessation of broadcasting by Radio Martí.[6] Cuba has indicated an interest in a resolution of the Radio Martí "problem" based on the principle of reciprocity. One possibility that has arisen in discussions is an arrangement whereby Cuba might broadcast on medium-wave frequencies to all of the United States, using several clear-channel frequencies for this purpose. To date, the Unites States has not agreed to this proposal, due in part to problems related to the statutory independence of the Federal Communications Commission (which allocates U.S. radio frequencies), the paucity of clear-channel stations that might be available for Cuban use, and perhaps the domestic opposition from broadcasters and others that such action might engender.

In principle, Cuba's clear-channel broadcasting to the United States would satisfy Cuban demands for reciprocity and treatment on the basis of sovereign equality and mutual respect. In practice, the gross disparities in the two countries' size, population, and number of radio stations will have to be taken into consideration in devising a solution that, while respecting the principle of reciprocity, also takes such practical considerations into account.

The problem of radio broadcasting on medium-wave frequencies on the basis of reciprocity illustrates a factor that may play an important role in the eventual improvement in, or failure to improve, U.S.-Cuban relations. Cuba, like other states in Latin America and the rest of the world, wants to be treated as the sovereign equal of the United States and other nations. Within the framework of international law, this is the basis on which relations in general, and negotiations on specific issues in particular, are generally conducted. Indeed, the sovereign equality of all states is a fundamental principle of international law.[7] Great differences in the size, population, wealth, and power of different states, on the other hand, dictate that agreements and relations do not and cannot produce equal results for each party in every case. When two states deal with each other on the basis of sovereign equality and mutual respect—i.e., within the framework of international law—they act as sovereign equals on the juridical plane. Each remains free, however, in exercising an attribute of its sovereignty, to enter into agreements that take important differences between countries into account.

Accommodation on both sides would help greatly to resolve differences relating to Radio Martí and radio interference on the medium-wave band. On the U.S. side, it would be advisable to avoid an aggravation of the problem by firmly resisting all proposals for direct television broadcasting to Cuba. The legality of such broadcasting appears to be considerably more dubious than that of direct radio broadcasting on medium-wave frequencies, particularly in view of the heated controversy that has attended debates and decisions in international telecommunications organizations regarding the permissibility of direct television broadcasting by satellite. Second, the United States might take into account the fact that Cubans find the name "Radio Martí" to be almost or more offensive than the broadcasts themselves. Cubans revere José Martí as a great national hero and as the father of their country. One accommodating step the United States could take would be to change the name of Radio Martí to that of "Voice of America: Cuban Service." Such a step is authorized by current law,[8] and might go far to defuse the issue.

On the Cuban side, some broadcasting arrangement short of full U.S. coverage on clear-channel frequencies might represent a reasonable accommodation that recognizes the technical and legal difficulties, and political opposition from broadcasters and others, that the federal government may face.

On the broader question of reducing interference on medium-wave frequencies resulting from transmissions from two countries in such close proximity, a number of highly technical issues are involved. Bilateral negotiations can usefully address these problems, while Cuba's return to regional telecommunications organizations would probably also help to minimize the problem of radio interference.

Other Areas of Possible Agreement on Technical Issues

Maritime Boundary Agreement. Recent changes in the law of the sea, including the establishment of a 200-mile exclusive economic zone, have made it necessary for all coastal states with overlapping zones to reach agreement on the delimitation of their respective maritime boundaries, and to regulate the exercise of certain rights by other states within these zones. The United States and Cuba initially signed a limited interim agreement in April 1977, which has been extended successively for two-year periods by specific agreement. The current extension became effective on January 1, 1988.[9] Since it is equally in the interests of the United States and Cuba to have these maritime delimitation issues clearly resolved, a definitive treaty should be negotiated and ratified by both parties.

Fisheries Agreement. A fisheries agreement regulating fishing off the coasts of the United States was signed at the same time as the maritime boundaries agreement, on April 27, 1977.[10] It remained in force until the United States decided to allow it to lapse in 1982, when it also blocked tourist travel to Cuba though the adoption of regulations prohibiting travel-related economic transactions.[11]

Conclusion of a new fisheries agreement would represent a small step forward in the process of establishing better relations, introducing some positive inducements into the U.S. relationship with Cuba. If possible, the agreement might be drafted so as to provide certain benefits to U.S. fishermen, in accordance with the principle of reciprocity.

Anti-hijacking Agreement. The 1973 anti-hijacking agreement in force between Cuba and the United States[12] was terminated by Cuba in the wake of the destruction of a Cubana de Aviación civilian air liner off the coast of Barbados in October 1976. Cuba accused the United States of responsibility for the terrorist bomb that caused the crash. This reaction to the tragic loss of life of the seventy-three persons on board appears more understandable today, particularly in light of the analogous conclusions that the United States drew following the Soviet downing of a South Korean air liner in 1983, and that Iran drew following the downing of one of its civilian air liners by U.S. naval forces in the Persian Gulf in 1988. In the latter two cases, the tragedies proved to be the result of error, while the charge of U.S. responsibility for the downing of the Cubana air liner is viewed, in the United States at least, as untrue.

Leaving aside the tragic events of 1976, it is clearly in both Cuban and U.S. interests to reinstate the old anti-hijacking agreement, or to negotiate a new one encompassing the hijacking of both aircraft and seagoing vessels.[13] The interest of both countries in such an accord is revealed by the fact that the terms of the lapsed agreement continue to be observed in practice, even if on an informal basis. Conclusion of an anti-hijacking agreement at an early date would implement policies reflected in the criminal law of both countries.[14]

Cooperation in the Control of Drug-trafficking. Numerous international conventions prohibit the traffic in narcotic drugs and psychotropic substances, and it is now generally recognized that all nations are under an obligation to cooperate in the suppression of such prohibited traffic engaged in by ships on the high seas.[15]

The U.S. interest in preventing the importation of illegal drugs is clear. Cubans have objected on occasion to what they perceive as use of the drug issue by the United States as an instrument of intimidation in order to secure unrelated foreign policy objectives. They have also stressed what they view as the structural causes of drug use in the United States, including factors related to gross disparities in wealth among nations and the lack of viable alternatives for crop production in certain drug-producing countries.[16] But, however complex and interrelated the causes of the problem may be, Cuba has no legitimate interest in refusing to take immediate steps in cooperation with the United States in order to effectively control and suppress actions that cause great human suffering, and that are contrary to fundamental tenets of socialist legality and morality.[17]

Cuba and the United States once cooperated in the suppression of smuggling under the terms of a 1926 treaty,[18] and through the exchange of information regarding drug trafficking pursuant to an agreement concluded in 1930.[19] More recently, between 1978 and 1982 the coast guards of the two countries cooperated in the suppression of the drug trade, in accordance with an informal understanding.[20]

Building on these precedents, conclusion of an international agreement for cooperation between U.S. Coast Guard and Cuban Border Guard forces to prevent the illegal importation of narcotics into either country would be helpful, both in controlling drugs and in affecting general perceptions of Cuba in the United States, where the drug issue has a deep impact on public opinion. Such an agreement would go far to reduce the potential for what is perceived by some Cubans as abuse of the drug issue to serve unrelated U.S. foreign policy interests vis-à-vis Cuba. Were it to become actively or even passively associated with drug-trafficking operations, Cuba could lose potential support in U.S. domestic circles. Even close relations with foreign heads of state or government officials with known ties to the drug trade are likely to produce negative reactions in the United States. Active cooperation in the suppression of drug trafficking, on the other hand, may have such a favorable impact on U.S. domestic opinion that it could help to improve the general atmosphere of relations between the two countries.

Visits to Cuba by U.S. Family Members. Visits by U.S. citizens or residents of Cuban origin to family members in Cuba are justified on humanitarian grounds alone. Beginning in 1979, some 100,000 visits to Cuba took place in a little over a year. While this number may have been excessive from Cuba's point of view, a return to the annual rate of the early 1980s (about 10,000 visits per year) would constitute an important step in modifying attitudes in the Cuban-American community regarding the desirability of improving relations between the two countries. As these relations improve, the United States might also ease further existing limitations on family visits by Cubans to relatives living in the United States.

Environmental Concerns. Technical agreements relating to environmental concerns should also be considered as subjects for negotiation. An agreement to regulate pollution in the Straits of Florida would serve the immediate interests of both countries, as would an agreement relating to the protection of migratory birds and other wildlife.

Nuclear Safety Issues. Cuban construction of Soviet-designed 440 Mw nuclear power reactors, including the one currently under construction near Cienfuegos,[21] represents a legitimate source of concern to citizens in the United States as well as in Cuba, particularly in light of the Three Mile Island emergency in Pennsylvania and the Chernobyl disaster in the Soviet Union. Traditionally, Soviet engineers have placed less emphasis on nuclear safety than their U.S. counterparts, though the situation has probably changed since Chernobyl. Both the United States and Cuba might benefit from cooperation on nuclear safety issues, which would address U.S. concerns regarding the Cienfuegos reactor and any concerns Cuba might have regarding U.S. reactors. The sharing of technical expertise in this area could benefit Cuba as it deals with such issues for the first time.

Tourism

Travel by U.S. tourists to Cuba was permitted from 1977 to 1982, when it was effectively halted due to stringent restrictions added to the U.S. Cuban Assets Control Regulations.[22] The U.S. ban on tourism could be lifted, perhaps gradually. This step would provide Cuba with hard currency, but might also contribute to a softening of antagonisms between citizens in the two countries. If the purpose of improving friendly relations between the two countries is to be served, tourists should have ample opportunities to move freely about the island and to interact with its people.

Diplomatic Relations

No linkage is necessary between the establishment of full diplomatic relations and a lifting of economic sanctions, although the former will create some pressure for the latter. The issues, however, may be separated. For example, the United States could restore diplomatic relations while retaining tight control over U.S.-Cuban trade.

Full diplomatic relations could legitimate the Cuban government in the eyes of some governments perhaps, but since most countries in South America, and Panamá, Costa Rica, and Mexico already maintain relations with Cuba, the legitimation effect would be largely limited to a few countries in Central America. Even these nations recognize Nicaragua. In a day in which the United States has diplomatic relations with China, the Soviet Union, and even Mongolia, the absence of full relations with Cuba seems anomalous.

The establishment of normal diplomatic relations, as opposed to the interests sections arrangement in force since 1977,[23] would be beneficial to both countries. It would, for example, help ensure that the views of the ambassador and other U.S. diplomats in Havana are included in the bureaucratic routines and action channels involved in U.S. decision making toward Cuba, reducing the likelihood that the views of U.S. specialists on the scene may not be taken seriously in reaching important decisions affecting Cuba, as has occurred in the past.[24] The views of the U.S. chief of the interests section in Havana may receive such consideration at present, but the risk of bypassing in-country experts and reaching decisions based on more abstract, or even ideological, considerations remains a potentiality.

Diplomacy is an important means for advancing each nation's interests. Routine face-to-face communications, personal familiarity with the individuals involved in decision making, and the slow accretion of confidence in the reliability of diplomatic representations can all contribute to a diminution of the hostility and mistrust that have so often characterized U.S.-Cuban relations in the past.

Agreement on International Security Issues

Agreement on international security issues might occur either prior to or concurrent with progress on the questions discussed above, or a gradual relaxation of economic sanctions. The following issues are salient:

Withdrawal of Cuban Troops from Angola. Major breakthroughs occurred during the summer of 1988 in negotiations aimed at securing the withdrawal of Cuban troops from Angola, the withdrawal of South African troops from Angola and Namibia, and final achievement of self-determination for the latter.

In an advisory opinion in 1971, the World Court held that South Africa's continued occupation of Namibia was contrary to international law. The possibility of a Namibia settlement in the near future thus illustrates the important influence of international law, if not always immediately, at least over the longer term. Clear and continuing violations of international law generally remain on the agenda of the international community of states, as revealed not only by the case of Namibia but also by the Turkish invasion of Cyprus in 1974, the Moroccan "unarmed" invasion of the Western Sahara in 1975 (in defiance of the terms of an advisory opinion by the International Court of Justice), and the 1979 Soviet invasion of Afghanistan. This phenomenon is also likely to occur with respect to continued U.S. support for the contras in

Nicaragua, in view of the World Court's 1986 decision condemning the United States for its actions against Nicaragua.

Nonetheless, it must be recognized that U.S. policy makers attach great importance to the withdrawal of Cuban troops from Angola, and it is to be hoped that the negotiations currently underway will lead to an agreed timetable for and successful implementation of such a withdrawal. A possible stumbling block could result from continued U.S. military assistance to the UNITA rebels in Angola, which, in the light of the ICJ's decision in the Nicaragua case, clearly violates international law. Given the attitudes of U.S. policy makers, some political accommodation between the MPLA government in Luanda and the UNITA forces, led by Jonas Savimbi, will probably be required to bring U.S. support of the latter to an end. This objective should be pursued vigorously, so that Namibian independence and the successful completion of the withdrawal of Cuban troops from Angola may be effectively achieved, bringing peace to the region.

The withdrawal of Cuban troops from Angola should make a significant contribution to improved U.S.-Cuban relations, while opening the way for the use of international law by both Cuba and the United States as a means of deterring and sanctioning future South African cross-border military actions. With the issue of the Cuban troops in Angola settled, it may be easier to persuade the United States to support more vigorous sanctions against South Africa if the latter continues to refuse to move rapidly toward dismantling the system of apartheid.

Halting Material Support of Revolutionary Groups. One issue on which the United States and Cuba have taken sharply opposing views is whether any state may provide material aid and support to revolutionary groups operating against or within another state. Cuba maintains that it has a right to provide such assistance to rebel movements, such as the FMLN in El Salvador, although it may for policy reasons decide to forego exercise of the right. In 1978 and 1979, it provided massive aid to the FSLN insurgency in Nicaragua, while from 1979 to 1981, it supplied similar assistance to the FMLN in El Salvador.

In sharp contrast, the United States has consistently taken the position that such aid violates basic norms of international law and is therefore impermissible. It has justified its own aid to the contras in Nicaragua, not by accepting the Cuban position, but rather by arguing that it represents a valid exercise of the right of collective self-defense in response to Nicaragua and Cuba's prior violation of the corresponding norms in providing material support to the guerrillas in El Salvador.

While this self-defense claim was firmly rejected by the World Court in the *Nicaragua* case, and while the United States has really offered no serious legal justification for its provision of material assistance to UNITA forces in Angola since 1985, the fact remains that the formal U.S. views on this principle are diametrically opposed to those of Cuba. These differences represent one of the principal stumbling blocks to a Central American peace settlement, and also have the potential for reversing any progress in U.S.-Cuban relations that might be achieved.

If a Central American peace settlement is to be obtained, some form of agreement must be reached that will assure the United States that neither Cuba nor Nicaragua will provide material aid to revolutionary groups in Central America, such as the FMLN, while the United States will have to give credible assurances that it will not resume military support of rebels seeking to overthrow the government of Nicaragua. Looking at the matter realistically, how might such objectives be achieved?

The 1986 judgment on the merits of the World Court established with new clarity that material aid to guerrillas violates fundamental norms of international law. Specifically, it held that the supply of weapons, materiel, or logistical assistance to revolutionary movements constitutes an illegal use of force, and that the mere supply of funds to revolutionary groups violates the principle of nonintervention in the internal affairs of another state. In short, the Court accepted the position consistently advanced by the United States in the past.[25]

Because the matter was not at issue in the present case, the Court explicitly refrained from addressing the question of whether such aid might be allowable in the case of a territory where decolonization has not occurred.[26] The United States, other western countries, and others have taken the position that the prohibitions of material assistance apply here as well, though Cuba might attempt to justify its assistance to SWAPO in Namibia and to the POLISARIO front in the Western Sahara on this ground. The Court simply did not address the issue. If ever called upon to do so, however, it appears doubtful that the ICJ would endorse such an exception to the prohibition of the use of force, particularly in view of its highly restrictive interpretation of this principle in the *Nicaragua* case.

The World Court has thus stated clearly that material aid to revolutionaries is illegal, with the possible exception noted above.

This authoritative clarification of the law offers a focal point for potential agreement, or a major narrowing of differences, on one of the most difficult security issues dividing the United States and Cuba.

Both Cuba and the United States derive much of their legitimacy from conduct consistent with (or at least assertions that they support and observe) basic principles of international law such as those referred to here. To maintain such legitimacy, and the influence that flows from perceptions of the legitimacy of state behavior—particularly among the developing and smaller countries of the world—neither Cuba nor the United States can afford to be seen as adopting defiance of international law as a basic tenet of national policy over the longer term. This means that, sooner or later, the United States will have to abandon material support of rebel movements, such as that of the contras in Nicaragua and the UNITA forces of Jonas Savimbi in Angola, while Cuba will have to reconsider and eventually change the doctrine according to which it has the right to provide material support to revolutionary movements in Central America and elsewhere.

Such shifts in policy are also required by the terms of peace efforts in Central America, including the Esquipulas II Agreement signed in Guatemala City by the five Central American presidents in August 1987. The essential point is simply that no settlement is likely to be reached, or, if reached, to endure, if its central provisions do not include a reaffirmation of the international law rules banning the provision of material support to any guerrillas or insurgent groups in the region.

The Limitation of Foreign Military Ties to Nicaragua and El Salvador. The World Court has confirmed in the *Nicaragua* decision that states are legally permitted to receive military assistance from other governments, unless such ties are limited by international agreement.[27] This legal principle means that the issue of Cuban military ties to Nicaragua, like that of U.S. military ties to El Salvador and other countries in the region, is essentially a political issue that needs to be resolved by negotiation and agreement between the parties.

A negotiated solution prohibiting or regulating the stationing of foreign troops or the establishment of foreign military bases in Nicaragua and El Salvador (or perhaps even any Central American country) would be consistent with proposals made within the framework of regional peace negotiations, and might logically form part of a Central American peace settlement. An agreement whose provisions applied only to Nicaragua and El Salvador might be easier to reach in practice than one generally applicable to all Central American countries, though the latter remains a possibility.

Other Security Issues. There are three additional security issues that deserve serious attention. While it would be a mistake to link progress on any of them to resolution of the security issues discussed above, agreement on them could contribute greatly to the long-term stabilization of U.S.-Cuban relations.

Cessation of U.S. overflights of Cuban territory: U.S. surveillance overflights of Cuba were suspended by President Carter in early 1977, but resumed in November 1978. If U.S. surveillance overflights of Cuba are continuing, it is clear that they violate Cuba's right to sovereignty under international law so long as they are conducted without Cuban permission. In principle, Cuba should not have to make concessions to secure the cessation of U.S. activities that violate fundamental principles of international law. In practice, given the importance attached to the 1962 U.S.-Soviet understandings, it may be necessary for Cuba to take U.S. national security concerns into account in resolving this issue.

If conducted with the consent of the Cuban government, freely granted in exercise of its own attributes of sovereignty, such overflights would be legal. Consequently, one possible solution would be for Cuba to authorize such overflights in exchange for some right of inspection or other confidence-building measure involving Cuban observance of U.S. military activities. The issue deserves priority attention.

Reaffirmation of U.S. noninvasion pledge: The cornerstone of the United Nations Charter is the prohibition of the threat or use of force against the territorial integrity or political independence of any state.[28] While the United States has violated this provision in various instances, it has never taken the position that it is not bound by what is perhaps the most fundamental rule of international law. Cuba, to be sure, has also violated the norm.

Article 2(4) remains a bedrock principle of international law, which the United States is solemnly obligated to uphold. A public reaffirmation of its commitment to uphold this norm, expressed in a bilateral agreement with Cuba, would reaffirm and strengthen one of the basic elements of the 1962 U.S.-Soviet understandings regarding Cuba, remind U.S. policy makers not familiar with international law of this obligation, and help assuage Cuban fears of a potential U.S. invasion. Significantly, such an agreement would go far to remove even the consideration of direct military actions against Cuba from the list of policy options U.S. decision makers are likely to consider in dealing with future difficulties in U.S.-Cuban relations. Such a bilateral agreement should, of course, contain a reciprocal obligation on the part of Cuba.

Cuban ratification of Treaty of Tlatelolco: An important long-term consideration that could disrupt normalization of U.S.-Cuban relations is the theoretical possibility that Cuba might join a consortium of Third World states in the construction of nuclear weapons. Cuban ratification of the Treaty on the Prohibition of Nuclear Weapons in Latin America ("Treaty of Tlatelolco") would go far to put this potential concern to rest, while gaining goodwill among its Latin neighbors for joining them in their efforts to establish a denuclearized Latin America. Cuban ratification of the Treaty would bring the treaty very close to entry into force for all parties. Such an action would greatly serve the U.S. nonproliferation interests, which are largely shared by the Soviet Union.

Also of great importance is the fact that Cuban ratification of the Treaty of Tlatelolco, if accompanied by waiver of the treaty's unusual unanimous ratification requirement, would immediately place the Soviet Union under a binding legal obligation not to introduce nuclear weapons into Cuba, even if under Soviet control.[29] Soviet transfer of such weapons to Cuban control is already prohibited by the Non-Proliferation Treaty.[30] Coupled with a reaffirmation of the U.S. noninvasion pledge, such action would go far to solidify and reaffirm the essential provisions of the 1962 U.S.-Soviet understandings. Certain elements of these understandings, such as the nonintroduction of nuclear-capable offensive weapons systems, would as a result remain subject only to the firm political commitment of the two superpowers. However, even these might eventually be covered in a formal agreement with the Soviet Union and/or Cuba dealing with these and other security issues.

Relaxation of Economic Sanctions

As explained above, in the United States the executive branch retains the authority to relax economic sanctions against Cuba without any requirement for legislative action. Sanctions could be lifted gradually, perhaps in the following sequence: (1) immediate lifting of all restrictions on trade in medicines and other goods destined for humanitarian purposes; (2) lifting the embargo on trade while retaining strict licensing requirements for exports, including, in particular, high-technology products; (3) easing or lifting restrictions on capital flows; and (4) full lifting of all economic sanctions. Removal of the ban on shipping and the establishment of an air-transport agreement might also be explored, though the inclusion of specific provisions in the agreement itself, or legislative action by Congress, might be required to prevent the attachment of Cuban ships, planes, and related assets by private litigants.

Negotiations on Human Rights Issues

Bilateral discussions and negotiations on human rights issues could be limited, at least initially, to issues of compliance with international legal obligations, the desirability of each country ratifying additional human rights instruments (treaties and optional clauses), and measures to be undertaken on humanitarian grounds. Public criticism would continue, though perhaps in a more focused manner.

The United States might press for Cuba to change its domestic policies relating to the incarceration of individuals charged with anti-state behavior, and for a relaxation of the legal definitions of such behavior. It might also press for greater freedom of expression. At the same time, the United States should recognize that certain progress on human rights issues may be possible within the framework of socialist legality.[31] Indeed, there are some indications that Cuba may be moving in this direction. Attention from the UN Human Rights Commission as well as the example of perestroika and glasnost may contribute to this movement. At the same time, Cuba might raise issues relating to U.S. observance of human rights, particularly certain economic and social human rights. The important point is that the issue of human rights should be used to promote effective observance by each government of universally recognized rights, thereby contributing to the freedom and welfare of individual human beings in both countries.

Deferred Issues

Settlement of Claims. The question of settling claims for U.S. property expropriated by Cuba is likely to be a thorny one, particularly in view of the fact that some $1.8 billion of pre-adjudicated claims exist, plus interest, against some $33 million in frozen assets. The final solution will probably be a lump-sum agreement and/or an agreement involving the sale of equity in joint ventures or similar enterprises, or possibly some kind of management and marketing agreements. The issue does not admit of easy solution in view of the amounts involved and the paucity of assets with which to pay outstanding claims. Innovative solutions will be required.

When this issue is reached, a number of lump-sum settlements that the United States has reached with socialist countries will constitute relevant precedents, as will U.S. settlements with Mexico, Peru, and Venezuela. Cuban settlements with France, Switzerland, Canada, the United Kingdom, and Spain will similarly serve as precedents that may be useful in devising a settlement.[32]

Cuba, for its part, also has claims against the United states for damages resulting from actions such as the Bay of Pigs invasion, other covert activities directed against Cuba, and the economic embargo. While it would be extremely difficult in domestic political terms for the United States to recognize these claims in any specific manner, an appropriate formula might be found that recognized, in general language, that all claims by both states had been taken into account and were considered settled.

Guantánamo. The Panama Canal Treaties provide an important precedent for the termination of perpetual treaties, as does the UK-PRC agreement relating to the future of Hong Kong.

While legal arguments can be made in favor of a right of termination by Cuba, these are not likely to be accepted by the United States, in part because there are also strong legal counterarguments.[33] The United States may have no overwhelming need for continued occupation of the base, although the matter could become a hot internal political issue.

The Extension of Trade Benefits. The granting of most-favored-nation (MFN) status will require legislative action by Congress repealing several provisions of law. Similarly, inclusion of Cuba as a beneficiary of the U.S. Generalized System of Preferences (GSP) would require action by Congress, though it need not be ruled out should relations be normalized. Both are domestic political issues. More problematic is the question of a domestic sugar quota for Cuba, which at present appears to be a remote possibility.

Conclusion

International law contains specific prohibitions on certain military, military-related, and other activities, a useful way of framing issues, and a large repertoire of agreed principles that can be drawn upon in devising specific agreements. It represents a lens through which each state might more objectively view the behavior of the other, and an indispensable tool in U.S.-Cuban negotiations.

As suggested above, the first approach to negotiations may help resolve immediate irritants in U.S.-Cuban relations, but is unlikely in itself to change the status quo. The second approach would attempt to relate U.S.-Cuban relations to the framework of international law, and to the broader interests of both states that the latter reflects. It holds considerably more promise in terms of achieving real accommodation on a number of the deeper issues that divide the two countries.

The recommendation of a gradual and sequential strategy of negotiations is not meant to preclude the possibility of breakthroughs on such thorny issues as the settlement of claims, Guantánamo, or the lifting of economic and trade restrictions. Such breakthroughs could occur. On the other hand, when sharp policy differences between the two countries do arise, continued adherence to the sequential strategy will be important to preserve existing gains, and to keep the process going.

International law should be used as a tool, but without losing sight of the reality that there are many individuals in the world—including some who may from time to time exercise considerable influence over U.S. or Cuban policy—who do not understand its provisions, appreciate its benefits, or take its constraints seriously. One of the challenges of U.S.-Cuban relations in the 1990s will be precisely to construct a web of legal and other relationships that will make it increasingly costly, and therefore unlikely, for policy makers in either country to undertake actions toward the other without regard for international law and the broader interests that it represents.

International law should be a useful language for discourse between Cuba and the United States about power, ends, and means. It is a language that should facilitate understanding. For societies in such essential disagreement as Cuba and the United States, international law represents a neutral ground nurtured by others, where new and more promising interactions and relationships might spring forth.

Notes

1. The author would like to express his appreciation for the comments and suggestions made by other participants in the workshop, the thoughtful written observations made by

Jorge Domínguez on earlier drafts, and the valiant research assistance of Audrey Baker.

2. Adopted under the Trading with the Enemy Act. See *The Cuban Foreign Assets Control Regulation*, 31 CFR (Code of Federal Regulations), Chapter 5 (July 1, 1987 version).

3. *Military and Paramilitary Activities in and Against Nicaragua (Nicaragua v. U.S.)*, 1986 I.C.J. Reports, p. 14, at p. 128 (para. 251) (Merits judgment of June 27) [hereinafter cited as *Nicaragua v. U.S.*].

4. "U.S.-Cuba Agreement on Immigration Procedures and the Return of Cuban Nationals," Dec. 14, 1984, reprinted in *International Legal Materials*, 24 (1985), pp. 32-37.

5. Press release reported by the Cuban News Agency *Prensa Latina*, and published in *Granma*, Nov. 21, 1987, p. 10. For an explication of the agreement by Ricardo Alarcón, Vice Minister of Foreign Relations, see *Granma*, Nov. 30, 1987, p. 13.

6. For a discussion of the technical issues involved, see Note, "Radio Martí and the U.S.-Cuban Radio War," *Federal Communications Law Journal*, 36 (1984), pp. 69-94.

7. See UN Charter, art. 2(1).

8. Broadcasting to Cuba Act, Public Law 98-11, 97 Stat. 749, Sec. 3(e) (Oct. 4, 1983).

9. U.S.-Cuba Maritime Boundary Agreement, April 27, 1977, 28 U.S.T. 5285, T.I.A.S. No. 8627; U.S.-Cuba Agreement Extending the Provisional Application of the Maritime Boundary Agreement of Dec. 16, 1977, Exchange of Notes of Dec. 16 and Dec. 21, 1987; effective Jan. 1, 1988 (two-year extension). See also U.S. Department of State *Digest of U.S. Practice in International Law, 1977*, pp. 557-559.

10. U.S.-Cuba Agreement Concerning Fisheries Off the Coasts of the United States, With Agreed Minutes, April 27, 1977, 28 U.S.T. 6769, T.I.A.S. No. 8689.

11. Wayne S. Smith, *The Closest of Enemies* (New York: Norton, 1987), pp. 102-109.

12. U.S.-Cuba Memorandum of Understanding on the Hijacking of Aircraft and Vessels, Exchange of Notes at Washington and Havana, Feb. 15, 1973, 24 U.S.T. 737, T.I.A.S. 7579, reprinted in *International Legal Materials*, 12 (1973), p. 370.

13. According to the former head of the U.S. interests section in Havana, U.S. failure to prosecute those responsible for the hijacking of Cuban seagoing vessels later taken to the United States was an important factor in the Cuban decision

to initiate the Mariel boatlift. See Smith, *The Closest of Enemies*, pp. 200-214.

14. See, e.g., Código Penal (Cuba), art. 117, Law No. 62 of Dec. 29, 1987, published in *Gaceta Oficial* of Dec. 30, 1987 (Edición Especial). Article 117 proscribes acts of both air and sea piracy.

15. See, e.g., United Nations convention of the Law of the Sea, signed Dec. 10, 1982, art. 108. For the text of the Convention, see UN Doc. A/CONF. 62/122 (7 Oct. 1982), U.N. Pub. No. E.83.V.5. (1983), reprinted in *International Legal Materials*, 21 (1982), p. 1261.

16. See, e.g., Luis Suárez Salazar, "El narcotráfico en las relaciones interamericanas: Una aproximación estructural," *Cuadernos de Nuestra América* (Cuba), vol. 4, No. 8 (July-December 1987), pp. 24-64.

17. See, e.g., Código Penal, art. 190.

18. See U.S.-Cuba Convention for the Suppression of Smuggling Operations Between Their Respective Territories, March 11, 1926, 44 Stat. 2402, T.S. 739, 6 Bevans, 1144, L.N.T.S. 383.

19. See Arrangement for the Direct Exchange of Certain Information Regarding the Traffic in Narcotic Drugs, Exchange of Notes at Havana, Feb. 12, and March 7, 1930, 6 Bevans 1157.

20. The understanding is recorded in U.S. Department of State, Minutes of Talks Relating to Search and Rescue Operations, Illicit Drug Trafficking, and Acts Endangering Maritime Navigation, Jan. 16-19, 1978. The understanding was not an international agreement, and had no binding force under international law.

21. See generally Jorge F. Pérez López, "Nuclear Power in Cuba: Opportunities and Challenges," in Irving Louis Horowitz, ed., *Cuban Communism* (6th ed., 1988), pp. 386-408.

22. In 1984, the Supreme Court upheld these restrictions on travel-related economic transactions. *Regan v. Wald*, 468 U.S. 222 (1984).

23. Agreement Relating to the Establishment of Interests Sections of the U.S. and Cuba in the Embassy of Switzerland in Havana and the Embassy of Czechoslovakia in Washington, respectively. Exchange of Notes, May 30, 1977, 30 U.S.T. 2101, T.I.A.S. 9313.

24. See, e.g., Wayne S. Smith, *The Closest of Enemies*, pp. 122-127, 167-169, 251, 253.

25. See *Nicaragua v. U.S.*, at pp. 101, 118, 124-125 (paras. 191, 228, 241-242).
26. *Ibid.*, p. 108 (para. 206).
27. *Ibid.*, p. 126 (para. 246), p. 135 (para. 269).
28. UN Charter, art. 2(4).
29. The U.S.S.R. has ratified Additional Protocol II to the Treaty of Tlatelolco, which obligates nuclear-weapons states to fully respect the Treaty of Tlatelolco "in all of its express aims and provisions" (art. 1) and to avoid contributing in any way to the performance of acts involving a violation of the obligations of article 1 of the treaty in the territories to which the Treaty applies in accordance with article 4 thereof" (art. 2). Treaty for the Prohibition of Nuclear Weapons in Latin America ("Treaty of Tlatelolco"), Feb. 14, 1967, arts. 1 & 4, 634 U.N.T.S. 281, reprinted in *International Legal Materials*, vol. 6 (1967), p. 521; Treaty of Tlatelolco, Additional Protocol II, Feb. 14, 1967, arts. 1-2, 22 U.S.T. 754, T.I.A.S. No. 7137, 634 U.N.T.S. 364. Protocol II has been ratified by all five nuclear-weapons states, and is currently in force. However, it would not apply to Cuba in unambiguous fashion until the latter ratified the Treaty of Tlatelolco, and Cuba either waived the unanimous ratification requirement, or all remaining ratifications required to bring the treaty into force were deposited. These include ratification of the treaty by Argentina, Cuba, and probably Guyana, as well as ratification of Protocol I by France.
30. Treaty on the Non-Proliferation of Nuclear Weapons, July 1, 1968, art. 1, 21 U.S.T. 483, T.I.A.S. No. 6839, 729 U.N.T.S. 161.
31. For a sophisticated theoretical analysis of the role of law and the importance of the principle of legality within the constitutional order of a state such as Cuba, see Raúl Gómez Treto, "El concepto marxista de la constitución y el sistema jurídico-normativo de la sociedad constituída en estado," *Revista Cubana de Derecho*, 16, 31 (1987), pp. 3-55.
32. To put the claims issue in perspective, it is worth recalling that the United States and the Soviet Union have never reached a general settlement of their claims, although the U.S.S.R. assigned certain assets to the United States by means of the so-called "Litvinov Assignment" in 1933, when the United States recognized the Soviet Union. For a discussion of the claims and other economic issues, see Note,

"Legal Impediments to Normalization of Trade With Cuba," *Law and Policy in International Business*, 8 (1976), p. 1007. See also Paul A. Shneyer & Virginia Barta, "The Legality of the U.S. Economic Blockade of Cuba Under International Law," *Case Western Reserve Journal of International Law*, 13 (1981), p. 451.

33. These counterarguments include the fact that certain norms relied upon by Cuba did not exist when the 1903 and 1934 treaties were signed, and have no retroactive effect. For Cuban views on Guantánamo, see Miguel A. D'Estéfano Pisani, *Cuba, Estados Unidos y el derecho internacional contemporáneo* (Havana: Editorial de Ciencias Sociales, 1983), pp. 141-171.

Index

314

324